The Non-Reality of Free Will

The Non-Reality of Free Will

RICHARD DOUBLE

New York   Oxford
Oxford University Press
1991

Oxford University Press

Oxford   New York   Toronto
Delhi   Bombay   Calcutta   Madras   Karachi
Petaling Jaya   Singapore   Hong Kong   Tokyo
Nairobi   Dar es Salaam   Cape Town
Melbourne   Auckland

and associated companies in
Berlin   Ibadan

Copyright © 1991 by Richard Double

Published by Oxford University Press, Inc.,
200 Madison Avenue, New York, NY 10016

Oxford is a registered trademark of Oxford University Press

Library of Congress Cataloging-in-Publication Data
Double, Richard.
The non-reality of free will / by Richard Double.
p. cm.   Includes bibliographical references.
ISBN 0-19-506497-6
1. Free will and determinism.   I. Title.
BJ1461.D67   1991   123'.5—dc20   90-33531

1 3 5 7 9 8 6 4 2

Printed in the United States of America
on acid-free paper

To My Mother

Acknowledgments

I gratefully acknowledge the editors of the following journals for permission to use in Chapters 2, 6, and 8, respectively, portions of articles that appeared in their journals: *Philosophical Studies*, 1989, "Puppeteers, Hypnotists, and Neurosurgeons"; *American Philosophical Quarterly*, 1988, "Meta-Compatibilism"; *The Southern Journal of Philosophy*, 1988, "Libertarianism and Rationality." I also wish to thank some very able philosophers who commented on chapters and on papers that became chapters: John Atwell, George Graham, Lilly Russow, George Schlesinger, Stephen Stich, and several referees who know who they are although I do not. A special debt is owed to Robert Kane for his considerable assistance with Chapter 8 and his valuable correspondence concerning the whole project. The book doubtless would have been better had I heeded the advice of these readers more conscientiously, but such is the strength of belief perseverance.

In addition, I am grateful to three people from the Philosophy Department at Indiana-Purdue University at Fort Wayne for help in producing the manuscript: David Fairchild, Paul Vorndran, and especially Janet Hoagburg, whose excellent typing, ceaseless encouragement, and good cheer were invaluable. Finally, I wish to thank Cynthia Read and the staff of Oxford University Press for their assistance in completing the book.

Edinboro, Pennsylvania   R. D.
October, 1990

Contents

The Non-Reality of Free Will

1

Introduction

1. The Problem of the Reality of Free Will

The ideas of free will and moral responsibility play a deep and central role in the way that we view ourselves. Because of this, almost all of the great figures in Western philosophy have addressed free will and moral responsibility, most of them attempting to vindicate these beliefs. In recent years, the importance of freedom and responsibility have been well documented. The belief that we often act freely and are at those times morally responsible for our behavior is an integral constituent of the Manifest Image of Man, the view of ourselves and the world that we hold before we entertain the postulation of theoretical entities that constitutes the Scientific Image (Sellars, 1963, Chapter 1). The belief that persons are capable of moral responsibility and deserve moral consideration comprises (along with the logically prior *intentional stance*) the *personal stance* that we take toward each other (Dennett, 1978, Chapter 12). This personal attitude is characterized by "reactive attitudes" such as gratitude and resentment, which stand in distinction to the "objective" attitude that we take toward beings that we believe are not endowed with free will (Strawson, 1962; Nagel, 1986). The capacity for free will has been alleged to be a criterion for distinguishing persons from non-persons (Frankfurt, 1971). And in law, besides the obvious issue of retributive justice, the ideas of free will and moral responsibility provide the moral rationale for legal responsibility.

It is important to appreciate the ontological presuppositions of free will and moral responsibility as they appear in the philosophical discussion. As much as anything, the need to "make room for"

3

freedom and responsibility led Kant to posit the possibility of a noumenal world beyond phenomenal appearances. Free will is understood to be that which ensures that anyone "who is the subject of justified punishment, blame or moral condemnation" will "really *deserve* it" (Strawson, 1962, 61). Free will is held to ground human dignity by allowing agents to be "ultimately responsible" for their actions (Kane, 1985, 47). Such deep responsibility, in turn, is held to justify looking at persons in visceral ways: For instance, when we think that we have been gratuitously injured "we blame, we remonstrate, we hate, we reflect on the futility of hate, we plan revenge . . ." (van Inwagen, 1983, 207).

Since our interest in free will primarily comes from a concern for moral responsibility, the notion of a deep sense of moral responsibility must be appreciated if the free will debate is to seem very important. For instance, if one views moral responsibility as societally dependent and pragmatically established, then the worry over giving *the* correct analysis of free will might well seem overdone. But moral responsibility cannot be viewed in this way if it is to play its role in philosophy and common sense. In contrast to the everyday notion of legal responsibility as something that depends upon changeable laws, customs, and norms, moral responsibility cannot depend upon such vagaries. Moral responsibility must be unified and basic if it is to provide a benchmark against which we measure the moral suitability of the laws of China, the United States, or Indiana.

It is not enough that the *concept* of moral responsibility is terribly useful (Dennett, 1984), since all sorts of fictitious concepts may be useful or even indispensable in practical life. If moral responsibility is to play the normative role that philsophers and common sense think it does, then it must have its existence grounded in firmer soil than pragmatic or conventional considerations. And for us to be really morally responsible, it seems that we need a similarly nonconventional, real capacity—the capacity of free will.

This is not to claim that the belief in freedom and moral responsibility is so deeply entrenched that no one has envisaged giving it up. Hard determinists have sometimes provided scenarios where these beliefs have lapsed into desuetude, to the benefit of all concerned. *Walden Two* sketches the beginnings of a Utopia where persons have largely risen above such beliefs (Skinner, 1948). Edgar Wilson (1979, Chapters 10–12) gives an explicit recipe for how legal systems might be redesigned so that crime is viewed as a "maladjustment disorder" that is subject to behavioral treatment, an idea reminiscent of Butler's *Erewhon*. Still, even if it is pragmatically possible for us to stop treating ourselves and others as free and responsible—and that is debatable—it looks as if doing so would involve an enormous revision in our prephilosophical view of ourselves.

In this book I shall argue that there can be no such thing as free will and moral responsibility. My argument is a metaphilosophical one that holds that neither concept can have discrete reference. Instead, these terms are merely honorific and subjective; they cannot be legitimized by appeal to the nature of extralinguistic reality. Free will and moral responsibility, as they are viewed in philosophical discourse and everyday life, are not to be counted as candidates among the class of real entities.

In outline, my non-realist argument looks like this. (1) There is nothing about extralinguistic reality that constrains our judgments about whether choices count as truly free or unfree. (2) Instead, our judgments about whether a choice is free or not must rely upon a variety of factors that cannot produce clear answers. These factors will be pragmatic, ideological, conventional, aesthetic, psychological, and/or idiosyncratic. (3) But any categorization of choices that relies on such an assortment of non-objectively grounded factors will necessarily fail to ground the deep, nonconventional sense of free will that is needed to support genuine moral responsibility, dignity, and all the rest that free will is supposed to guarantee. (4) Therefore, there can be nothing that answers to the deep senses of *free will* and *moral responsibility*.

I have come to the non-realist position grudgingly. Several years ago at a meeting of the American Philosophical Association a very prominent incompatibilist commented on a paper delivered by a younger, less prominent, but very sharp compatibilist. The exchange between the two lasted the entire hour, and toward the end it became clear that neither speaker could understand at all why the other held the position that he did: as one spoke, the other just shook his head in disbelief. I remember that I was surprised that these two very bright people could find so little of value in what the other said, and it seemed implausible to me that their predicament could be explained by way of disagreements over terminology, logical blunders, or differing estimates of empirical probabilities. Instead, I thought, something deeper had to be at stake.

At the time I thought that the deeper disagreement must lie in the fact that they differed on some metaphilosophical intuition, the sort of thing that separates realists from phenomenalists or people who accept physical–nonphysical interaction from those who find it incredible. But recently something happened that suggested to me that the disagreement between the compatibilists and incompatibilists involves intuitions that are more 'visceral' than those that separate philosophers on many other metaphysical issues. I was reading a defense of compatibilism at an APA meeting and was astonished by the degree of emotion that it stirred in my incompatibilist commentator. The commentator not only pointed out that my argument was deeply confused (a charge that I expected), but suggested that compatibilists may suffer from a personality disorder that tries to derive satisfaction from the ugliest of scenarios (determinism), something analogous to the concentration-camp syndrome. At the same time, I remembered the vituperative tones used by many compatibilists who denounce the wickedness of the retributive rationale for punishment sometimes used by libertarians. It occurred to me that when emotions intrude into the philosophical debate, it is probably because each side is appealing to some inchoate image or paradigm that drives their intuitions— paradigms that probably have strong moral overtones, perhaps involving what Hilary Putnam (1987) calls "moral images of man." This would scarcely be surprising, given that one's view of freedom is an important constituent of any explicit moral image.

Before reaching the non-realist conclusion, I vacillated between compatibilism and incompatibilism. During my compatibilist periods, my principal motivation was that indeterminate decisions could not be free. Because I was convinced that we (sometimes) enjoy free will, I was sure that compatibilism must be true. At those times when I accepted incompatibilism, my motivation was from the other direction. I held that we could not be free in a deterministic universe, and, given my conviction that we are free, I therefore concluded that freedom must somehow lie in indeterminism. During those years of vacillation I never took seriously the option of accepting the negative claims of both the compatibilists and incompatibilists at the cost of denying the existence of free will. Since I could not bring myself to reject the intuitive belief that we are sometimes free, I could not accept both negative claims and was left to vacillate.

I finally began to question my conviction that we are free by asking myself just what freedom and moral responsibility were and why I thought we enjoy them. These two lines of inquiry—philosophical analysis and amateur psychology—began to converge on the conclusion that there is not anything that answers to the prephilosophical notions of "free will" and "moral responsibility." At this point, the option of accepting the negative morals of the compatibilists and incompatibilists seemed exactly right. The conclusion I reached was not that of the *skeptic*, who questions whether free will and moral responsibility exist, but that of the non-realist, who affirms that they do not because the two respective concepts cannot be satisfied.

This is not a conclusion for which I have a general bias. On the contrary, metaphilosophically I am a scientific realist, committed to a realistic conception of truth, and I respect the enterprise of constructing metaphysical theories to answer questions about what exists. I regard the distinction between the epistemological question "Do we know that p is true?" and the ontological question "Is p true?" to be basic and inviolate in the face of pragmatist and verificationist attempts to blur it. Accordingly, I am incredulous of linguistic arguments that metaphysical problems—whether the mind–body problem, the existence of God, or the free will question—are pseudo-problems, since such arguments usually depend on verificationist theories of meaning or, at least, verificationist ideas about what a viable philosophical alternative might be. So, for example, regarding the mind–body problem, I am a materialist who rejects dualism because I think that a dualist ontology is less plausible than a materialist one, not because I find dualistic minds conceptually incoherent. My suspicion of linguistic arguments that are designed to undermine ontological theories extends to the area of metaethics, where I take the unverifiability of ethical claims to have no particular weight against the moral realist's claim that there are moral truths.

So, in general, I do not hold that the difficulty of answering a philosophical question provides grounds for thinking that there is something wrong with the question. Rather, I think that proposing the most plausible answers we can to questions that do not admit of confident answers is the proper role of the philosopher. That's why we get paid the big bucks. The problem is that, in the case of *this* metaphysical problem, it seems to me that all the standard positions are wrong. The usual answers are given by two groups, one that affirms that we have free will and the other that denies it. The former are the libertarians and compatibilists, the latter are the hard determinists and an unlabeled camp that holds that free will is incompatible with both determinism and indeterminism. The view that all four groups share, irrespective of their positions on whether humans in fact enjoy free will, is the belief that free will is a sensible and desirable sort of commodity. It is my rejection of the belief that "free will" is even logically coherent that separates my position from all the others.

My non-realist view of free will must be distinguished from the easily conflated position that we are all *un*free. My aim is not to subsume one part of the free–unfree dichotomy under the other but rather to undermine the distinction altogether. I do not, for instance, argue for the non-reality of free will via the incompatibilist strategy used by hard determinists, since incompatiblism, like compatibilism, is committed to the coherence of the free will notion. I do not claim that we are all unfree, but that we are neither free nor unfree in the important sense that the standard positions presuppose.

This is not to say that all persons equally enjoy the capabilities that we typically associate with freedom of the will, i.e., rational decision making, the ability to act as we desire, the ability to make choices noncompulsively, and so on. People experience these to different degrees, and it would be absurd to propose an a priori argument to try to show that we do not. I also grant that there are paradigms of unfree agents—prisoners in chains, drug addicts, kleptomaniacs, persons who are radio-controlled by the Martians, etc. If we did not have both positive and negative exemplars of freedom, it is doubtful that the concept of *free* would be learnable, and certainly we do know, at least roughly, how to wield the vocabulary of freedom. My position is that if we go beyond the clear exemplars of free and unfree agents to ask whether these exemplars stand for distinguishable non-linguistic classes of types of entities, there is ample reason to conclude that there can be no such classes. Not all exemplars that enable us to use terms stand for objective classes of things.

The claim that there is no free will and moral responsibility might seem to be equivalent to the claim that "free choice" (and "moral responsibility") do not denote anything, but that formulation needs slight amendment. That amendment is that these terms do not denote any well-behaved, principled, philosophical 'natural kinds' that make discussions of freedom and responsibility truth-valued in even the loose sense in which common sense takes claims about persons' beliefs and desires to be truth-valued. Instead, the denotata of "free choices" and "morally responsible agents" constitute heterogeneous instances for which there is no more reason to put them in those classes than the unprincipled impressions of those who wield the respective terms. Thus, the extension of *free choice* for various speakers will skew widely, and there will be no truth to the matter of whose usage is correct. In this sense, saying that there is no free will and moral responsibility is not like saying that there are no Zeus thunderbolts or caloric fluid, because in these cases there are principled replacement kinds that can serve as the real denotata of the original terms.

The assumption that there is a 'central core' of cases underlying the proper use of the terms *freedom* and *moral responsibility* is understandable given the intellectual predilections of philosophers. Philosophers characteristically attempt to extend conceptual rigor in very ambitious ways, by giving analytic definitions and by attempting to map out logical relations between diverse concepts, all the while assuming that the world contains 'natural kinds' that we can uncover if we are clever enough. This effort to organize the disorganized has many sources. The personality types of philosophers and the way that many philosophers are enamored of the success of deductive logic, mathematics, and science are two. The desire to make the really hard things—like life and death and good and evil—understandable and hence psychologically more controllable also contributes to the aim of clearing away the clutter and seeing into the heart of terribly messy issues.

Even if one were dubious about the ultimate success of this type of enterprise, it is hard to argue against the proposal that some group of thinkers should be in the business of trying to organize those areas of thought that are most resistant to being organized. At any rate, it is hard for a *philosopher* to argue against it, since organizing the disorganized is the most basic thing that philosophers do. There is a pitfall, however, that is inherent in such attempts. Sometimes the apparent disorder will be genuine, in which case the philosophical attempt at organization will be more distortion than hygiene. Science cannot exist in virtue of scientific method alone, since it requires the cooperation of a subject matter that at least roughly conforms to scientific laws. Likewise, the attempt at a rigorous understanding of philosophical subject matter requires more than keen analytical skills. The philosophical subject matter must cooperate also.

My conclusion that in abstracting to a philosophical conception of free will philosophers have tried to organize the unorganizable is similar to one that could be drawn in several other areas of philosophy. In epistemology, the attempt to arrive at a true definition of *knowledge* (and the corresponding problem of answering skepticism) has been venerated since Plato, and yet it is possible to view this entire tradition as based on a too-narrow view of our cognitive mechanisms (Goldman, 1978). In normative ethics, consequentialists and formalists have seemingly forever tried to produce formulas that will systematize our moral intuitions in such a way that we will have a completely adequate theory of ethics couched solely in their preferred terms. But the failure of either side to produce an entirely satisfactory account of normative ethics suggests that our moral phenomenology is not amenable to such attempts at rational reconstruction. Similar points could be made regarding philosophical attempts to provide the rational bases of political obligation or aesthetic value. I do not claim to have a proof that the attempted idealizations in these various areas fail, but, in the case of free will, this book constitutes my argument.

2. Definitions of Terms

There are several perplexing questions about free will that cry out for answers. (1) Is determinism compatible with it? (2) How is free will even conceivable, given that both determinism and indeterminism seem unpromising candidates for producing freedom? (3)

Does moral responsibility require it? (4) Do we, in fact, have free will very much of the time?

These questions, as important as they seem, risk being frivolous unless we are able to say what we mean by *free will*. This is clear from the general logical point that if you do not know the meaning of a term *R*, then you cannot answer whether S is compatible with R, how R is conceivable, does T require R, or whether we in fact exercise R.

The logically primary task, therefore, is to produce a theory or account of free will and moral responsibility before we can address these questions. This task will be a conceptual one and has parallels to other philosophical issues. Consider the mind–body problem. Until one gives clear senses to *physical* and *nonphysical*, the debate over whether persons are completely physical is doomed to being a merely emotive exchange. Or take epistemology. Without a clear sense of *knowledge* or *justification*, the problem of knowledge cannot be clearly discussed.

The fact that the first step is conceptual has advantages and disadvantages. The good news is that if we reach agreement on an account of free will and moral responsibility, then three of the four just-listed questions can be expected to fall right out of that account. That is, the a priori questions concerning the compatibility of free will and determinism (1), the conceivability of free will (2), and the relation of moral responsibility to free will (3) should be answered by satisfactory analytical work on the key terms. The fourth question of whether we actually have free will is empirical and cannot be settled by philosophical means, but at least we will have some idea of what to look for, as it were.

The bad news is that in our attempt to produce a coherent account of free will (in the formal mode, analysis of "free will"), we may find grounds for thinking that there cannot be any such thing to be found. Philosophy teaches us not to take anything for granted. And it is not as if we have not been reminded of the potential danger here. A familiar complaint against libertarianism has been that "supporters of free will have rarely been prepared to elaborate on the nature of free will" (Young, 1984, 43). It has also been suggested that "the Free Will issue, in large measure, *is* a linguistic tangle" because "the parties involved do not fundamentally agree on what . . . 'rationality' and 'freedom' mean . . . and, as a result, much of the discussion is unfocused" (Bernstein, 1989). The danger is that once we go beyond the ceremonial use of the key terms in expressing our various *feelings* about the free will issue and try to produce focused accounts, we may see that the free will debate is a tangle simply because the key notions themselves are confused.

Let me now explain what I will mean by certain key words in this book:

Free choice (decision), *freedom, free, free will, free act, free agent*—Because the aim of this book is to see whether any theory of free will is acceptable (what "free will" really means), I cannot produce a complete definition here prior to that investigation. It is clear, though, that free will has to do with making choices that have the desirable property of being *free*, which enables agents who make such choices to be more worthy of dignity than agents who cannot. Free will seems, at first blush, to be something without which our moral responsibility for our actions will be jeopardized. At the same time, free will has connections with other highly desirable things like independence, autonomy, activeness rather than passivity, and rationality. The libertarian Isaiah Berlin gives a description of free will that few compatibilists would reject:

> I wish my life and decisions to depend on myself, not on external forces of whatever kind. I wish to be the instrument of my own, not of other men's, acts of will. I wish to be a subject, not an object; to be moved by reasons, by conscious purposes, which are my own, not by causes which affect me, as it were, from outside. . . . I wish, above all, to be conscious of myself as a thinking, willing, active being, bearing responsibility for my choices and able to explain them by reference to my own ideas and purposes. (Quoted in Lindley, 1986, 6)

There is reason to believe that these general desiderata might be generated by the satisfaction of three basic conditions that have produced much of the historical debate between the compatibilists and incompatibilists. The first conditon is the requirement that free agents have the ability to choose and to act differently than they actually do. The point here is that free agents do not have to make the choices they do; they have the ability, in a sense to be established, to choose otherwise. The second condition, often subsumed under the first, is that free agents *control* what their choices shall be. The intuitive idea, accepted by compatibilists and incompatibilists, is that if I choose freely the choice that I make is 'up to me', again in a sense to be established. The third component of free will is rationality. Free choices are reasonable and sensible in the light of a belief-desire psychology where we choose in order to maximize the likelihood of achieving our goals.

Interesting questions about these three fairly innocuous conditions arise when one tries to interpret them either within the context of determinism or indeterminism. Compatibilists think that all three conditions can be met by deterministic persons and have worked hard to show how that can be done. Concerning the first, a great deal of effort from G. E. Moore (1911) on has been expended to show that the concept of "could have chosen otherwise" is analytically definable in terms of our having the freedom to choose otherwise *had* we so wanted. Concerning control, many compatibilists have argued that free agents can control their choices only if determinism is the case. For instance, R. E. Hobart argues that if "the self" experiences indeterminate volitions, then

> [t]he self, considering the alternatives beforehand, is not in a position to say, "If I feel thus about it, this volition will take place, or if I feel otherwise the contrary will take place; I know very well how I shall feel, so I know how I shall will." The self now existing has not control over the future "free" volition, since that may be undetermined, nor will the self's future feelings, whatever they may be, control it. Hence the sense expressed by "I can," the sense of power inhering in one's continuous self to sway the volition as it feels disposed, is denied to it. All it is in a position to mean by "I can" is, "I do not know which will happen," which is not "I can" at all. (1934, 77)

Even the libertarian Roderick Chisholm sees indeterminism as potentially destructive of control:

> Perhaps there is less need to argue that the ascription of responsibility also conflicts with an indeterministic view of action—with the view that the act, or some event that is essential to the act, is not caused at all. If the act—the firing of the shot—was not caused at all, if it was fortuitous or capricious, happening so to speak out of the blue, then, presumably, no one—and nothing—was responsible for

the act. Our conception of action, therefore, should be neither deterministic nor indeterministic. (1964, 27–28)

And, concerning rationality, compatibilists have similarly argued that indeterminacy within human choices would diminish the rationality of those choices. A. J. Ayer expresses the argument this way:

[I]f it is a matter of pure chance that a man should act in one way rather than another, he may be free but can hardly be responsible. And indeed when a man's action seems to us quite unpredictable, when, as we say, there is no knowing what he will do, we do not look upon him as a moral agent. We look upon him as a lunatic. (1954, 17)

The upshot of all this is that compatibilists have interpreted the requirements regarding the ability to do otherwise, control, and rationality to be 'one way', deterministic requirements. Since on determinism we have only a hypothetical ability to choose otherwise than we do, the compatibilist is forced to argue that these three requirements can be satisfied by agents who lack the categorical ability to choose otherwise, provided that the determinism occurs in a benign way.

Because the libertarian is committed to showing how these three conditions could be satisfied by indeterministic free agents, for the libertarian these conditions must be interpreted as two-way, or dual. This means that libertarians will have to show what it would be like for free agents to possess the dual, categorical ability to choose otherwise, to enjoy dual control, and to make choices that are dually rational. Consider first the categorical sense of "could have chosen otherwise" that libertarians impute to free agents. According to that sense, when I freely select one alternative, I possess the categorical freedom to choose otherwise in exactly that same circumstance. Both options are equally available to me, given my condition at that moment, and, indeed, given my entire psychological history. Chisholm holds that this condition is necessary in order for us to be responsible for our actions:

Let us consider some deed, or misdeed, that may be attributed to a responsible agent: one man, say, shot another. If the man *was* responsible for what he did, then, I would urge, what was to happen at the time of the shooting was something that was entirely up to the man himself. There was a moment at which it was true, both that he could have fired the shot and also that he could have refrained from firing it. And if this is so, then, even though he did fire it, he could have done something else instead. (1964, 24–25)

Peter van Inwagen expresses this condition this way:

When I say of a man that he "has free will" I mean that very often, if not always, when he has to choose between two or more mutually incompatible courses of action—that is, courses of action that it is impossible for him to carry out more than one of—each of these courses of action is such that he can, or is able to, or has it within his power to carry it out. (1983, 8)

Van Inwagen provides an explicit example of what this would be like. Sometimes while stealing money a thief remembers the face of his dying mother when he promised her he would lead an honest life. Just once when this happens the thief decides not to complete the crime, and "this decision was undetermined." By this van Inwagen means

there are possible worlds in which things were absolutely identical in every respect with the way they are in the actual world up to the moment at which our repentant thief made his decision—worlds in which, moreover, the laws of nature are just what they are in the actual world—and in which he takes the money. (128)

Let us now consider the libertarian's notion of dual control. Libertarians seem to be committed to the idea that free agents not only control which choices they actually make, but counterfactually *would* control alternative choices *had* they manifested their categorical ability to choose otherwise. Although one could imagine a libertarian maintaining that we would not have control over our choices had we chosen otherwise, this looks very bizarre and appears at odds with our commonsense assumption that our control is dual. This commitment to dual control is one that libertarians will welcome, given their almost unanimous conviction that deterministic, one-way control is a sham. For instance, van Inwagen objects that determinism would undermine our control of our actions in what he calls "the Consequence Argument":

> If determinism is true, then our acts are the consequences of the laws of nature and events in the remote past. But it is not up to us what went on before we were born, and neither is it up to us what the laws of nature are. Therefore, the consequences of these things (including our present acts) are not up to us. (1983, 56)

Finally, consider the libertarian notion of dual rationality, a requirement whose importance to the libertarian I did not appreciate until I read Robert Kane's *Free Will and Values*. As with dual control, the libertarian needs to claim that when agents make free choices, it would have been rational (reasonable, sensible) for them to have made a contradictory choice (e.g., chosen not A rather than A) under precisely the conditions that actually obtain. Otherwise, categorical freedom simply gives us the freedom to choose irrationally had we chosen otherwise, a less-than-entirely desirable state. Kane (1985) spends a great deal of effort in trying to show how libertarian choices can be dually rational, and I examine his efforts in Chapter 8.

Given my non-realist conclusion regarding free will, it is no surprise that I shall find neither the one-way nor two-way interpretation of these three conditions satisfactory. I think that compatibilist and incompatibilist interpretations of each condition have significant intuitive appeal, and sometimes I feel myself drawn into the compatibilist's web. But even at those times, I find that one view provides a neutralizing antidote to its opponent, as I hope to show in this book.

Having said this much about the concept of "free choice," let me explain the interconnection between the various *free* words that I shall use. *Freedom*, as I shall use it, is a nominative for the ability of exercising free choice. So, to say that S lacks freedom shall simply mean that S fails to have that ability. *Free* is the adjective that I apply severally to choices, decisions, acts, persons, and agents who enjoy freedom. *Free will* is the archaic term of art designating the 'faculty' for making choices and decisions freely.

The term *free act* has come to do double duty. The sense in which I shall most commonly use it is to denote actions that are the immediate causal results of agents' free choices. It is useful to have this term available, since we are typically held morally responsible for our acts rather than our choices. It would sound odd to say that I hold you responsible for your choice rather than your act, since if your choice had 'misfired' and produced no action, then I would not have held you responsible. Some philosophers prefer to treat free acts as primary for this reason and also because not all free actions are caused by explicit, conscious choices, and emphasis on free will seems to ignore this commonplace. The way that I defend my selection of free will as the primary subject for discussion is by allowing choices to be both conscious and unconscious. For the latter variety, choices are unobserved entities whose existence is inferred from the presence of action, although, metaphysically speaking, the choice is the cause of the action. Cognitive psychology is full of subcognitive mental events, and I see no reason why choice should not be counted as one of them.

The second sense of *free act*, which I use only in Chapter 2, stems from Harry Frankfurt's distinction between free acts, as cases where we are able to get our behavior to accord with our intentions, and free will, where we get our intentions into accord with our reflective judgments about our intentions (1971). In Frankfurt's sense of *free act*, a free act need not be caused by a free choice, since some creatures who act freely in his sense lack the capability for free choice. Finally, *free agent* is an imprecise term for a person who manifests free will a non-negligible number of times. One might unpack this by saying that S is a free agent with respect to choice C at t if and only if S has the ability to choose C freely at t, but this has the disadvantage of surrendering the dispositional nature of "free agent," which I assume is more or less the reason for using it.

Moral responsibility—At this stage it will suffice to use this term as it is generally used, that is, S is morally responsible for *a* if and only if S is an appropriate candidate if praise or blame for *a* is warranted. In Chapter 4 I discuss some of the different senses applied to "moral responsibility" by compatibilists and incompatibilists and try to find a sense that both satisfies prephilosophical intuition and can be reasonably ascribed by a compatibilist.

Determinism—The intuitive idea that I have in mind when I use this term is the thesis that all events, states of affairs, conditions, etc., of the universe (including any nonphysical parts of it, if there are any) are made necessary by preceding events, states of affairs, and so on. Using the notion of possible worlds, determinism expresses the view that at any one time there is only one physically possible future world (van Inwagen, 1983, 3). Expressing the intuitive idea by appeal to the notion of causation, determinism is the claim that for every event there is a sufficient causal condition that results in that event (Chisholm, 1976, 59).

Although the notion of determinism appears frequently through this book, the free will discussion is concerned only with a tiny subset of what might be determined, *viz.*, those events that affect human decision making. Whether there is, e.g., indeterminacy in quantum physics is an empirical matter outside of philosophers' ken and, by itself, does not bear on the free will debate, although some libertarians have argued that quantum indeterminacy *could* bear on human choices (see Chapter 8). This book is primarily about free will, though, and about determinism only incidentally.

Compatibilism—The view that the theses of free will and determinism can both be true.

Incompatibilism—The view that they cannot both be true.

Soft determinism—Technically, compatibilism plus the belief in determinism, but in fact, the view that we have free will not as a result of indeterminism, whether or not determinism is true.

Hard determinism—Technically, incompatibilism plus determinism, but in fact, the view that humans lack free will because their decisions are determined, again, whether or not determinism in its fullest generality is true.

Libertarianism—The view that humans have free will as a result of indeterminism in their choices.

Intuitions—By this term I mean reflective judgments about what we would say about a particular instance—in this book, intuitions about whether a person would manifest free will or be morally responsible in such and such circumstances. Intuitions may be prephilosophical, that is, the sort of judgment that might be expressed by first-year college students, or they may be philosophically sophisticated. I do not believe that having intuitions requires any special 'faculty' of the human mind, nor that intuitions are unequivocal. Sometimes we do not know what to say because we are pulled in opposite directions. Moreover, often two philosophers will experience conflicting intuitions, and neither will be able to sway the other, despite the ingenious use of "intuition-pumps" (Dennett's word) to attempt this. Perhaps the non-philosophical use of intuitions that is closest to mine is the practice of linguists when they ask subjects to make judgments about the grammaticality of sentences.

Since I shall frequently refer to what I claim are prephilosophical or commonsense intuitions about free will (many of which I collected unscientifically in classroom discussions in Philosophy 101), I should say something about what I take their epistemic status to be. I do not take statements of untutored judgment concerning freedom to be highly accurate to the meaning of *freedom* generally, or to "freedom" in the speaker's idiolect, or, for that matter, to what the speaker really believes. First-person reports of any sort deserve skepticism, especially when they concern such a rarified topic, where there is no clear demarcation between pristine, non-philosophically based intuitions and ones that are shaped by incipient theory and ideological bias. And I concede the general Quinean point that speakers have no privileged access to the meanings of the words they use (Stich, 1983, 77–78). But, admitting this, the fact remains that intuitions—prephilosophical and those sophisticated by theory—remain the basis against which analytical discussions such as those in this book must be tested. In this sense, intuitions are bedrock, although they are not infallible and not privileged—a sort of "bedrock by default." Theorizing may suggest which intuitions we have to give up, but if we do not start from them we will never get anywhere (Putnam, 1987, 28).

3. Overview of the Text

The text has two major sections. Part I, which includes Chapters 2 through 4, represents the positive development of the most reasonable theory of free will that I can devise. That theory is compatibilistic; my account aims to develop the "hierarchical" account of free will of Harry Frankfurt et al. in a strongly normative way and defend it from incompatibilist objections, including objections made concerning the compatibility of determinism and moral responsibility. In Chapter 2, I develop what I call an autonomy variable account of free will that is designed to save compatibilism from incompatibilist counterexamples such as those based on Martian remote-controllers, hypnotists, ingenious neurosurgeons, and so forth. My account has a strong rationality component, in effect making its demands so stringent that the hypothesized controllers would be otiose if the account were satisfied. This account is based on a belief-desire psychology that can be realized by materialistic beings, but if nonphysical minds can have intentional states, then they can satisfy this account also. Chapter 2 broaches some serious questions about a compatibilist theory of free will, especially those regarding the normative requirements placed on a free agent's cognitive states and what I view as compatibilism's probable commitment to an internalistic view of free will. These questions are not entirely resolved until Part II.

Chapter 3 defends and further refines the Chapter 2 position by addressing the connection between freedom of the will and morality. Specifically, I ask whether free agents need, to any degree, to be moral, a question whose positive answer seems at least prima facie acceptable. This is a serious problem for my autonomy variable view, since my account does not entail that free agents are moral, and, hence, stands in jeopardy of a positive answer to this question. In justifying a negative answer to the question, I argue that the increased morality of actions is actually a contingent by-product of the underlying source of free will, *viz.*, satisfaction of the cognitive requirements from Chapter 2, especially those pertaining to increased reflectiveness about one's choices.

Given the account of Chapter 2, one might wonder whether it can be extended to moral responsibility to produce a complete compatibilist picture. This is attempted in Chapter 4 where I argue that a compatibilist can (1) assign a strong *content* to ascriptions of moral responsibility, i.e., can maintain that a person is truly *blameworthy* for an act, and (2) justify the ascription of moral responsibility on non-utilitarian grounds. This defends compatibilism from criticisms based on the notion of justice. Thus, it looks as if the compatibilist account makes determinism not only compatible with free will but with a strong prephilosophical sense of moral responsibility. If this is correct, then compatibilists can claim a total victory over the incompatibilists by defending genuine moral responsibility and not a weakened version.

The compatibilist account of Part I sometimes seems so plausible to me that I am tempted to attend to it by simply looking for confirming instances and treating my nagging doubts about it as mere 'slippage,' something to be expected in any theory. But in Part II I show that my best efforts are not good enough; I argue that by asking a few pointed questions we can quickly see that the compatibilist account succeeds only if we ignore serious problems with the concept of free will. I develop this line in Chapters 5 through 7 by giving two arguments against the very idea of free will. Then I argue in Chapter 8 that even if one ignores the general criticisms of free will given in the previous three chapters, libertarianism is unable to capture anything like a plausible sense of "free will." This independent argument against incompatibilism is directed to libertarian readers who may accept my earlier arguments as criticisms of compatibilism but believe that they do not count against libertarian theories, especially those that have been very ably defended in recent years.

The arguments of Chapters 5 through 7 rely on two related themes. The first non-realist argument is that "free will" (and, by extension, "moral responsibility") are paradigm or exemplar concepts whose application is governed by conflicting paradigms. I try to show this in Chapter 5 by citing five issues in which intuition yields radically different judgments on whether individuals are free and responsible. I then try to explain why intuition diverges so radically by proposing that our beliefs about these topics are dictated by various exemplars that compete for our allegiance. On the line developed in Chapter 5, the free will concept resembles a concept like "a good baseball game," where there is no way to adjudicate between the conflicting paradigms that are typically appealed to when we make judgments about whether X is a good baseball game. The conclusion of Chapter 5 is that free will is one of those topics where philosophers have tried to organize the unorganizable through selective attention to some of our paradigms of freedom at the expense of ignoring the rest.

A second non-realist argument is given in the next two chapters. In Chapters 6 and 7, I argue that the notions of *free* will and *moral* responsibility are irretrievably value-laden, and that there can be no fact of the matter whether an agent satisfies them. In Chapter 6, I show how the debates between the compatibilists and incompatibilists depend on the premise that ascriptions of moral responsibility and free will express objective moral properties. Thus, if there are no such properties, then the whole question of the compatibility of determinism and free will (and moral responsibility) degenerates into the obvious compatibility of determinism and individuals' subjective attitudes to use free will and responsibility ascriptions (as compatibilists may) or to completely renounce their use (as hard determinists do). Indeed, given the subjective nature of freedom and responsibility ascriptions, it is easy to account for our ambivalence about whether to apply such ascriptions to determined persons. On this subjectivizing view it is therefore possible to rationally hold a person responsible *and* to completely exonerate that person of all responsibility for the same act. I devote all of Chapter 7 to arguing for moral non-realism to support the major premise of the argument begun in Chapter 6. On the line developed in Chapters 6 and 7, the claim that an agent is free or is morally responsible is assimilated to subjective attitudes, which depend upon whether one is prepared to view things from a compatibilistic or incompatibilistic perspective.

In Chapter 8 I turn away from the general criticism of the notion of free will to examine libertarianism directly. Here the question is whether any libertarian theory of free will—including the views suggested by Roderick Chisholm (1976), Peter van Inwagen (1983), Robert Kane (1985), and others—can manage to make consistent the dual interpretation of our ability to choose otherwise, to control our choices, and to choose rationally. I conclude that none of the libertarian accounts succeed because these three conditions are collectively inconsistent. If I am right about this, then the reader who has accepted the earlier criticisms of compatibilistic free will has no avenue open except the non-realist conclusion of this book.

In sum, Part II represents an attack on compatibilist and libertarian theories of freedom and responsibility. Chapters 5 through 7 provide two criticisms of any attempt to explicate free will, especially the hierarchical view of Part I. Chapter 8 gives independent grounds for rejecting libertarianism. Chapter 9 adds some final touches to the argument of Part II and examines the implications of accepting the non-realist argument of this book.

Although my position is neither compatibilistic nor incompatibilistic, there are individual arguments that should appeal to traditional theorists. Compatibilists might like Chapters 2 and 3, where I defend the hierarchical view from several familiar incompatibilist objections that many thinkers believe vitiate any compatibilist program. Chapter 4 defends a much stronger sense of moral responsibility than compatibilists usually do and may be of special interest to compatibilists for this reason. Compatibilists may also like my criticism of libertarianism in Chapter 8, particularly my debate with Robert Kane over the rationality of libertarian choices. Libertarians might like Chapter 5, where I show how compatibilism prospers by selective attention to certain prephilosophical intuitions at the expense of others, although libertarians certainly will not like the non-realist conclusion of that chapter. Readers who are sympathetic to moral non-realism may find my metaphysical argument against moral realism in Chapter 7 interesting, and I hope that even moral realists will agree with the conclusion of Chapter 6 that the viability of the free will problem logically implies moral realism. Finally, hard determinists should be sympathetic to the overall conclusion of the book, even if my way of reaching that conclusion is at odds with their incompatibilistic views.

I

Hierarchical
Compatibilism Defended

2

A Compatibilist Account
of Free Will

ABSTRACT I begin by examining the hierarchical accounts of free will provided by Frankfurt and Watson, which can be viewed as improvements of the classical compatibilist views of Hobbes, Locke, and Hume. The hierarchical views are shown to face several serious objections. I divide these into what I call *local* and *global challenges* and then show how to answer them. First, I distinguish between those challenges that a compatibilist account must meet and those illegitimate challenges that it may safely ignore. This will make the compatibilist's task somewhat more manageable. Next, I argue that the compatibilist needs to produce a hierarchical account that makes stringent demands on the cognitive capabilities of free agents. Such a view, which I call *the autonomy variable account*, is couched in terms of five factors that I call *autonomy variables*. After explicating and defending this account of free will, I show how it may be used to answer the legitimate local and global challenges. My strategy is disjunctive. In counterexamples where intuition dictates that we are not free, it turns out that one or more of the autonomy variables have not been met. But in cases where all the autonomy variables are satisfied, I argue that agents are free despite our incompatibilist intuitions to the contrary. Finally, I show how my defense of compatibilism depends upon viewing free will from an internalistic perspective and conclude by defending that perspective.

1. Two Hierarchical Accounts

Traditional compatibilism's solution to the free will question was that freedom is the ability to act as one wishes. Since acting as one wishes is clearly compatible with determinism, freedom was seen as possible within a determined universe.

Hobbes expresses that compatibilist view in a famous exchange with Bishop Bramhall:

> [H]e is free to do a thing, that may do it if he have the will to do it, and may forbear if he have the will to forbear. And yet if there be a necessity that he shall have the will to do it, the action is necessarily to follow; and if there be a necessity that he shall have the will to forbear, the forebearing also will be necessary. (Hobbes, 1841, 42)

Locke gives his notion of freedom this way:

> [S]o far as a man has a power to think or not to think, to move or not to move, according to the preference or direction of his own mind, so far is a man *free*. Wherever any performance or forbearance are not equally in a man's power, wherever doing or not doing will not equally follow upon the preference of his mind directing it, there he is not *free*, though perhaps the action may be voluntary. So that the *idea of liberty* is the *idea* of a power in any agent to do or forbear any particular action, according to the determination or thought of the mind, whereby either of them is preferred to the other; where either of them is not in the power of the agent to be produced by him according to his *volition*, there he is not at *liberty*: that agent is under *necessity*. (Locke, 1974 [1690], II, XXI, 8)

Hume also sees liberty as the ability to make one's actions match one's desires:

> [W]hat is meant by liberty when applied to voluntary actions? We cannot surely mean that actions have so little connection with motives, inclinations, and circumstances that one does not follow with a certain degree of uniformity from the other, and that one affords no inference by which we can conclude the existence of the other. For these are plain and acknowledged matters of fact. By liberty, then, we can only mean *a power of acting or not acting according to the determinations of the will*; that is, if we choose to remain at rest, we may; if we choose to move, we also may. Now this hypothetical liberty is universally allowed to belong to everyone who is not a prisoner and in chains. Here then is no subject of dispute. (Hume, 1748, VIII, Part I, 104)

The problem with accepting the Hobbes–Locke–Hume line as proof that free will is compatible with determinism lies in the fact that "freedom" and "liberty" may be applied to either actions or choices. As accounts of actions, their view is unexceptionable, since it is more or less a verbal truth that you act freely to the extent that you do as you please. It is doubtful, though, that free action in this sense implies free *choice*, since it is easy to imagine cases where one is able to act according to one's choices that are themselves unfree due to kleptomania, drug addiction, phobias, and so on. The compatibilists' assurances that action, and not the will itself, is the only logically appropriate subject of the term *free* (Hobbes, 42) seemed implausible to anyone—compatibilist and incompatibilist alike—who insisted that the free will question was, after all, a question about the will. As Roderick Chisholm puts it, following Aquinas: the real issue is not whether we bring about what we will, but whether our willing is free (Chisholm, 1976, 66).

In recent years, spurred by a seminal paper by Harry Frankfurt (1971), compatibilists have developed a more subtle account of free will than those of Hobbes, Locke, and Hume. These new accounts extrapolate from the basic compatibilist intuition that freedom is the ability to act as one desires to a more stringent requirement on the nature of the desires that control behavior. These accounts are sometimes called "hierarchical" because they (1) presuppose some principle for ranking the desires that motivate choices, and (2) claim that behavioral control by the higher ranking desires constitutes free will. I shall use the well-known hierarchical accounts of Frankfurt and Gary Watson (1975) as a springboard for giving the best hierarchical account that I can manage, but other hierarchical accounts are extremely appealing and deserve serious examination in their own right.[1]

Frankfurt draws an analogy between free *action* and free *will*: Just as acting freely is being able to act as one wants, having free will is being able to have the will one wants (1971, 75). Thus, only creatures capable of having wants concerning their wills are capable of free will. Nonhuman animals act freely when they are unrestrained, yet they do not have free will because their wills are not subject to their higher level control. "Wantons" include nonhuman animals and humans who, for whatever reason, take no position regarding the desirability of their desires (1971, 71). In contrast, free persons manifest free will by dictating what their wills shall be, whereas unfree persons are unable to bring their wills into line with their "second-order volitions" concerning them:

> . . . [T]he statement that a person enjoys freedom of the will means
> . . . that he is free to will what he wants to will, or to have the will he
> wants. . . . [I]n securing the conformity of his will to his second-order
> volitions . . . a person exercises freedom of the will. (1971, 75)

According to Frankfurt, a necessary condition of being free is
caring about the nature of one's lower order states:

> The wanton addict cannot or does not care which of his conflicting
> first-order desires wins out. His lack of concern . . . is due either to
> his lack of the capacity for reflection or to his mindless indifference
> to the enterprise of evaluating his own desires and motives. (1971, 73)

Thus, for Frankfurt, the hierarchical desires that produce freedom
of the will are those higher level ones that dictate which lower level
desires will be satisfied.

Watson, for reasons we shall discuss shortly, replaces Frankfurt's
hierarchy of levels with what might be called a hierarchy of valua-
tion. Watson's 'hierarchy' is actually horizontal, since he wishes to
explicate free *action* rather than free *will*, and his account involves
distinguishing between those acts one desires without valuing and
those one values. Rather than appealing to a higher level reflection
on a lower level mental state to produce free will, Watson requires
that one's actions conform to one's overall value scheme. Thus,
agents are free when they bring their actions into line with their
valuational system or reflective conception of the good:

> The *valuational system* of an agent is that set of considerations
> which, when combined with his factual beliefs (and probability esti-
> mates), yields judgments of the form: the thing for me to do in these
> circumstances, all things considered, is *a*. To ascribe free agency to a
> being presupposes it to be a being that makes judgments of this sort.
> (1975, 91)

Frankfurt and Watson are thus able to show that the familiar
counterexamples (kleptomania, drug addiction, and so on) do not
count as instances of freedom on their accounts. For Frankfurt, the
unwilling addict, e.g., is unfree despite the correspondence between
taking drugs and the desire for them, provided the addict has a
second-order desire that disapproves of the first-order desire but is

inefficacious in preventing satisfaction of the lower order desire. Watson's way out of the addiction counterexample would be similar: the drug user who *values* the consumption of drugs is free, whereas the user who simply desires drugs without valuing them (which includes positively rejecting them) is unfree. So, both the solutions of Frankfort and Watson enable the compatibilist to reject problematic counterexamples without departing from the deterministic context.

2. Problems for the Accounts of Frankfurt and Watson

Although the hierarchical accounts mark an important improvement over the traditional accounts, one might naturally wonder whether the same *sort* of criticisms that counted against the latter can be adapted to those of Frankfurt and Watson. The counterexamples may have to be more subtle than those of kleptomania and addiction (which the latter accounts handle admirably), but if we are ingenious enough, perhaps we can devise thought-experiments that do the trick.

Many critics have tried. Most of the philosophical counterexamples involve thought-experiments in which the hierarchical accounts are satisfied in a case where an agent remains unfree due to control by some other agent. Such examples can be usefully divided into two types. *Global challenges* are typically philosophers' thought-experiments where controllers are hypothesized to dictate all of the subject's choices. (Daniel Dennett calls such cases as the Nefarious Neurosurgeon, the Cosmic Child Whose Dolls We Are, and the Peremptory Puppeteer "incompatibilist bugbears."—1984, 7–10) The second type, which I call *local challenges*, runs the gamut from fanciful thought-experiments to real-world cases of manipulation and even non-manipulative cognitive failure. In local challenges there is something untoward about some, but not all, of our choices. Thus, local challenges range from the Brave New World sleep-teaching of the value that "a gramme is better than a damn" (Huxley, 1932), to subliminal advertising's production in me of the desire to eat popcorn at the movie theater, to some examples from recent social psychology where we seem to be victimizing our own decision-processes with motivated cognitive failure.

Here are some examples of global challenges. Robert Kane imagines the existence of an omnipotent, omniscient "covert non-constraining controller" who makes a totally controlled agent "a means and not an end in himself because he does not ultimately determine his own purposes or ends" (1985, 34). Peter van Inwagen considers the case of Martian remote control of volition-determination devices in our brains (1983, 109). Richard Taylor hypothesizes an "ingenious physiologist" who induces volitions in us by pushing buttons (1974, 50).

Examples of local challenges include Michael Slote's counterexample involving hypnotism:

> Robert, who is genuinely undecided between two conflicting first-order desires X and Y, is visited by a hypnotist who decides to "solve" his problem by putting him in a trance and inducing in him a second-order volition in favor of X; as a result of having this second-order volition, Robert then acts to satisfy X, never suspecting that his decisiveness has been induced by the hypnotist. The example . . . seems adequate . . . to point up the conceptual insufficiency of "rationality" conditions of free action. For we would all surely deny that Robert acts of his own free will. (1980, 137)

I take Slote's argument to be this: (i) The hypnotist makes Robert unfree, despite the fact that Robert satisfies any plausible hierarchical account of free will. (ii) But, having accepted (i), we see that the hypnotist can be detached in the example so that we have the same freedom-defeating conditions produced by impersonal determinism instead of a hypnotist. (iii) Hence, there are situations where the satisfaction of hierarchical accounts will not produce free will in the face of determinism per se. (iv) Hence, the satisfaction of hierarchical accounts does not ensure free will.

But local challenges need not be limited to fanciful hypotheses like those of Slote and Huxley. Questions arise over real-world cases where our beliefs and desires have problematic origins, whether as the result of manipulation or not. Imagine, for instance, that choices are made on the basis of desires that are uncritically imbibed from the environment, e.g., desires to live in a certain way that are created by advertisers who play upon our susceptibility to favorable schemas and *personae* (Nisbett and Ross, 1980, 36–41).

Or consider the desire to lead lives that *reduce* the demands on us to make decisions, the so-called desire to submit or escape from freedom (Fromm, 1941). And what if choices are made on the basis of beliefs that are motivationally suspect? For instance, suppose I decide to continue to submit to "insufficiently justified" laboratory shocks because I believe that the shocks are not so painful, and *that* belief results from the fact that admitting that the shocks are painful would create the dissonant thought that I am a fool for allowing the experimenters to give me painful shocks for insufficient rewards (Nisbett and Wilson, 1977, 233–234). Or, to consider Watson's evaluational view, suppose my values are uncritically gotten from religion, the media, or pop culture?[2] Finally, local challenges abound to the extent that the Freudian theory is correct. It seems that all these examples—both the philosophical thought-experiments and the psychological cases—create doubt that Frankfurt's and Watson's accounts capture all that we require of free will, inasmuch as free choice must meet normative standards. Choices, so we think, must be 'good enough' to qualify as free.

There is another way that this difficulty with the accounts of Frankfurt and Watson can be expressed. This difficulty, recognized by both thinkers (we may call it the *identification problem*) is this: How can a hierarchical account explicate what it is for a higher order volition to be truly *mine* in such a way as to make the resulting act one that *I* perform freely? What is to distinguish my decisions from decisions that happen 'in me'? Watson raised this objection by pointing out that one could satisfy Frankfurt's account even if one were wanton regarding all of one's higher order volitions (1975, 93). Watson continues:

> Since second-order volitions are themselves simply desires, to add them to the context of conflict is just to increase the number of contenders; it is not to give a special place to any of those in contention. (94)

Frankfurt allows the possibility that his account could be satisfied by someone with wanton second-order volitions:

> [A] person may be capricious and irresponsible in forming his second-order volitions and give no serious consideration to what is at

stake. . . . There is no essential restriction on the kind of basis, if any, upon which (second-order volitions) are formed. (1971, 73)

In a more recent paper Frankfurt agrees that the possibility of wanton second-order desires creates the problem of how to specify which decisions really belong to the person:

> It appears that the hierarchical model cannot as such cope with this difficulty. It merely enables us to describe an inner conflict as being between desires of different orders. But this alone is hardly adequate to determine . . . where (if anywhere) the person himself stands. (1987, 35)

Frankfurt tries to solve this problem by developing his original answer that a free agent's second-order volitions are truly reflective of who that agent is when the agent "decisively identifies" with a first-order volition (1971, 76). For Frankfurt, this decisive identification entails refusing to entertain further challenges to the volition. Such decisive identification "eliminates the conflict *within the person* to which . . . desires he prefers to be his motive" (1987, 40), thereby integrating the person, ensuring an active rather than passive stance toward one's volitions, and guaranteeing autonomy. Frankfurt thus appears to admit that although a free agent *might* be a wanton regarding second-order desires, one need not be: When agents decisively identify with their volitions they have accepted responsibility for their choices and *are* responsible for them.

My objection to Frankfurt's way of addressing the identification problem is that it at best provides only a subjective criterion for determining when choices 'belong' to agents. And it may not even do that. Frankfurtian decisive identification may be sufficient for establishing that choices are *psychologically* free, that is, that agents *feel* free in making them. But decisive identification seems to go no distance toward establishing that agents are really or *normatively* free, since one can easily imagine such decisiveness exemplified by grossly irrational, unfree agents. Psychological freedom, whether explicated in terms of Frankfurtian decisiveness or Watsonian value-conformity, does not imply genuine free will any more than believing x implies knowing x. The serious problem for hierarchical accounts raised by the possibility of non-reflective second-order volitions is not: How shall we ascertain which volitions psychologically reflect who the agent really is? Rather, the problem is that the mere satisfaction of a hierarchy, whether vertical or horizontal, goes no way toward establishing the rationality of the choices. This is a general logical point: If we want our account to require satisfaction of normative criteria of rationality, then we must explicitly build those requirements into the account. A hierarchy of purely psychological conditions will not suffice.

Here is why I believe that hierarchical accounts must require a strong rationality component. For Frankfurt's account, suppose I decisively identify with my first-order desire for drugs or my desire to sacrifice my life if my religious leader asks me to. If I do so in a completely non-reflective way, it is difficult to see how I have more freedom than a wanton, despite the fact that according to Frankfurt's psychological account these decisions are clearly mine. To consider Watson's account, suppose that both of these decisions accord with my valuational system. We might even embellish the case by imagining these desires had been produced in a Brave New World scenario via sleep-teaching, and that I could even recite prepackaged justifications for them that agree with my value system. Nonetheless, if I lack the fallibilistic, Mill-like attitude of self-criticism toward my decisions, then I seem *normatively*, that is, *actually*, unfree despite my psychological integration (Lindley, 1986, 44–48). To the extent that hierarchical accounts do not require this sort of self-critical attitude, they appear vulnerable to counterexamples not only due to esoteric philosophical thought-experiments but to any examples in the real world that approximate Huxley's dystopia in psychologically relevant ways, e.g., brainwashing, subliminal advertising, use of mood-altering chemicals, etc. Let us call this species of local challenge to the hierarchical accounts *rationality based challenges*.

3. The First Line of Reply: Let's Distinguish between Intrusive and Non-Intrusive Controllers

Among the three types of objections to hierarchical accounts so far considered—global, local, and, a subset of the latter, the rationality-based challenges—the global challenges are the easiest to handle, despite their considerable rhetorical impact. How, it might be wondered, can we be free if our every belief, desire, and choice were traceable to the machinations of a diabolical controller! In this section, I begin to address that worry by distinguishing between the sort of controllers who would be a threat to our *freedom* (these are easily imagined) and those who would be a threat to a compatibilist *account of freedom* (these are not so easily imagined).

The global challenges gain an unwarranted dialectical advantage, I believe, because incompatibilists advance them without regard to the following distinction. First, consider global controllers who are completely 'remote' from agents in the sense that, although they stand at the causal origin of agents' choices, they never interfere with the law-like interaction of agent and environment. Such 'puppeteers' set the show in motion, but never pull any individual strings. (In a theological context, they would be gods who never interfere with their creations.) The choices of agents under the reign of such remote-controllers would be in the same boat with the choices of determined agents in a world where there are no controllers. Let us call such controllers *non-interveners* or *non-intrusive controllers*. Now, contrast to these non-interveners a second category of controllers, *viz.*, those who sometimes interfere with the law-like interaction of agents and their environments. I call these *interveners* or *intrusive controllers*. The difference between the non-interveners and the interveners is that the 'handiwork' of the former results in a deterministic world, whereas the result of the latter is momentary lapses from determinism.[3]

Using this distinction, I want to argue that it is only the intrusive controllers who clearly make us unfree; it is not clear that non-intrusive controllers do. Hence, the failure to distinguish between the two unfairly tars the non-intrusive controllers with the same brush that is correctly applied to intrusive controllers.

To see this, consider the following dilemma. A hypothesized global controller either actively intervenes in the life of its subject or it never intervenes. If the latter, then the controller is no more a threat to the subject's freedom than is determinism per se, and the force of the controller hypothesis is shown to be merely rhetorical. The hierarchical account will have to be evaluated on its own merits, and the fact that there is an agent standing as the remote cause of the agent's choices does not impugn the account. On the other hand, suppose that the global controller sometimes produces in the agent mental states that are not nomological consequences of the interaction between the agent and its environment. That is, suppose that the controller is intrusive. In this case, the threat to the subject's freedom is greater than the threat from the non-intrusive controller (i.e., the "controller-*qua*-determinism"), and it is unreasonable to view the subject's subsequent loss of freedom as a criticism of the hierarchical account. This is so because the compatibilist can plausibly attribute the loss of freedom to the *intervention*. After all, the compatibilist wishes to show that free will is compatible with agents' deterministic decision making; the aim is *not* to show that free will is compatible with being manipulated by an intervener who falsifies the supposition of determinism.

Hence, it is reasonable to demand that the hierarchical accounts work only in the normal cases, i.e., determinism, including nonintrusive global control. To the extent that the hypothesized global controllers are intrusive, the compatibilist may correctly rule them out by fiat. We might, thus, add to hierarchical accounts the proviso that there is no *intrusive* global controller who interferes with our choices.

4. The Second Line of Reply: The Autonomy Variable Strategy

Having handled the problem posed by intrusive global controllers, we still need to defend hierarchical accounts against non-intrusive global controllers. We also need to meet the local challenges, including the rationality based challenges. Here is how I believe that the hierarchical theorist should try to deal with these objections. The hierarchical thinker can address all of them by building a strong cognitive requirement into the account. I call the version I shall develop the *autonomy variable account*. This account will reply to the local challenges by explaining why the examples that illustrate a lack of freedom count as unfree by citing which autonomy variable has been violated. It will not be an easy task to formulate the autonomy account so that it eliminates all and only the challenges that intuition takes to be unfree. There may be some slippage, but to the extent that we succeed, we will have accomplished something worthwhile. In a similar fashion, in order to meet the rationality based challenges, the account will try to demand enough critical reflection to rule out the unfree counterexamples, without making its demands so great that it picks out some rarified subclass of free choices (e.g., "highly intellectualized free choices").

This leaves last, but certainly not least, the objection that is most important to the incompatibilists, *viz.*, the non-intrusive global challenges, which are equivalent to the problem posed by determinism per se. My approach will address this worry by showing that if an agent satisfies the account, then that person is free irrespective of whether determinism is true or even whether our decisions trace back to a Kanian covert non-constraining controller. It is now time to provide the autonomy account.

5. Five Autonomy Variables

In this section I describe and justify five autonomy variables for my account in order to show how a hierarchical account can capture the normative aspect of free will. As a first approximation, let us understand the variables as follows: *Self-knowledge* includes the knowledge (true belief) of what one's mental states are. *Reasonability* is the motivation to critically evaluate one's beliefs, desires, and choices; it is the desire to be both a good epistemic agent and a reflective person.[4] *Intelligence* is skill at gaining, retaining, and using knowledge, both about oneself and about the world. *Efficacy* is the power to control our mental states (including our choices). And *unity* implies that there is a single agent underlying free choices (as opposed to the possibilities that there are no agents, or multiple agents, or multiple recalcitrant cognitive subsystems).

The picture of freedom that emerges from these five variables is as follows: A self finds itself at a time T with a certain battery of mental states (beliefs, memories, desires, fears, goals, values, and so on). Free will consists in a rationally controlled transition to a condition at T+1 that contains a choice. Self-knowledge allows the self to have an accurate representation of its states at T. Reasonability is the motivation to submit those states to objective evaluation, and intelligence provides the likelihood that the evaluation is accurate. One manifests efficacy if one is literally able to perform the evaluation and bring the choice into accord with one's reasonable and intelligent efforts. And unity has been presupposed, since the account assumes that a single self was responsible for bringing about the transition.

A fair question to ask regarding the autonomy variables is: How much satisfaction of each am I claiming is required for free will? I believe that minimal satisfaction of each condition is necessary for free will. But beyond this threshold, I think that trade-offs are possible in that a greater satisfaction of one variable might compensate for a lesser satisfaction of another. The reason for this degree of imprecision is that since "free will" does not denote a discrete entity but simply decisions that meet a normative standard of freedom, more precise specifications cannot be given. One should expect a certain number of borderline cases within the individual variables and for freedom overall. If Stephen Stich is right about the failure of 2500 years of analytic philosophy to reductively define *any* philosophically interesting concepts (1983, 77), then this result is a virtue of my account. After all, not all choices need to satisfy our rationality requirements as fully as others need to: some free choices can be made without conscious reflection upon alternatives at all, whereas others demand substantial criticial wherewithal. For instance, I can freely choose one pencil instead of another to begin writing without any deliberation at all and may even be prepared to defend my "liberty of indifference" as constitutive of my freedom in this case. Yet if my choice of a vocation is equally mindless, then my freedom is almost certainly at risk.

(i) Self-knowledge

Self-knowledge, understood as true belief about one's commonsense psychological states, is a standard desideratum in hierarchical accounts, since the evaluation of desires and intended actions presupposes that we know what they are. Dennett nicely captures the flavor of this presupposition:

> Among the questions facing a sophisticated self-controlling agent are: Could I revise my basic projects and goals in such a way as to

improve my chances of satisfaction? Are there grand strategies or
policies that are better than my current ones? Is there a style of
operation that would suit my goals better than my current style? . . .

In order to engage in this process of meta-level reasoning, the
aspirant to a high order of self-control must have the capacity to
represent his current beliefs, desires, intentions, and policies in a
detached way, as objects for evaluation. (1984, 86)

Self-knowledge is intimately bound up with reasonability, intelligence, and efficacy, given the cognitivist thrust of the autonomy
variable sketch. This demonstrates how ignorance, or, more interestingly, self-deception provides a problem for free will. On the
autonomy sketch it is crucial that one's reasoning process be part of
the causal mechanism that drives behavior. Suppose that you are
about to make a deliberate choice to do A because you wish to do
A, and you think that you have this wish because it is supported by
considerations B and C. Suppose further that, as the reasonability
variable requires, you go on to evaluate B and C. It is important
that B and C are in fact causally responsible for that wish. If the
cause of your wish to do A is actually an entirely unrelated factor Z,
then considering B and C will be merely an intellectual exercise, a
gear not attached to anything. Thus, as long as Z's role is out of
your awareness, you do not satisfy the account's requirements for
free will, since you lack rational control over your decision to do A.

Michael Levin raises the interesting question of whether gaining
knowledge in general (and we may narrow that down to self-
knowledge here) increases one's freedom. For instance, when I learn
that I have a dime in my pocket, do I gain a freedom to spend the
dime that I lacked before I gained that knowledge (1979, 242)?
Levin argues that the compatibilist should say that I have not
gained freedom. Rather, Levin suggests, we should say that I had
the freedom to spend the dime even when I did not know about it;
what I gain upon learning that I have a dime is an increased *horizon*
of causally possible choices. For Levin, our range of freedom out-
strips the range of physically possible choices available to us.

I think that we should reject this conclusion for the autonomy
account since it has some bizarre consequences. As Levin notes, on
this view we have to conclude that we decide freely while under
neurotic delusions whenever it is true that if we had been apprised

of our delusions we would have decided freely (242). Moreover, it looks as if we could never exonerate persons of blame for decisions on the grounds that ignorance destroyed their free will, but sometimes we wish to do this. The most problematic aspect of Levin's claim is its diminution of the importance of knowledge among the necessary conditions for freedom. One wonders why self-knowledge is less important than reasonability, efficacy, or for that matter, having the requisite brain cells to make the decision. Suppose that neurotics are free to choose X simply on the strength of the counterfactual that if they wanted to choose X (which is in fact physically impossible owing to their ignorance), then they would. Then by parity of reasoning, persons lacking the necessary neurons to choose X are also free, provided they would choose X had they possessed those neurons.

Although I reject Levin's reduction in the importance of knowledge (and self-knowledge) to freedom, I gladly accept his claim that increased self-knowledge often enlarges the range of choices that one can make. Freedom conceived positively as the opportunity to pick among many options seems a function of the increased span of all the autonomy variables, and self-knowledge seems no exception.

(ii) Reasonability

The second autonomy variable, *reasonability*, marks the motivation of someone who satisfies the historical philosophical model of rationality. This motivation, adeptly chronicled in Nathanson (1985), is the desire for objective knowledge irrespective of the consequences in terms of pleasure and pain. Exemplars include Socrates, Goethe's Faust, Mill, with his famous dictum that it is better to be a Socrates dissatisfied than a pig satisfied, and Russell, who offered indignant criticism of William James's freewheeling theory of belief.

The knowledge desired by someone who satisfies the reasonability variable includes self-knowledge as well as knowledge about the world. Thus, reasonability includes the desire to take a critical stance toward one's mental states. The degree of one's reasonability is a function both of the range of one's states that one is prepared to submit to scrutiny and one's depth of self-evaluation. (*Prepared to submit* allows us to avoid the charge of infinite regress.) Concerning beliefs, the reasonable person's desire to ascertain truth has greater efficacy than less high-minded motivations in belief formation, e.g., the desire to confirm one's existing beliefs (Nisbett and Ross, 1980, Chapter 8) or the desire to reduce cognitive dissonance (Brehm and Cohen, 1962). In desiring objectivity one recognizes that "our knowledge is often limited . . . by personal inclinations as well as by contingent facts about our perceptual capacities" which need be overcome "to arrive at a true picture of . . . reality" (Nathanson, 1985, 47). The reasonable person wishes to evaluate evidence for and against preexisting beliefs impartially. Reasonability seeks fairness in evaluating evidence that conflicts with one's beliefs: the person whose behavior is motivated by reasonability can be "reasoned with" and won't appeal to the "informal fallacies," e.g., argumentation *ad hominem, ad baculum*, and appeal to authority, which reveal a lack of respect for reason. The same traits involved in taking a reasonable stance toward one's beliefs also apply to desires, fears, and other affective states, since these are also subject to evaluation. The reasonable person is a counterexample to Swift's saw that "[n]o man will take counsel, but every man will take money: therefore money is better than counsel."

Including the reasonability variable in the autonomy account reveals the normative intuition that within limits (see Frankfurt, 1971, 76, on the danger that excessive reflection may destroy the will by producing a Hamlet-like syndrome), people are *better* the more they are motivated by reasonability. This theme is present in Sartre's claim that persons who accept what sort of persons they have to be stand in "bad faith" (Sartre, 1956, 63–67). It is echoed in Charles Taylor's view that "radical questioning" of oneself marks one of the most basic characteristics of human beings, and that "[w]e consider people deep to the extent, *inter alia*, that they are capable of this kind of radical self-reflection" (Taylor, 1976, 126).

I have already given support for including reasonability in the autonomy account when I claimed that I am unfree in the case where I uncritically accept my programmed desires for drugs and self-sacrifice. Other cases of psychological manipulation also support the reasonability variable. The idea is that without reasonability to motivate us, we will not initiate the critical process required to be evaluators and controllers of our desires, rather than receptacles through which the desires operate. The importance of this process is emphasized by Lindley:

> The person who fails to consider properly alternative opinions to his own is either led by authority, in which case the principles to which he appeals for guidance in choosing a way of life, are *external* to him, or they are simply principles given by inclination—those he just feels attracted to—for no reason. In either case, although there may be no errors of reasoning, there is a lack of self-determination. (1986, 51)

(iii) Intelligence

Even if we could know what our mental states are (self-knowledge) and we desired to evaluate them as fairly as possible (reasonability), our rational control over them would extend no further than our third autonomy variable, *intelligence*, permits. One needs the intellectual ability to carry out reasonability's good intentions, just as it is a good thing for Superman to be strong. By *intelligence* I mean the ability to learn facts about the world, retain that information, and draw inferences from it. I also include the ability (rather than the desire) to reason well about ourselves and our mental states.

The degree of intelligence required for free will is not exactly specifiable. It seems pretty uncontroversial that, *ceteris paribus*, the greater one's ability to learn about the world by perceptual and inferential means, the better one can rationally control oneself. Conversely, a very stupid entity will lack plasticity of behavior, in Dennett's terms, will be "sphexish." And, as a limiting case, it seems clear that a *free* agent must have at least some ability to draw inferences, on pain of not being an *agent* at all (Cherniak, 1986, 10–11). On the other side, there is a danger of making this demand too stringent.

Although the question of the exact amount of intelligence required for free will is a thorny problem for me, I think that it is a problem for any hierarchical theorist, whether it is explicitly recognized or not. This is because intelligence is already presupposed by the standard accounts. For instance, Dennett argues that reflectiveness will increase self-knowledge, but only if the reflective person has the intellectual skill to bring this about.

Why are we inclined to think, then, that further levels of reflection, further bouts of self-evaluation *tend* to lead to improvements in the "character" of the agent? Suppose there are two agents, *A* and *B*, born to similar circumstances and with similar endowments, except that agent *A* engages in considerably more self-reflection and subsequent self-choosing than agent *B*. Is there any reason to suppose that *A* will tend to be a "better" agent? There is, it seems, if *A* and *B* are both members of the class of learners, that is, beings designed to have a propensity for gathering truths. For then their bouts of self-evaluation will *tend* to create self-knowledge, and how could more self-knowledge fail to be better than less? (1984, 87)

Frankfurt's account also presupposes intelligence. To see this, suppose that one's Frankfurtian second-order volitions are the products of really stupid inferences. Suppose, for example, that I have a first-order desire to smoke a cigarette. I reflect on the acceptability of that desire, remember my belief that cigarette smoking causes lung cancer, and remind myself of my desire to avoid lung cancer. Running all these premises through my (defective) practical reasoning generator, I arrive at the conclusion that I approve of my first-order desire to smoke, and choose accordingly. In such a case it seems clear that the mere fact that I have second-order volitions is simply impotent with respect to rational self-control: I am no better off than I would be if I lacked them altogether. The same conclusion can be drawn regarding Watson's demand that one bring one's decisions into consistent accord with one's valuational system. Thus, it looks like intelligence must be reckoned as one of the autonomy variables, despite its imprecision.

(iv) Efficacy

Even if agents satisfy the first three variables, they will be unfree unless they satisfy the control variable, *efficacy*. Efficacy is the power to actually make self-knowledgeable, reasonable, and intelligent choices. This requires, as Frankfurt and Watson have shown, not the ability to 'turn off' our fears and desires, but the ability to choose contrary to them. This entails the ability to resist non-rational factors in our choices, such as threats and bribes from the external world, as well as non-rational motivations from within the cranium. Conscious emotions are a historical favorite, but also important are unconscious motivations such as the desire to reduce the cognitive dissonance that results from recognizing unhappy facts about oneself, the desire to conform to the views of those around us, and our bias for defending preexisting theories in the face of contrary evidence.

Efficacy is a traditional assumption of compatibilism. Locke expresses the view that freedom requires the power to resist our desires this way:

> For, the mind having in most cases, as is evident in experience, a power to *suspend* the execution and satisfaction of any of its desires; and so all, one after another; is at liberty to consider the objects of them, examine them on all sides, and weigh them with others. . . . This seems to me the source of all liberty; in this seems to consist that which is (as I think improperly) called *free-will*. For, during this suspension of any desire . . . we have opportunity to examine, view, and judge of the good or evil of what we are going to do. . . . (Locke, [1690] 1974, II, XXI, 47)

Clearly, the accounts of Frankfurt and Watson presuppose efficacy. Dennett insightfully sees a lack of efficacy as a species of fatalism (understood as impotence of the will):

> Here is an instance of yet another variety of local fatalism: the man who is madly and helplessly in love, but who sets out, with paper and pencil, to make a list of his beloved's shortcomings—as an aid to helping him decide whether or not to propose marriage to her. . . . We know this fellow is just going through the motions; we already know the outcome of his pathetic effort at deliberation. This is not because the outcome is determined, but because of the way it is determined: a simple, informationally insensitive way, . . . [T]here is a compensating mechanism at work that will convert any supposed blemish into a virtue: she's not stupid, she's down-to-earth; she's not selfish, she's spirited. . . . Our lover will arrive at a positive verdict no matter what evidence is placed before him. (1984, 105)

Dennett's example raises the interesting question of whether our account should require efficacy over not simply our choices but over the beliefs that go into them. I think that intelligence does presuppose this sort of efficacy to some extent in order for us to meet minimal standards of competence in our reflections concerning our choices. That is, successful reflection seems to require not only the intellectual wherewithal to distinguish between warranted and unwarranted inferences, but the efficacy to suspend, alter, and dismiss belief under appropriate epistemic circumstances. Otherwise, intelligence and the other variables will not do us much good. To see this, consider the earlier case where I evaluate my first-order desire to smoke cigarettes by reflecting on my belief that smoking causes lung cancer and my desire to avoid lung cancer. Suppose that I correctly infer that I have a prima facie reason to disapprove of my first-order desire. But suppose also that I cannot bring myself to accept that conclusion because I have a preexisting belief that all of the first-order desires that I have that day are good ideas, irrespective of the conclusion I reach about them by reflection. For my intelligent inference to help make me free in this instance, it seems I must not be a victim to belief-perseverance here, and, thus, efficacy must extend to beliefs, too, at least in some cases.

(v) Unity

The final autonomy variable, *unity*, represents the commonsensical assumption that for each human body there is a single agent who is the subject of all the mental states associated with that body. In terms of our account, unity is the requirement that the other four variables apply to the same agent.

To clarify this assumption we might consider what it excludes. Challenges may fall anywhere on a continuum between an extreme and a mild form: (i) there are multiple agents within the cranium, and (ii) although there is only one agent, the agent's cognitive subsystems are largely out of the agent's control. Some challenges to unity come from the brain-bisection discussion. For instance, Roland Puccetti (1981) suggests that normal, non-commissurotomized human beings contain two conscious persons, one associated with each cerebral hemisphere, each with different areas of control. Thomas Nagel (1971) argues that brain bisection experiments show that the entire notion of countable persons should be rejected for the notion of the brain as a depersonalized center of mental activity. A less dramatic challenge to the unity assumption comes from

Stich's interpretation of studies in attribution theory and dissonance reduction (1983, 230–242). Stich argues in favor of what might be called the two-sets-of-books theory of quasi-belief. On this view each of us possesses two distinct belief-like subsystems that often disagree: The verbal-belief system governs our conscious thought and speech, whereas the non-verbal system governs our nonverbal behavior. A still less radical, but problematic, view for free will would be the view that many of our cognitive subsystems are "modular" and immune to our higher cognitive control (Fodor, 1983).

My reason for including unity as an autonomy variable is that, without unity, a committee of homunculi or subsystems each satisfying a different autonomy variable would be possible. Now, such a committee could be either anarchist or harmonious. If the former, then unfree choices would be likely, since the efficacious homunculus might disregard the desires of the reasonable homunculus or the beliefs of the intelligent homunculus. But even if the homunculi, or, less fancifully, the separate subsystems that are not ascribable to a single agent, interacted in a harmonious way, free choices would not result. This is because the prephilosophical notion of *free choice* that compatibilists seek to explicate requires that *agents* make free choices; it does not allow that choices 'emerge' from underlying non-personal sources. This view is supported by the intuition that "responsibility" and "moral responsibility" require a unified agent as their subject.

Unity seems to me to be an uncontroversial variable, since it has already been presupposed by hierarchical theorists. Watson mentions the possible danger that results from a lack of decisiveness:

> [I]t does not follow from the fact that one must assume some standpoint that one must have only one, nor that one's standpoint is completely determinate. There may be ultimate conflicts, irresolvable tensions, and things about which one simply does not know what to . . . say. . . . [T]hese possibilities point to problems about the unity of the person. . . . [W]hen the split is severe enough, to have more than one standpoint is to have none. (1975, 92)

Frankfurt also emphasizes the challenges to unity that are possible on his account.

If there is an unresolved conflict among someone's second-order desires, then he is in danger of having no second-order volition. . . . This condition, if it is so severe that it prevents him from identifying himself in a sufficiently decisive way with *any* of his conflicting first-order desires, destroys him as a person. . . . [H]e becomes, like the unwilling addict . . . , a helpless bystander to the forces that move him. (1971, 75–76)

6. The Autonomy Variable Account

Having elaborated and justified the five variables individually, the resulting account of free will looks like this:

S's choice *c* is free just in case:

  1. S knows the nature of S's beliefs, desires and other mental states that bring about *c* (self-knowledge).
  2. S desires to perform a critical and nondogmatic evaluation of *c* and the mental states that bring about *c* in cases where such evaluation is appropriate (reasonability).
  3. To the extent that reasoning is appropriate, S's reasoning concerning *c* and those other states meets normative standards of intellectual skill (intelligence).
  4. S possesses the power, at each step in the decision-making process, to produce subsequent deliberations in accordance with 1, 2, and 3 (efficacy).
  5. There is a single agent to whom variables (1) through (4) apply (unity).

Now that we have the full account in front of us, we can consider one of the most important aspects of this view of free will, *viz.*, the efficacy of the reasoning process. Although the autonomy account does not require that a free agent go through explicit ratiocination in all or even most cases, in those cases where such a process is undergone the choice must be a causal product of the reasoning process. Post facto justifications of choices are insufficient for free will. So, e.g., if your choice is literally indeterministic with respect to the totality of your physical and psychological states at the instant of choice (van Inwagen, 1983, 140–141), then the fact that you are clever enough to confabulate reasons why you chose as you did cuts no ice with respect to the autonomy variables. Your reasoning, on this variety of libertarianism, did not control your choice, and you have violated the efficacy variable.

The autonomy account shows how the issue of fatalism arises as an empirical threat to free will: failure among any of the five autonomy variables raises the possibility that one's choices are not under one's reasoned control. Thus, our autonomy view takes what Dennett calls "local fatalism" seriously; fatalism is not viewed as a hypothesis about the complete loss of control of our lives (Goldman, 1968), but as a clear and ever-present danger. If the decisions involved in our attempt at self-control are as liable to fail to meet the autonomy variables as some of the recent social psychological literature suggests, then cognitive shortcomings often preclude our having free will.

7. How the Autonomy Account Handles the Local and Global Challenges

As previewed earlier in this chapter, my strategy is disjunctive. I argue that legitimate local challenges are cases where one or more of the autonomy variables is violated. Similarly, I argue that the rationality-based local challenges can be eliminated by the strong normative component built into the account. Finally, the global challenges of determinism and non-intervening controllers are addressed by the reply that the stringency of the autonomy account makes determinism irrelevant to the free will of anyone who satisfies it.

Let us begin with the local challenges, first considering cases where we are manipulated by others. Consider Slote's case of the hypnotist who produces in Robert a second-order volition that produces a choice. To address this counterexample, we must answer two questions: (i) Does Robert satisfy the five autonomy variables in making his choice? and (ii) Is Robert's choice the one that he would have made without the hypnotist's intervention?

Because I take Slote's example to be intended as a general criticism of hierarchical accounts, I shall assume an affirmative answer to (i). Otherwise, the case is not really a counterexample, since the compatibilist can maintain that the reason that Robert is unfree is that he fails to satisfy the hierarchical account. But an affirmative answer to (i) strongly suggests an affirmative answer to (ii). Suppose that Robert's choice satisfies the autonomy variable account. Then even the "induced" second-order volition would be subject to Robert's reasoned control. Now, since Slote's counterexample is designed to show that the satisfaction of compatibilist conditions does not guarantee free will, it seems that Slote should not dispute the important compatibilist thesis (defended at length in Chapter 8) that in rational decision making there is no libertarian "liberty of indifference." That is, I assume that all choices that equally satisfy the autonomy variable account, given the same psychological conditions, will be qualitatively identical. Thus Robert's choice would have to be the same whether the hypnotist interfered or not, given that Robert satisfied the autonomy account. But if the choice would have been the same irrespective of the hypnotist's role, then the case is one of overdetermination, and the compatibilist can safely view Robert as free, despite the hypnotist's role.

There is an analogy between the case of Slote's hypnotist and the earlier discussed distinction between intrusive and non-intrusive global controllers. With the latter, it was important to distinguish between controllers who falsify and those who do not falsify the deterministic hypothesis. With a Slotian hypnotist, it is crucial to distinguish between those who prevent satisfaction of the autonomy variable account and those who do not. As with the former distinction, it is important not to let the irrelevant counterexamples confer persuasive force upon the relevant, but innocuous, examples.

Another manipulative local challenge that might be offered to show that the autonomy variable account is not sufficient for free will is the case of choices under duress. Suppose, for instance, that I have the 'forced option' of surrendering my wallet or risking being shot by a mugger. In this case I might satisfy the autonomy variables, yet I choose unfreely.[5]

Threats constitute an interesting type of example, since it is possible to evoke both the intuition that threats clearly destroy our freedom and the intuition that although threats may radically change the *utilities* that we assign to our options, they do not reduce the freedom of our choices. Perhaps this ambivalence stems from the fact that cases of duress are typically underdescribed: in some imaginable situations we would be almost certainly unfree, while in others we would retain a large measure of freedom. Slote (1980) demonstrates this point in offering a friendly amendment to compatibilist solutions to the problem of duress, which is broadly consistent with the answer our autonomy variable approach will take. On Slote's suggestion, if agents are capable of viewing the threat in a calm, detached, Spinozistic-Stoical way, then they can choose freely despite the threat. Conversely, if a threat leaves agents in psychological turmoil because they desire to resist but do not dare, then they have lost freedom.

The distinction that Slote draws by comparing the Stoical vs. the emotionally ambivalent ways of perceiving threats is captured, on my view, by reference to what I have called the efficacy of the reasoning process. If an agent's choice is the product of a reflective process that satisfies self-knowledge, reasonability, and intelligence, then that choice is under the agent's reasoned control, despite the unhappy circumstances. We can then hold, as Slote does, that a decision to submit to a threat can be as free as a decision to accommodate a non-personal obstacle (like deciding to walk around a large lake that stands in your way) (129). Yet if, as is likely, the threat short-circuits the efficacy of the reasoning process by terrorizing the victim, then free will is almost totally lost. Efficacy is also lost if the victim becomes completely muddled in a Hamlet-like state. Moreover, since one can imagine a graduation of cases that lie between the various extremes, the autonomy variable account, like Slote's, produces the conclusion that there will be grey areas where we are partially free when deciding under duress.

This leaves the non-manipulative local challenges. Self-knowledge (as well as reasonability and efficacy) is violated in many cases in which we are not manipulated by others, but are 'victims' to our own cognitive foibles. Consider the unconscious reduction of cognitive dissonance, the psychological distress caused by having conflicting beliefs or attitudes. In one series of experiments involving the effects that dissonance-reduction has on the perception of pain, subjects were given an initial round of electrical shocks while attempting to perform a learning task. After receiving the first round of shocks, the subjects were then divided (unbeknownst to them) into two groups, depending on whether the experimenters provided the subjects with "sufficient" or "insufficient justification" to continue the experiment. The individuals who had been given sufficient justification were asked to undergo a second round of shocks in order to validate the data collected during the first round of shocks. The insufficient-justification group were asked to undergo a second round for a frivolous reason (e.g., to satisfy the idle curiosity of the experimenters). Judging by their superior performance on the learning task and lower galvanic skin responses during the second round of shocks, it seems that the insufficient-justification subjects experienced the shocks as less painful than their sufficient-justification counterparts. The interpretation of these results given by dissonance theorists was that the insufficient-justification group found the thought that they were undergoing painful shocks 'for no good reason' so dissonant that they unconsciously experienced the shocks as less painful than the sufficient-justification group did. That is, these subjects, without knowing that they were doing so, acted out the 'sweet lemons' (rather than 'sour grapes') version of dissonance-reduction (Nisbett and Wilson, 1977).

If the claims of the dissonance theorists are correct—and there is a growing body of supporting evidence (see Brehm and Cohen, 1962, and Harvey, Ickes, and Kidd, 1976)—then there are many instances that resemble manipulation, where the only 'manipulator' to be found resides in the agent's cranium. In such cases, the nature of beliefs, desires, and even sensations is dictated by a mechanism whose motivation is often unknown to us. Besides the obvious loss of self-knowledge, other variables are threatened, including unity. But do these cases mark reductions in our free will? Not always, since failure to satisfy the autonomy variables bears on freedom of the will only when it affects our ability to choose. Cognitive failings may be isolated in such a way as to not influence choices. Nonetheless, when cognitive failings such as dissonance-reduction influence decisions, they do reveal lessened freedom. For instance, in the above experiment, an insufficiently justified subject's perception of the second round of shocks as less painful does not bear on the subject's freedom. Yet if that perception leads to a belief upon which a decision is based (e.g., the decision to undergo a third round of shocks), then the freedom of the agent becomes a risk, basically in the same way one's freedom is at risk in a Brave New World scenario.

A final non-manipulative local challenge would be choices made on the basis of beliefs maintained through biased motivations. For instance, there is a literature that describes how we maintain existing theories at the cost of unfairly evaluating competing theories and disconfirming evidence. That is, once we arrive at a particular belief or theory, our allegiance to it makes us partial to finding confirming evidence and biased against looking for disconfirming evidence (Wason and Johnson-Laird, 1965). An example of such bias comes from showing two groups of subjects with strong ideological differences (e.g., on whether capital punishment deters murder) two purportedly authentic studies, one of which gives evidence that capital punishment is a deterrent and the other that provides statistically equivalent evidence that capital punishment is not a deterrent (Lord, Ross, and Lepper, 1979). One would expect that subjects exposed to such mixed data would modulate their opinions. Instead, the subjects assigned great weight to the studies that supported their previous position, and ignored the countervailing studies, so that the result was a polarizing of opinion.

This sort of case raises an interesting question of classification for the autonomy variable account. On the face of it, subjects fail on reasonability, understood as the *desire* for objectivity. But one could argue that the subjects really *want* to be objective, and that the problem is created by that fact that their fondness for their views overpowers their desire for objectivity. On this interpretation, it is efficacy that is lost. Or, one could view the case as a conflict between a reasonable subsystem that wants to be a fair epistemic agent and a hedonistic subsystem that wants the gratification of believing that it is right at the cost of objectivity. On this interpretation unity is imperiled. I do not know which framework is better for understanding theory-maintenance bias, and maybe it is not important which one we choose. What is clear is that all three interpretations represent the violation of some part of the autonomy variable sketch. The autonomy account poses the model of the unified, reasonable, and efficacious agent thoroughly in control of decisions, and all three interpretations violate that model in one way or another.

I now turn to the global challenges. We can begin to appreciate this approach by considering an example from Dennett's *Brain-*

storms. There Dennett asks whether a neurosurgeon could implant just one belief into our heads. Dennett answers,

> [O]ne cannot directly and simply cause or implant a belief, for a belief is essentially something that has been *endorsed* (by commission or omission) by the agent on the basis of its conformity with the rest of his beliefs. . . . A parallel point can be made about desires and intentions. Whatever might be induced in me is either fixed and obsessive, in which case I am not responsible for where it leads me, or else, in MacIntyre's phrase, "can be influenced or inhibited by the adducing of some logically relevant consideration," in which case I am responsible for *maintaining* it. (1978, 252–253)

The dilemma Dennett poses for intentional states seems, *a fortiori*, applicable to decision making in the case of determinism: if my desires are not amenable to rational consideration and revision, then my decision is not sufficiently rational, and I am unfree. Yet, if my desires are amenable to rational self-evaluation, then I have endorsed them, they 'are mine' irrespective of their etiology, and I am free. Either way, the truth of determinism is irrelevant to my freedom.

One might object that this compatibilist line is nearsighted because it overlooks the question of the causal origin of subjects' self-critical or obsessive stances toward their desires. "Don't you see," it might be objected, "that one's 'rational' evaluation of one's desires is still the product of determinism? This shows that even allowing the distinction between taking reasonable and obsessive stances toward them, we cannot reach a point where the rationality at stake is truly the subject's. Your volitions (of whatever order), irrespective of their apparent rationality, are not really *yours* if they can be traced back deterministically. You cannot control your decisions if they come from an outside source."

This objection takes us to the heart of the issue. The compatibilist must allow that our rational reflections about our desires, our reflections about *these* reflections and so on would be determined. But the aim of hierarchical accounts (including the autonomy variable account) is not to reach some point where our rationality stands outside of determinism. The compatibilist's point is that if the ultimate result of determinism is rational decisions, then the fact that the mental states involved are determined is simply irrelevant to the rationality and, thus, the freedom of the decisions.

This reply rests on the intuition that if you knew that your decisions satisfy the autonomy variable account, then you should regard yourself as free whether determinism is true or even if a non-intervening controller resides at the front of the causal sequence that ends in your decisions. To paraphrase Frankfurt, you would have everything you could want by way of rational control. Since I have argued ealier that compatibilists need not face objections based on intrusive controllers and that non-intrusive controllers are no more of a problem for hierarchical accounts than is mere determinism, my answer to the global challenges of Kane, van Inwagen, and Taylor is clear: If the autonomy variable account is satisfied, we have all we need for free will.

8. The Third Line of Reply: *Free Will* as an Internalistic Concept

Having said all this in behalf of my hierarchical account, I realize that incompatibilist intuitions are quite strong (I feel them myself). I would like to address them directly and try to neutralize them to the degree that I can.

An incompatibilist might object to everything that I have stated in this way: "Look. If determinism is true, then it is not physically possible for people to decide otherwise than they do. So, rationality, sprationality, determinism makes us unfree. So much is clear and does not need to be proved. The hypotheses involving global controllers are not designed to *prove* this, but to simply *illustrate* the unpalatable consequences of determinism."[6] Another expression of incompatibilist intuition comes from Robert Kane:

> [T]he controlled agent is not free in the dignity-grounding sense. It is the controller and not the controlled agent who is ultimately responsible for the outcome. . . . The controlled agent is a means and not an end in himself because he does not ultimately determine his own purposes or ends. He has a "kind of freedom," but not the true

freedom of being an end in himself, which confers dignity on human beings. (1985, 34)

These expressions of incompatibilist intuition can be understood within the context of the general debate discussed in Chapter 1 over whether our abilities to choose otherwise, to control one's choices, and to choose rationally should be understood as one-way or dual capabilities. The compatibilist's aim historically has been to specify conditions whose satisfaction makes the one-way interpretation of these three conditions so attractive that critics will stop demanding that free agents possess dual capabilities. A highly cognitive account like my autonomy variable view uses its emphasis on the rationality of determined choices as a lever to gain acceptance for the compatibilist's view of one-way control and ability to choose otherwise: If one-way rationality is acceptable, then why not one-way control and one-way ability to choose otherwise? The incompatibilist's strategy is to reverse this emphasis by focusing on control and on our commonsense belief that we have a dual or categorical ability to choose otehwise. Who cares about one-way rationality if we have lost the other two? It is important for the compatibilist to reply to the incompatibilist's attempt to turn the argument around.

I think that the difference between compatibilist and incompatibilist intuition is largely explained by the fact that compatibilists take "free will" to be an internalistic concept, whereas incompatibilists do not. That is, there is an analogy between the compatibilists' way of looking at free will and the methodological solipsism of Descartes and Jerry Fodor, who hold that psychological states are the types of states they are because of their internal and functional characteristics, irrespective of their connection to the external world (Fodor, 1981). So, for instance, the belief that cats eat fish would still be that belief, even if there were no cats or even if, due to an Evil Genius, there were no physical objects. The case would be likewise for other psychological states such as desires and choices.

On this way of looking at psychological states, one's choices remain choices irrespective of the nature of the world that surrounds them. And, by analogy, the degree of *freedom* that one's choices enjoy is unaffected by the way that they are situated in the physical world, provided those choices satisfy the normative requirements of the autonomy variable account. According to this internalistic perspective, the freedom of one's choices is a function neither of their causal background, nor of the freedom of the *actions* that the choices produce. In particular, given the internalistic nature of free will, determinism logically *cannot* reduce the freedom of an agent's choices any more than determinism can make one's pains more or less hurtful.

The internalistic view is implicit in compatibilism. For one thing, compatibilism has not a chance of plausibility without it, since otherwise the incompatibilist abhorrence of determinism will destroy it. For another, Frankfurt's insightful distinction between free *will* and free *action* helps the internalistic position by shifting the primary focus to where it belongs, i.e., to the purely psychological realm of free choice and away from that hybrid of the psychological and external world, free action.

I have no definitive proof that the internalistic view is better than the non-internalistic view of the incompatibilists, but some considerations can be adduced. If psychological states in general should be typed solipsistically, as I am inclined to believe they should (for a dissenting view, see Burge, 1979), then it seems that choices should also be viewed solipsistically. But then it becomes very difficult to see why the addition of *free* should make free choices depend upon the cooperation of the external world. One can understand why this would be the case for a semantic predicate like *true* when attached to a solipsistic concept like "belief," but *free* does not seem to me to operate this way. So, if we are predisposed to accept methodological solipsism for psychological states generally, I think that the internalistic view of free will looks attractive.

But even if we are not prepared to endorse methodological solipsism in its fullest generality, the internalistic view of free will still looks attractive. This is because the anti-solipsistic case derives its plausibility when aimed at *beliefs* (cf. Burge's example about the patient whose belief that he has arthritis is determined by social factors and not by any of his psychological states solipsistically construed—1979, 77). The internalist can concede that beliefs may be typed non-solipsistically, but insist that choices are solipsistic. Using a distinction from Searle (1983, 7–9), the internalist can argue that whereas beliefs require a "mind-to-world" fit and, thus, may be somewhat vulnerable to anti-solipsistic arguments, choices require a "world-to-mind" direction of fit. Although it is the 're-

sponsibility' of a belief to match reality, for a choice it is not the
fault of the choice but the world (including the chooser) if the
choice is not satisfied. This difference conveys upon choices a
greater degree of independence than beliefs enjoy and allows inter-
nalists to maintain their view on choices even if they are not
prepared to defend the solipsistic view for beliefs.

As a test case for the internalistic view, the compatibilist should
be prepared to defend the logical possibility that brains-in-vats
which satisfy our autonomy account could enjoy free will. I am
happy to accept that implication. We must, of course, keep in mind
the distinction between free will and free action, since brains-in-vats
fail on the latter score inasmuch as they produce no actions. But
once that point is settled, the internalist should ask: Assuming that
brains-in-heads and brains-in-vats both satisfy the autonomy account, how *could* their differing causal connections affect the freedom of the choices they reach? Would you conclude that you have
never made a free choice if you came to believe that your brain
resides in a vat instead of a head?

Let me continue my support for the internalistic view with a
thought-experiment designed to support an internalist interpretation of dignity, and, thus, address Kane's worry. Imagine that on
Earth and on its molecule-for-molecule replica, Twin Earth, there
are two persons who are likewise qualitatively identical (including
the states of their Cartesian minds, if they have them), call them
"Jim" and "Twin Jim."[7] Imagine also that (i) all of Jim's and Twin
Jim's choices are qualitatively identical, as are their entire psychological histories, and (ii) some of Jim's choices satisfy the libertarian notion of freedom (that is, there are other causally possible
Earths where Jim's choices are different given the conditions that
hold on Earth), whereas all of Twin Jim's choices are determined.
Now, if the dignity objection to determinism is sound, it seems that
Jim, but not Twin Jim, is sometimes worthy of dignity. But how can
that be? They have done all the same things for the same reasons—
they are qualitatively indistinguishable physically, intellectually,
emotionally, and so on. If Jim and Twin Jim differ with respect to
freedom or dignity, then these characteristics are 'doubly super-
venient'. That is, freedom and dignity would have to supervene not
on the actual states of Jim and Twin Jim, which are, after all,
qualitatively identical, but on the modal status of the actual states

of the two. Although this is not incoherent, I think that it is problematic enough to send us searching for a deterministic interpretation of dignity.

We need to get clear about what we are supposed to risk losing if determinism is true. Although Kane does not define the notion of "dignity-grounding," it seems that Kane is relying on the intuition that dignity is something we lose if we are unmasked as "big foolish clocks." This makes dignity something that is in part *relational* in that one might lack dignity not because of the intrinsic nature of oneself and one's choices, but in virtue of one's causal background. Against this intuition, I would suggest a view of human dignity wherein those qualities that confer dignity are intrinsically valuable and, hence, are not at all subject to diminution by relational properties. Consider some of the wide range of traits whose criteria are neutral with respect to the determinism/indeterminism distinction. *Pace* some libertarian thinkers (Popper, 1965), it seems that one's line of reasoning is logically valid or not due to its adherence to valid rules of logic, irrespective of whether the reasoning is determined or not. Or consider a moral quality such as compassion: are one's actions and feelings less compassionate if they turn out to be determined? Or take a non-moral virtue such as the diligence to stay with a difficult task until completion. In all these cases, which I think represent the sort of intrinsic qualities that give humans dignity, I think that determinism is logically irrelevant: the criteria of logical validity, compassion, and diligence are neutral with respect to whether the actions and character traits involved are determined or not. But since these sorts of things seem to be constitutive of human dignity, I think human dignity has nothing to fear from determinism per se.

Whether the universe is constructed such that one's choice is the only one that is physically possible or such that one's choice might have been different is not an intrinsic characteristic of the choice itself. Thus, if one's ability to make choices can possess intrinsic value, something I also take to support human dignity, then that ability can be intrinsically valuable whether or not determinism is true. Thus, I do not think that determinism is demeaning to human dignity.

Finally, I want to defend the internalistic view against a line of criticism that has a strong appearance of plausibility. One way this criticism might be pressed is by likening the internalistic view to the dubious Paradigm Case strategy. According to such a strategy, "only . . . superficial features of people and their acts . . . can be relevant to determining whether to apply the term 'free'" (van Inwagen, 1983, 110). For those of us with a penchant for deep, microstructural analyses, this is a serious accusation. A similar way to develop this criticism is to compare the internalistic view of free will to O.K. Bouwsma's argument in "Descartes' Evil Genius" that a perfect illusion is really not an illusion if there is no way for those persons having the experience to detect that it *is* an illusion (Bouwsma, 1965). If the variety of free will that I have been defending is on a par with the veridicality of the perceptions of Tom and Milly, then it looks as if it is a sham.

The best reply to this forceful line is to point out that it is question-begging. Paradigm Case arguments are clearly suspect where there are microstructural properties in addition to the "superficial" characteristics that serve (in the parlance of Putnam and Kripke) to fix the reference of terms. But the dispute between those who take an internalistic and those who take a non-internalistic view of free will just is over whether the distant causal antecedents to one's choices are important. For the incompatibilist to simply assume that an indeterministic background is important (and that the satisfaction of hierarchical accounts marks merely superficial characteristics of free will) is question-begging, because the compatibilist has the type of reasons adduced in this chapter for claiming that the causal history is a superficial characteristic. Certainly neither side is entitled to an easy victory in this dispute.

The compatibilist can resist the comparison of the internalistic view to Bouwsma's view by pointing out the conceptual differences between free will and perception. For non-phenomenalists, perception is an inherently causal process: conceptually speaking, one perceives veridically only if, in some sense, the external world that causes your perceptions 'agrees' with your perceptions. So, *ex hypothesi*, illusions created by the Evil Genius are logically different from veridical perceptions. But there is no reason to think that the concept of free will carries any causal (or acausal) implications regarding the world. *Free* when modifying *will* does not require any particular relationship between the will and the world in that way that *veridical* does when applied to *perception*. This is not to deny that the incompatibilist may be ultimately correct in rejecting internalistic free will; the point is that compatibilism has not committed the logical blunder that the Paradigm Case criticism says it has.

There is one innocuous similarity between the view of free will defended in this chapter and Bouwsma's view. As already noted, the compatibilist must allow that a controller could be hypothesized to reside at the causal origins of our choices. Such a controller, by hypothesis, has the power to change our choices, even in ways of which we would be unaware. Such a controller also knows before we do what we will choose, and such a controller could make us choose in erratic ways. But although the controller could take away our freedom, the controller could not do so without violating our satisfaction of the autonomy variable account. Hence there is a similarity between Bouwsma's Evil Genius and the covert controllers from this chapter. Just as the Evil Genius could not *convince* its subjects that they were experiencing an illusion while maintaining the perfect illusion intact, so the controller cannot remove our freedom while letting us satisfy the autonomy account. Both would have to interfere with their handiwork to accomplish their aims.

9. Conclusion

The challenge for the compatibilist is to provide a way of distinguishing between free and unfree choices without relying upon indeterminism to make the demarcation. This limitation creates a natural tendency to emphasize the 'internal quality' of freedom: e.g., whether we are acting as we wish (Hume), whether we are choosing as we think best (Frankfurt, Watson), or whether we are actually doing a good job with our choices, as the autonomy variable view stresses. When we focus on the internal integrity of our choices, the eventual success of *some* compatibilistic program appears to enjoy an air of 'inevitability', since it is difficult to imagine how indeterminism could contribute anything to the quality of free choices. Although the task of arriving at the *best* compatibilist account may be indefinitely perplexing, the compatibilist's strategy promises to ever more closely approximate the best account.

3

Does Freedom
Require Morality?

ABSTRACT In the last chapter, I tried to provide the best compatibilist account of free will that I can. In this chapter, I wish to demonstrate the strength of that compatibilist view by showing how it permits us to give a decisive answer to the title question of this chapter. That question expresses the intuition that in some deep sense people cannot be really free unless they are moral. This claim poses a serious problem, not only for my autonomy account of free will but for any account that tries to explicate freedom in non-evaluative terms. This is so because the satisfaction of a non-evaluative account will not guarantee the moral quality of the actions that satisfy the account. So if freedom requires morality and some particular account does not, then that account cannot be sufficient for freedom.

In the first section, I provide three cases that appear to support an affirmative answer to the title question. These include the neo-Kantian line that morality liberates the "heteronomous" will, an existentialist theme about taking responsibility for one's choices, and an argument from Susan Wolf (1987) that free will requires sanity, and sanity requires morality. In the second section I explain why I think that morality has no necessary connection with free will, and in the third I use this view to provide alternative explanations of the cases cited in Section 1.

1. Three Arguments for the Affirmative Answer

The autonomy variable account of Chapter 2 expressed normative requirements for 'how good' our practical reasoning processes must be if we are to choose freely. But there was no hint in that account that free choices must be *moral*. On the autonomy variable sketch, both moral saints and moral cretins have an equal opportunity of choosing freely provided they enjoy self-knowledge, reasonability, intelligence, efficacy, and unity. On the face of it, it seems desirable to not require morality of free choices, since otherwise immoral choices become, ipso facto, unfree. (See Sidgwick, 1907, 58–59 and 511–516 for a discussion of this problem for Kant; also see Wolf, 1987, 61–62.) But there is a long philosophical tradition that takes morality to be a part of freedom. Susan Wolf reiterates this view when she claims that "the condition of freedom cannot be stated in terms that are value-free. Thus, the problem of free will (is not) a purely metaphysical problem" (1980, 234). If Wolf is correct, then any compatibilistic view that holds that freedom can be defined without reference to morality is doomed.

In addition, it may be tempting to think that compatibilist accounts that emphasize the importance of rationality to free will are ultimately committed to the view that free will requires morality. Socrates and Kant held, for very different reasons to be sure, that rationality implies morality. So, if free will implies rationality, and rationality implies morality, then free will implies morality. But I do not accept the second premise, and showing why will be an important part of my strategy in this chapter.

Finally, compatibilistic views are not committed to the libertarian phenomenology of moralistic selves opting for the dictates of duty over the temptations of inclination. A completely free agent for Kant (1785) is one that is self-governing due to its perfect receptivity to the unconditioned dictates of the moral law. For C. A. Campbell, the conflict between duty and inclination constitutes the only arena where freedom of the will is likely to be manifested, since otherwise determinism operates through our inclinations to make us unfree: "[I]t is precisely that small . . . sector in which strongest desire clashes with duty—that is crucial for moral responsibility. It is . . . with respect to such situations . . . that the agent himself recognises that moral praise and blame are appropriate" (1951, 131). And, although Kane expands the realm of 'struggle' to include our attempt to remain open to new alternatives in practical decision making and our attempt to be concerned with our long-term best interest in prudential choices, the notion of making a moral effort plays a central part in his conception of free will (1985, Chapter 8). If freedom is dependent upon morality in this way, then compatibilism is in serious trouble.

Despite all this, I believe that the compatibilist can successfully deny that freedom requires morality. Given the complexities of the notions "freedom" (which severally denotes free will, free action, free agency) and "morality" (the morality of intentions, actions, and agents), the title question admits of numerous interpretations. Happily, I do not have to disentangle all the logically different interpretations that the title question has before I can address the deep intuition that it addresses. My aim is to reject all variants of the theme that there is *any* necessary relationship between freedom and morality. Positively expressed, my thesis is that, theoretically, a completely immoral agent can exercise completely free will in performing immoral actions wittingly done with immoral intentions. For the sake of the argument, I assume that there is no metaethical problem about "moral." Also, although my larger aim is defending my autonomy account from the objections cited above, I intend my argument in this chapter to hold irrespective of whether one opts for a compatibilist or incompatibilist view of free will.

Let me begin the three arguments for the conclusion that freedom requires morality. The first argument, a neo-Kantian line, goes like this. Autonomy of the will, a necessary condition for free agency, stands in constant danger from heteronomy of the will, understood as the natural condition of a human being whose decisions are made in order to satisfy desires, rather than because they satisfy the moral law (Kant, 1785, second section). It is only through respect for morality (the categorical imperative and its variants for Kantians, taking "the moral point of view" for someone who wants to adopt the neo-Kantian line without committing to Kantian specifics) that an agent can be truly self-governing. In doing so, free agents overcome heteronomy, thereby becoming able to resist the various desires that seduce and even control the heteronomous will.

This neo-Kantian line has some purchase on commonsense intuitions about freedom, since we think that in certain instances morality can liberate us. Take the case of a person who is obsessed with resentment toward some other person and whose perceptions and actions are colored by that feeling. Actions that are motivated by resentment can be as obsessive and unfree as actions grounded in textbook psychological disorders like neuroses, inferiority complexes, or learned helplessness. Getting the agent to adopt the moral point of view (i.e., to ask "Am I *right* to act out of resentment?") may be as liberating here as successful therapy is for standard psychological disorders. Or consider persons who decide how to behave on the basis of emulating peer groups, media celebrities, and various salient individuals. One might say, in psychological parlance, that their behavior is "controlled" by various external variables because of their several desires to be like those other individuals. Here also, agents' autonomy may be enhanced by getting them to take seriously the question of how they *should* act, thereby deemphasizing the heteronomous influence of desiring to be like this individual and that individual.

A second, existentialist, theme counterbalances the neo-Kantian line, while also supporting the affirmative answer. This view emphasizes the danger to one's freedom that can arise if one takes morality to 'dictate' only one possible decision. On this line, if you think (as Luther *said*) that you literally "can do no other," then you have abdicated your freedom and lapsed into Sartrian "bad faith." There are two aspects to this. Free agents need to realize that they *can* act contrary to the dictates of morality, if they so choose. As Sartre says, you are not wedded to any choice in the way that a table is wedded to being a table (Sartre, 1956, 64). Besides realizing that you are free to give up the moral point of view, this existentialist theme also requires that you realize that your assessment of what the dictates of morality *are* is subject to self-evaluation and correction. A free person is alive to the notorious vagaries of morality, and anybody who is dogmatic about moral choices looks more tropistic than free. Since each time you act according to your moral principles you are assenting to them, to be free you need to realize that you are taking responsibility for the moral principles and for being the sort of person that following these principles helps to make you (C. Taylor, 1976).

The existentialist theme can be illustrated by appeal to the classical obedience studies performed by Stanley Milgram (1974). Subjects in fake learning experiments were asked to apply what they took to be extremely painful electrical shocks to persons they thought were other subjects (but were, in fact, experimenters pretending to be shocked). Although the experiments were run in many different ways, the most remarkable results were found in cases where the experiments were held in the laboratories at prestigious Yale University, while the experiment director was present with the subject, and where the subject could see and hear the fake reactions of the 'subjects' whom they believed they were shocking. In these cases, approximately two-thirds of the subjects continued to 'apply' the 'shocks' to even the highest reading on their machines, despite the fact that in their pre-experiment predictions of how they would behave, no subjects predicted that they would apply shocks to the highest degree on the scale (35; 29).

Afterwards, some of the subjects who had obeyed the instructions to apply the shocks to the highest intensity on the machine justified their behavior by formalist reasoning. Such reasoning included the points that they had been paid to perform the experiment and that in accepting payment they had implicitly promised to complete the experiment. Although it is an empirical question to what extent these formalist explanations represented actual causal factors in the subjects' decisions, it seems that to the extent that subjects elected to continue to cooperate because of such formalist considerations, they were less free than those (few) who questioned the cogency of such considerations, thereby taking responsibility for their actions.[1]

A third theme to support the affirmative answer, provided by Wolf (1987), is that if we perform immoral actions in a cool and reflective way because we wish to be the sort of person who does such things, then we are "deeply insane" and, hence, not morally responsible for those actions, nor free in performing them. Wolf supports her view by imagining the case of JoJo, son of a cruel dictator, who grows up to be like his father. JoJo's acts of cruelty, in Wolf's example, are not the products of 'temporary insanity' inspired by uncontrollable emotions, but the products of *deep insanity*, since JoJo's perverse upbringing precludes his gaining "the ability to know the difference between right and wrong" (56). JoJo satisfies the free will accounts of hierarchical compatibilists; the problem is that his defective "deep-self" (50) makes him unfree.

Wolf supplements the JoJo example by reference to the McNaughten Rule, the criterion used in English criminal law for determining when the accused is sane enough to stand trial. According to Wolf, this principle states:

> [A] person is sane if (1) he knows what he is doing and (2) he knows that what he is doing is, as the case may be, right or wrong. (55)

Given this principle and the JoJo case, Wolf concludes that freedom requires sanity, which is "the minimally sufficient ability cognitively and normatively to recognize and appreciate the world for what it is" (56). Thus, for Wolf, any compatibilistic account that does not include conditions concerning moral value is inadequate.

2. The Case for the Negative Answer

To begin, it is worth noting that doing what is morally right can be as non-reflective as acting out of blind passion. (See Wolf, 1980, 231.) Although many moral philosophers, including Aristotle and Mill, advised that doing what is moral without reflection is a desirable goal of moral education, it is not clear that 'knee jerk' morality squares well with freedom. (Don't you question the rationality of someone you know to whom the opportunity of 'free riding', whether regarding public television or membership in the teachers' union, has *no* attraction?) By my lights, a free person remains alive both to the variegated nature of morality and to the question "Shall I be moral in this instance, or even at all?" A free person is not a "moral robot."[2]

One might reply, quite correctly, that even if moral actions may be robotic, this at most shows that morality is not sufficient for freedom, not that it is not necessary. Nonetheless, the above point suggests to me that the morality of actions may not even be a necessary condition because there is something more basic at stake that is the real determinant of freedom. This is the possibility that I shall exploit.

I am conceding in this chapter the controversial assumption that some variety of moral realism (objectivism, absolutism) is correct, and that it makes sense to talk about the literal morality of actions and agents. (In Chapter 7, I shall call that assumption into doubt.) While conceding this, the negative answer maintains that there is a better explanation of the examples used in behalf of the affirmative answer than saying that free will requires morality: It is not the *morality* of one's choices that increases free will, but the increased reflectiveness that often, but not necessarily, comes with adopting the moral point of view. This increased reflectiveness often leads to increased control of the will and results in greater freedom. What increases freedom of the will is the rationality of the *process* of decision that the agent performs; but the rationality of the process does not imply any particular moral *content* of the decision.

In Chapter 2, I spell out in detail one version of a rationality account of free will. In that view, freedom positively correlates with the rational reflection to which one submits one's decisions. A positive correlation between freedom and the morality of one's decisions exists only if one's moral decisions turn out to be more reflective than immoral ones, something that is not always true. Extreme cases that serve as endpoints illustrate this fact: On the end of unfree morality there is the previously mentioned 'moral robotics'. On the other end, there is the free immorality of, e.g., a highly reflective suicide or act of euthanasia when the deed is morally wrong.

In effect, I am rejecting the claim that morality itself has any role in determining whether the will is free, since the latter issue is entirely a function of nonmoral psychological factors. One might express this view by saying that compatibilistic free will is indifferent to morality in a way that is analogous to its indifference to the general metaphysical fact that it is determined. That is, the morality of choices is extrinsic to the nonmoral factors that dictate freedom.

3. Replies to the Three Arguments

Having stated my view in the last section, it is time to argue for it by showing how it does a better job at explaining the data in Section 1 than the affirmative answer does. I begin by acknowledging the neo-Kantian point that adopting the moral point of view may liberate one from the grasp of a heteronomous will. This admission will provide no support for the affirmative answer if it can be shown that it was not the morality per se of the viewpoint that increases freedom in such cases but instead some morally neutral aspect of it. This answer, in accordance with the analysis given above, is that what liberates the otherwise heteronomous person is the adoption of *any* viewpoint that enables reflection to counteract the force of one's varying desires.

Imagine, for instance, a case in which someone who suffers from heteronomy of the will adopts 'the epistemic point of view' (the view that one should always act in such a way as to maximize knowledge in the universe). The adoption of such a viewpoint, improbable as it may be, would be as effective in combatting heteronomy as would be a view that aimed for morality, because it would equally provide a check against the multiplicity of one's desires. The loss of freedom due to heteronomy could even be combatted by adoption of a selfish viewpoint, e.g., 'the egoistic epistemic point of view', which maintains one should always act to maximize one's own knowledge. Faust may have been immoral to make a deal with the devil, but he retained his freedom. One can be as single-minded toward a non-moral goal as one is toward following the dictates of morality; indeed, it may turn out to be easier to discern the path dictated by the former.[3]

Concerning the existentialist theme, I agree that in the Milgram experiments subjects who took responsibility for their actions were freer than those who felt that they had no alternative than to complete the experiment. But here, too, we can imagine an equally liberating nonmoral viewpoint that the subjects might adopt. Suppose that a subject subscribes to a particularly forthright religion that states that its adherents should always act in such a way as to maximize the glory of its god, while acknowledging that such glorification is often at odds with morality. Suppose further that this religion produces few guidelines concerning what sort of behaviors maximize the glory of its god, thereby placing a heavy burden on the individual to figure out how to achieve this end. Also, let us suppose that an adherent does not have to act in the way that the god prefers all the time in order 'to get to heaven,' but only needs to do so in some unclear majority of the times that the god thinks are important. Finally, let us assume that the subject wishes to do whatever it takes to get to heaven.

A non-moral subject with such views, I think, would be as undogmatic in proceeding with the experiment as would the morally conscientious existentialist who constantly rehearses the thought "My promise to participate in this experiment does not bind me; I am responsible for all of humanity." The nonmoral consideration "Does my continuing this experiment contribute to the greater glory of my god?" would keep the religious subject from manifesting the blind obedience that was destructive to the free will of Milgram's subjects.

Let us next turn to Wolf's argument, taking the JoJo example first. I think that Wolf's argument is this:

    a. Assume that JoJo's immoral world view and the behavior that follows from it are the determined consequences of his morally defective upbringing.
    b. Therefore, JoJo is not morally responsible for those actions.
    c. Therefore, JoJo is unfree with respect to those actions.

I shall offer a disjunctive strategy for rejecting this argument. First, I shall present the case for saying that JoJo is 'morally blind' on the analogy with color-blindness. I then show that on this way of viewing JoJo, the inference from (a) to (c) becomes untenable. Finally, I argue that if one rejects the color-blind analogy, then one should also reject Wolf's argument, since the inference from (a) to (b) would be unacceptable.

Let me present the analogy in the first person, making the assumption of moral realism. Suppose that one of my most deeply felt moral beliefs is that it is wrong to cause suffering to human beings for anything less than very strong justification. So, what do I say about a person like JoJo, who sees nothing wrong with torturing innocent people? That he is a moral monster, to be sure. But that is the *explanandum*, not the *explanans*. One way that I might view JoJo is similar to the way that I view color-blind persons. Whether I view moral blindness as an inability to see the moral qualities that reside in actions and agents (on the analogy with a direct realist theory of perception) or as an inability to form accurate moral 'qualia' (on the analogy with critical realism), I see JoJo as morally blind—that is, suffering from an important perceptual impairment. (The analogies between moral theories and theories of perception are discussed at length in Chapter 7.)

Such moral blindness *could* result in a loss of freedom for JoJo, if, e.g., it was the product of one of the problems already discussed such as heteronomy or rule-worship. (And I have argued that the negative answer could handle those cases.) But, as Wolf gives the example, it is JoJo's moral blindness that creates the immoral actions. And it is difficult to see how moral blindness per se could reduce freedom. First, the route to this conclusion through the notion of insanity as commonly understood seems blocked, since perceptual failures do not typically reduce one's sanity. Since "color-blind" does not support "insane," it is difficult to see why "morally blind" would. Second, the direct route from moral blindness to diminished free will seems blocked, since perceptual failures do not typically reduce free will. Just as color-blind persons remain free to make choices that presuppose color discrimination (doing a poor job to be sure), JoJo's moral blindness makes him *unreliable* with respect to choosing between right and wrong without reducing his ability to choose freely. Color-blindness makes one unable to respond to certain dimensions of one's environment in making choices without reducing one's free will; moral blindness would seem to impoverish the moral quality of one's decisions without undermining their internal structure wherein their freedom resides. Hence JoJo acts freely, although wrongly. Whether one wishes to say that JoJo is morally responsible for those wrong acts is something compatibilists and incompatibilists may wish to debate, but I do not here need to enter that debate.

Thus, *if* the moral blindness analogy holds, then we should reject the inference from (a) to (c). But consider the objection that the analogy is no good. How might the analogy be resisted? I think that the most plausible way to criticize the analogy is by pointing out that morally blind people are really more culpable than the analogy suggests. For instance, we do not blame someone for being color-blind, but it is very tempting to blame JoJo, determined environment notwithstanding. After all, JoJo wishes to have the sort of deep self that he has. So, maybe JoJo *is* morally responsible. But, of course, this claim will not do Wolf any good, since it rejects (b) and prevents the argument from even getting started. In sum, if you like the perceptual analogy, then you should resist the inference from (a) to (c), and if you don't like the analogy you should reject the inference from (a) to (b).

There is a final avenue available to Wolf: the moral blindness analogy does not hold, but the reason that it fails has nothing to do with JoJo's moral culpability. There is something *sui generis* about having a degenerate moral character like JoJo's that impairs the operation of our choices, even if the impairment fails to manifest itself in errors in gathering information, in drawing inferences, or in the structure of its practical reasoning. But it is difficult to see the principled grounds for maintaining this, especially for compatibilists working within a materialist framework who do not locate free will in a non-physical entity. The neo-Kantian and existentialist arguments that freedom requires morality could be appreciated within the context of a materialist psychology, but it is difficult to do so with Wolf's argument. And making freedom depend upon the morality of one's choices seems to bring with it an additional problem.

Wolf acknowledges the objection that her theory entails that decisions that we now *think* are free might prove unfree, provided our moral beliefs turn out to be wrong. I think that this is a serious problem for Wolf, since it demonstrates the danger of making freedom of the will depend upon a factor, like morality, that I think is external to it. Wolf replies to this objection by pointing out that "our judgments of responsibility can only be made from here, on the basis of the understanding and values that we can develop by exercising the abilities we do possess as well and as fully as possible" (61).

I doubt that citing the fallibility of our moral views touches the objection that the freedom of the will should not be held hostage to the fallibility of morals. To see this, let us contrive a situation in which our moral views prove to be grossly erroneous and ask whether we believe that our freedom would be diminished. Because Wolf has used racism and sexism as cases where we once saw the world incorrectly, let us imagine a case of 'kingdomism'. Suppose that, contrary to current biological theory, garden weeds have rich mental lives, full of contemplation, love for their peers, and constant dread of the sound of lawn mowers. Now, consider a weekend gardener who is asked to decide between controlling the weeds in the backyard by using a weed-killing poison and by using a chemical that makes the existent weeds infertile while permitting them to live out their natural lives. After reflection, which includes the thought "Why, they're just weeds—who cares if I kill them?", the gardener decides to use the former method. Although the gardener's moral responsibility is reduced in this instance, I see no reason to believe that the gardener's moral insensitivity reduces freedom of choice. After all, the gardener has gone through as much ratiocination as we go through in paradigmatically free choices. Since the example can be generalized, it seems that if the gardener's choice could turn out to be unfree due to moral truths that are revealed later, then few human decisions are safe from the potential loss of freedom. Although this conclusion is not absolutely untenable, I think that it is preferable to allow that the morality, but not the freedom of our actions, remains out of our hands. On my interpretation of this case, if garden weeds do not possess rich mental lives, then we are 'morally lucky' not to lapse into immorality by treating them as mere things. And if they do, we are unlucky in that we are unwittingly immoral in our dealings with them. Either way, our freedom is unaffected.[4]

Finally, let us consider Wolf's use of the McNaughten Rule to support the thesis that sanity requires that one see the difference between right and wrong. To begin, one might doubt that one can support a substantial ethical conclusion by appeal to a legal principle. Thus, it seems to be good strategy to look for an interpretation of the McNaughten Rule that captures its legal import without philosophical extravagance. Suppose the McNaughten Rule were rewritten to say that the accused must know the difference between what is considered right and considered wrong in England, rather than the difference between right and wrong per se. Thus understood, the McNaughten Rule makes a cognitive demand of responsible agents, without maintaining that sanity requires "that one's *values* be controlled by processes that afford an accurate conception of the world" (Wolf, 1987, 55).

This is not a recommendation for rewriting the rule, because it admittedly conveys an undesired subjectivist connotation. Still, it seems that this interpretation does the job that the actual rule is meant to do, without needlessly presupposing controversial philosophical theses. After all, the point of the rule is to exempt from prosecution persons who are not alive to the issue of morality due to impaired cognitive faculties, not sociopaths who have no moral consciences or ideologues whose moral views are radically at odds with society's. Moreover, Wolf's strong interpretation of the rule allows criminals the ready-made insanity plea that they accept the metaethical views of A. J. Ayer and Charles Stevenson, an unhappy consequence to be sure.

4. Conclusion

I believe that free will is a normative concept, but it is not normative in the sense that free agents need to be moral. Free will is normative in the way that any human excellence is normative—*viz.*, to exercise it, one must satisfy qualitative standards, in this case, standards of rationality. But, since the morality of the resulting actions depends upon different variables than the norms for free choices, the strong conclusion of this chapter follows. Free will does not require morality, not even a little bit. Libertarians, as well as compatibilists, should welcome this conclusion, inasmuch as it spares everyone the burden of specifying conditions that guarantee that free choices will be moral ones. This should greatly simplify the free will realist's chore. We shall see in Part II, however, that free will has another important connection with morality, a connection that cannot be severed as easily as was the connection discussed in this chapter.

4

Compatibilism and Moral Responsibility

ABSTRACT Moral responsibility is a general term covering a wide range of specific contents such as approbation, indignation, pride, guilt, praise, blame, punishment, reward, and retribution, to name a few. The question of the appropriate grounds for the ascription of moral responsibility may be addressed by appeal to consequentialist or formalist grounds. In this chapter I consider the range of possible contents of "moral responsibility" and the grounds for its ascription while asking the following questions: (1) What sense of *moral responsibility* should compatibilists have in mind when they claim that determinism and moral responsibility are compatible? (2) On what grounds can compatibilists justifiably ascribe whatever sense of moral responsibility they recognize in answer to (1)? After examining some well-known compatibilist answers to these questions, I argue that for the compatibilist who adopts the autonomy variable account of free will there is a plausible sense of *moral responsibility* available and reasonable grounds for its ascription.

1. Introduction

The account of the compatibility of free will and determinism that I have given in the last two chapters seems correct to me, as far as it goes, but I think that it is of little interest unless it can be extended to moral responsibility. It would not be too strong to say that, for many philosophers, the whole point of trying to explicate the *free will* concept is to show how it is possible for persons to be morally responsible. This is not to deny that some philosophers who write about the free will issue try to hold questions concerning moral responsibility in abeyance, since that concept raises enormously messy metaethical problems. But the concept of moral responsibility is so crucial to the way we view ourselves and others that any account of compatibilism that does not demonstrate how moral responsibility is possible is, at best, woefully incomplete and, at worst, a sleight-of-hand trick that fails to yield what we want most.

My objection to most compatibilist treatments of responsibility is that they endorse the compatibility of determinism with a variety of moral responsibility that is far too weak to provide what most non-philosophers want. For instance, on two issues—the *content* of ascriptions of moral responsibility and the *grounds* on which that content is ascribed—compatibilists like Moritz Schlick, J. J. C. Smart, and Dennett produce answers that drastically revise prephilosophical notions of moral responsibility. These thinkers, in effect, give accounts of this central notion that are not importantly different from the notions of moral responsibility given by hard determinists. If this is the strongest form of moral responsibility that compatibilism can accommodate, then I think that compatibilism is a failure. Peter Strawson (1962) produces a compatibilist account of moral responsibility that is more robust and closer to our prephilosophical views about its content and grounds for ascription, but he does not do enough to show that moral responsibility in this rich sense is warranted at all, let alone in a deterministic universe. Yet this is exactly what the compatibilist needs to do.

In this chapter I call on some themes from each of the just-mentioned thinkers and add to them a heavy reliance upon my autonomy variable account of free will, to suggest how we can be morally responsible in a strong sense in a determined universe. To the extent that my account succeeds, we will have a complete compatibilist picture at hand.

2. The Content and Ascribability Issues

What I call the *content* and *ascribability issues* concerning "moral responsibility" are retrievable from practically any account of the concept one might care to select. Here are two:

> [A] person is a morally responsible agent when he is an *appropriate candidate* for the reactive attitudes and for such activities as praise and blame and punishment and reward. (Fischer, 1986, 12)

> To say that someone is morally responsible for what he does may be
> to say that he can legitimately be praised or blamed if either of these
> responses is appropriate to the action in question. (Glover, 1970, 19)

The content issue involves the intensity of the view that may be
appropriately taken toward a morally responsible agent. Glover
and Fischer agree that praise and blame belong in that content,
with Fischer going further than Glover by including punishment
and reward, as well as what Strawson calls the "reactive" or personal attitudes such as resentment, indignation, gratitude, and forgiveness (P. Strawson, 1962, 62). The content issue may be high-
lighted by considering some of the attitudes and actions that are
possible candidates, starting with the least emotionally charged
ones: moral approval and disapproval, pride, respect, gratitude,
regret, smugness, hurt feelings, compunction, remorse, demand,
guilt, forgiveness, reproach, resentment, indignation, shame, praise
and blame, condemnation, self-condemnation, vindictiveness, re-
crimination, punishment and reward, and vengeance.

Since there is a considerable range of the possible contents of the
term *moral responsibility*, it is important that compatibilists be
explicit about what type of moral responsibility they think is possible in a deterministic world. That is, compatibilists should reply:
"*In what sense* can determined persons be morally responsible?"
Compatibilists have disagreed on the degree of intensity of content
that is appropriately applied to determined persons, some like
Smart and Schlick preferring to stay near the non-vituperative end,
whereas others like Strawson venture much further into the 'personal' attitudes. Needless to say, given the wide range of possible
senses with which the term may be intended, there is an ever-present
danger that disputants may use different senses of "moral responsibility" without realizing it.

The ascribability issue is broached by Fischer's talk of "an *appropriate* candidate" for ascriptions of moral responsibility, and
Glover's expression "can legitimately be praised or blamed." Other
terms that bring out the ascribability issue are those involving
deserts (e.g., "the agent *deserves* praise or blame") and the notion of
fittingness ("the agent is a *fitting* subject for praise or blame"). The
concept "moral responsibility," unlike a non-normative concept
such as "being held morally responsible," involves the difficult
normative problem of deciding when someone is appropriately or

fittingly subject to its ascription. This problem cries out for a principled account of what the correct grounds for ascription are. On the assumption that those grounds will not be straightforwardly empirical but will require some moral justification, the relevant candidates appear to be consequentialist and formalist justifications. That is to say, moral responsibility may be ascribed on the grounds that doing so, either in the individual instance or as a general rule, contributes to certain favorable non-moral consequences, such as promotion of the public good. Or moral responsibility might be ascribed on non-consequentialist (formalist, deontological) grounds, for instance, by someone who took the notion of deserts as fundamental. Of course, someone might be torn between ascribing moral responsibility on consequentialist or on formalist grounds, just as someone might vacillate between applying both objective and personal contents in those ascriptions. (This is discussed at length in Chapter 6.)

The grid below shows how I view the content and ascribability issues as analytically distinguishable:

Grounds for Ascribability

Consequentialist ← - - - - → Formalist

(grey area)

Content

Objective,
Impersonal,
Detached
Attitudes
↑
⋮
⋮   (grey area)
⋮
↓
Personal,
Reactive,
Emotionally laden
Attitudes

Despite the fact that one probably could find philosophical views to fill in all the grey areas on the grid, there is a natural tendency for one's answer to the ascribability issue to dictate one's answer to the content issue. In particular, it seems that the consequentialists wind up further 'up' on the content axis than do the formalists. In the next section, I consider the most frequently told compatibilist story about moral responsibility, where the content of the ascriptions are non-impassioned and the grounds for ascription are consequentialist.

3. Reduced Content and Consequentialist Ascribability

Smart distinguishes between what he takes to be a reasonable, deterministic content to ascriptions of moral responsibility and an unwarranted, libertarian content. In arguing for our acceptance of the former, Smart claims that "a clear-headed man" will see that

> to praise . . . or to blame a person for an action is not only to grade it (morally) but to imply that it is something for which the person is responsible. . . . Blame in this sense can be just as dispassionate as dispraise of a woman's nose. It is just a grading plus an ascription of responsibility. (1961, 212)

Smart points out that grading is consistent with believing that those whom we grade are determined agents who lack the libertarian ability to have decided differently under those exact circumstances. Yet, for Smart, blame, as it is typically used by most people, is not consistent with determinism:

> The appropriateness of praise and blame, is bound up in the eyes of the ordinary man, with a notion of free will which is quite metaphysical. (212)

These two claims, plus the premise that libertarian free will is incoherent, lead Smart to recommend a less intense content for our ascriptions of moral responsibility:

> We should be quite as ready to *grade* a person for his moral qualities as for his nonmoral qualities, but we should stop *judging* him. . . .

Moreover, if blame in general is irrational, so must self-blame or self-reproach, unless this comes simply to resolving to do better next time. (213)

Smart's view is a paradigm of the reduced-content, consequentialist-ascription position at the upper left side of the grid. For Smart, content is reduced to a non-recriminative, non-adulatory level far removed from the Strawsonian reactive attitudes. The rationale for such a reduction seems to be Smart's utilitarian theory of ascription:

[T]he ascription of responsibility and the nonascription of responsibility, have . . . a clear pragmatic justification which is quite consistent with a wholehearted belief in metaphysical determinism. (209)

The implication that Smart draws is that any degree of content that is not justified on utilitarian grounds is unwarranted, an exercise in confused metaphysics.

The rejection of retribution by determinists is, of course, a familiar theme. Schlick claims that the view of punishment as retaliation for wrong acts

ought no longer to be defended in cultivated society; for the opinion that an increase in sorrow can be "made good again" by further sorrow is altogether barbarous. (1939, 152)

Dennett shows an attraction to reduced content in defending a "naturalized institution of guilt":

[I]s our regret, remorse, and self-condemnation any less incoherent than the thwarted wish to undo the deed? . . . What attitude might we . . . take as an alternative? The attitude that goes with an embarrassed shrug? Or perhaps the impassivity of a disengaged spectator? Or rage at the unfairness of having been determined to be such a nasty and contemptible member of the human race?

How should one respond to the idea that one is guilty? If the concept of guilt . . . is the traditional, absolute concept of guilty-before-the-eyes-of-God, then . . . (n)o one, not monsters like Hitler or Eichmann, not ordinary sane criminals like Agnew or Vesco, and not you when you last broke a law, or broke a promise, is or could be guilty in that sense. For that sense of guilt has been screwed so tight by philosophical and theological tradition that the condition it purports to name defies description. (1984, 166)

Dennett, like Smart, provides a utilitarian justification of the ascription of moral responsibility. He begins by asking:

[W]hy do we want so much to hold others responsible? Could it be a streak of sheer vindictiveness or vengefulness in us, rationalized and made presentable in civilized company by a gloss of moral doctrine? (154)

Dennett answers his question this way:

The distinction between responsible moral agents and beings with . . . no responsibility . . . matters: the use we make of it plays a crucial role in the quality and meaning of our lives. (155)

[W]hatever responsibility is, considered as a metaphysical state, unless we can tie it to some recognizable social desideratum, it will have no rational claim on our esteem. Why would anyone care whether or not he had the property of responsibility . . . ? [W]e simply *hold* people responsible for their conduct (within limits we take care not to examine too closely). And we are rewarded for adopting this strategy by the higher proportion of "responsible" behavior we thereby inculcate. (163–164)

4. Problems with Consequentialist Ascribability

In this section I argue that the upper left-hand position of consequentialist reduced-content is too weak to yield the strong sense of moral responsibility that common sense requires. This view gets both the content and ascribability issues wrong relative to our prephilosophical views about what moral responsibility is. It also falls into a serious trap concerning justice. Once the ascribability issue is settled, we will be able to see how we may justify a more full-blooded content of moral responsibility for the compatibilist.

In discussing ascribability it is important to distinguish between rationales for (i) the general practice of holding persons morally responsible and (ii) assigning moral responsibility to particular individuals rather than others. We must agree with Dennett that the practice of holding persons morally responsible has obvious pragmatic advantages. For example, the utilitarian value of holding people morally responsible is clear. Yet this point does not touch the second issue. Although the general practice of holding persons morally responsible is supported on utilitarian grounds, that practice needs to be done in a morally acceptable way in individual instances if it is to avoid being morally repugnant. So, the compatibilist who seeks to justify ascriptions of moral responsibility must produce reasons that speak to (ii) as well as (i).

My objection is simply an application of the problem that utilitarian theories of moral obligation have with justice. Suppose that the only rationales for assigning moral responsibility to individuals were the utility of the practice in general and the utility of making the particular ascriptions. In this case, it would be easy to concoct thought-experiments where a preponderance of utilitarian considerations (deterrence, expression of communal condemnation, prevention of communal retaliation, etc.) would dictate that an individual should be held morally responsible (in whatever sense we choose) for an act performed by someone else. The same sort of moral repugnance seems to hold here as holds in the examples of scapegoats who are punished for crimes they did not commit. Thus compatibilism needs a principled means to overcome the charge that consequentialist justifications for the ascription of moral responsibility are morally wrongheaded. The compatibilist needs to produce an account of moral responsibility in which the agent's freedom in acting makes it *morally important* that the agent, rather than some innocent stranger, be held responsible for the agent's act.

Without explicitly raising the justice issue, Strawson also criticizes the consequentialist rationale for ascribing moral responsibility. Strawson imagines an incompatibilist objecting:

> [W]hy does freedom in this sense (freedom that is compatible with determinism-RD) justify blame, etc.? . . . The only reason you have given for the practices of moral condemnation and punishment in cases where this freedom is present is the efficacy of these practices in regulating behaviour in socially desirable ways. But this is not a

sufficient basis, it is not even the right *sort* of basis, for these practices as we understand them. (1962, 61–62)

For Strawson, consequentialist rationales for moral responsibility require that persons are viewed "objectively" and impersonally. Yet to the extent that we view persons in this way, our responses to them no longer qualify as holding them *morally* responsible (76). The only way we can do this is to continue to take the personal, reactive stance:

> [T]o speak in terms of social utility alone is to leave out something vital. . . . The vital thing can be restored by attending to that complicated web of attitudes and feelings which . . . are quite opposed to objectivity of attitude. Only by attending to this range of attitudes can we recover . . . a sense of . . . *all* we mean when . . . we speak of desert, responsibility, guilt, condemnation, and justice. (78)

The good news for compatibilism is that Strawson's suggestion saves compatibilism from the utilitarian's problem with justice. Utilitarian theories are impersonal, viewing persons as 'receptacles' for utility, and, hence, have inherent problems with the vantage point of the individual. Attempts to save utilitarian theories by stipulating that only the agent who performed the action may be held responsible for it (as Hart does for punishment—1968, 9) succeed only by admitting an additional, non-utilitarian principle. The 'logic' of the reactive attitudes, on the other hand, dictates that they are correctly directed at an individual only if that individual performed the act that prompts the reactive attitude. Resentment, for example, directed at someone who did not perform the resented act is simply misdirected resentment. So if the compatibilist can show that the reactive attitudes are warranted, the justice problem is solved.

The bad news is that the incompatibilist will object to Strawson that if determinism is true, then, despite 'the logic' of the reactive vocabulary, the reactive attitudes are not philosophically justifiable. "How," it might be objected, "can we justify resentment in a determined universe any more than we can justify moral responsibility per se?" Strawson provides two answers, neither of which looks terribly compelling:

i. Reactive attitudes are deeply embedded in "the general frame-work of human life" (70), which is impossible, practically speaking, for us to give up. And "it is *useless* to ask whether it would not be rational for us to do what it is not in our nature to (be able to) do" (74).

ii. Suspension of the reactive attitudes is appropriate for specific, aberrant causes, like insanity, being a child, and ignorance, but is "*never* the consequence of the belief that the piece of behavior in question was determined in a sense such that all behavior *might be*" (74).

A heroic objection to (i) would be to hold that even if we are psychologically unable to give up the reactive attitudes, they are still philosophically unwarranted, a regrettable psychological residuum of the sort that most people view jealousy and greed. A less heroic objection is to deny that viewing ourselves as persons psychologically requires that we hold reactive attitudes. It is not obvious that Smart's proposal to treat ascriptions of moral responsibility as moral grading would destroy our ability to see each other as persons; in *Walden Two*, Skinner (1948) sketched a seemingly coherent scenario in which certain reactive attitudes (resentment, gratitude, jealousy) were greatly reduced by behavioral engineering. Strawson's second point invites the charge of paradigm-casism: the fact that we normally allow only aberrant circumstances to undermine the warrant of reactive attitudes is not enough to show that they are warranted generally. Strawson's second point, however, may be subject to a more promising interpretation that may help solve the compatibilist's problem. I attempt to provide this in the next section.

5. Formalistic Moral Responsibility

I have argued that the compatibilist needs to specify (1) a content for ascriptions of moral responsibility that is stronger than those given by Smart and Dennett, and (2) provide a nonconsequentialist justification of that content's ascription. I shall try to do this, calling on Smart's theme of moral grading, Strawson's notion of reactive attitudes, and the autonomy variable conception of free will from Chapter 2.

I shall attempt this by arguing for the following progression: It is reasonable to morally approve or disapprove of the actions of agents who one believes are determined. But if those actions are indicative of the agent's character in a way that I shall elaborate, then one may approve or disapprove of the agent's character for having the disposition to act in such ways. Finally, it is reasonable to approve or disapprove of persons for their characters, even allowing that one can trace the ultimate causes of a person's character to factors that were not 'up to' the person. Thus, I shall be arguing for the compatibility of holding reactive attitudes toward persons in a deterministic universe.

I begin the argument this way. Smart is correct in pointing out that there is in principle no difficulty for a determinist who wishes to practice moral grading. We can, for instance, give an unfavorable grade to a particular action while ignoring the question of determinism altogether. In doing so, we need not be making a mere judgment of taste; we can say that the action is immoral in the strongest normative sense. Suppose that determinism is true and S performs some action *a* that is morally repugnant on consequentialist and/or formalist grounds. In this case we may justifiably grade *a* accordingly:

(A) S's action *a* is morally reprehensible.

I now add a premise that I intend to be analytic, *viz.*, that morally reprehensible actions deserve moral disapprobation. Since my use of *deserve* here simply means *warrants*, to prevent unnecessary qualms about its use, I express the premise this way:

(B) All morally reprehensible actions logically warrant moral disapprobation.

From (A) and (B) I deduce:

(C) Therefore, S's action *a* logically warrants moral disapprobation.

I now wish to specify conditions under which we may currently move to disapprobation of S's character. This is important, because ultimately I wish to justify applying moral predicates to the *agent* who performs the action, and character will be the transitionary step. The relevant empirical claim would be that *a* is reflective of S's character. But under what circumstances are actions reflective of one's character? To answer this, I appeal to the hierarchical conception of free will given by my autonomy variable account in Chapter 2. If the conditions of that account are satisfied, then the action that S's decision produced will reflect S's character. I express this as:

(D)   If S's action *a* satisfies the autonomy variable account of free will, then *a* reflects S's character.

Then an empirical premise is needed

(E)   S's action *a* satisfies the autonomy variable account of free will.

To allow us to deduce

(F)   Therefore, S's action *a* reflects S's character.

We next need to connect the evaluation of *a* and the fact that *a* reflects S's character to the evaluation of S's character. We do that with:

(G)   If (C) and (F), then S's character logically warrants moral disapprobation for performing *a*-like actions.

Note that now S's character is being viewed as disapprobational not for one specific act, but because S's best reflective effort produces *a*-like actions. We now are ready to connect disapprobation of character with disapprobation of the person:

(H)   If S's character logically warrants moral disapprobation for performing *a*-like actions, then S, the person, logically warrants negative reactive attitudes for having the sort of character that *a* reflects.

The whole argument can be telescoped together this way:

(I) Therefore, if (A) and (E), then S logically warrants negative reactive attitudes for having the sort of character that *a* reflects.

Now that the whole argument is set before us, let me try to show why I find it plausible. The argument tries to take us along a slippery slope, from moral disapprobation of actions, to disapprobation of the characters of the persons who produce the actions, to the justification of reactive attitudes toward the agents who manifest those characters. As with any slippery-slope argument, the problem for the critic is to find exactly the right place to object, and in this case I think there is no obvious point. Consider steps (A), (B), and (C). The claim that there are morally reprehensible actions is likely to be conceded by all sides, irrespective of anyone's particular views on the free will issue. (B) is simply analytic (or, at any rate, an uninteresting truism) because saying that morally reprehensible acts logically warrant disapprobation says nothing more than that such acts are reprehensible. As long as we are speaking about the moral quality of actions and not agents, any hypothesized incompatibilist pleas for the exoneration of determined agents would be off the mark, since we are not affixing blame at this point. Step (C) follows validly from (A) and (B). So, I do not see that the incompatibilist can very plausibly object to the argument through the first three steps.

The objection could be made that in a determined universe no actions could be morally reprehensible—if determinism is true, then all is permitted. Such an objection would seem to me to conflate the enormously different issues of moral realism (objectivism, absolutism) and determinism and have very little to recommend it. A more subtle objection might be the linguistic point that *actions* are not correctly said to be morally reprehensible or morally commendable, since only *agents* are. Such an objection, though, strikes me as needlessly fastidious—my linguistic intuitions do not grate at the thought of calling actions themselves reprehensible.

So, let us turn to step (D). I do not claim that (D) is obviously true, and I can imagine even a compatibilist having qualms about

whether actions that are the results of choices that meet the autonomy account genuinely reflect the character of the agent. The
reason (D) seems correct to me is that the satisfaction of the
autonomy account demonstrates a high degree of reflectiveness,
and reflective decisions seem to me to reveal the nature of the
decider. I hasten to mention that my use of the autonomy variable
account here is much less ambitious than my use of it in Chapter 2,
where I argued that its satisfaction is sufficient for free will. In (D) I
claim only that the account's satisfaction reveals the character of
the agent, not that the agent is free. Finally, even if one does not
think that the autonomy account shows how actions can be reflective of agents' characters, it seems likely that *some* non-libertarian
account of how actions reflect the characters of the agents who
perform them will be possible. So, if one does not think the autonomy account does the trick, then one may fill in a substitute
candidate.

Step (E) is simply an empirical premise stating that some act
satisfies the autonomy account (or whatever replacement account
the reader prefers). Assuming the account is coherent, there is
reason to suppose that it could be satisfied. And step (F) is validly
deduced from (D) and (E), so it will pose no problem if those
premises are acceptable.

This brings us to (G), the claim that if the agent's action is
morally disapprobational and if that action reflects the agent's
character, then the agent's character is disapprobational for producing actions of this type. This premise seems correct to me, as is
shown by this illustration. Suppose that little Johnny sometimes
engages in morally repugnant behavior such as harming small
animals. One day Mother notices Johnny tormenting the neighbor's
cat and immediately calls Johnny inside the house for a stern
reprimand. When Mother points out that cats, too, are capable of
suffering from such mistreatment, Johnny replies: "Of course they
are, Mom. I'm not stupid. That is exactly why I torment animals—
to create as much suffering as I possibly can, without leaving
evidence that might get me in trouble."

If Johnny's reply is accurate to the motivation of his behavior
(e.g., he has not performed a faulty self-attribution or is not just
saying this to tease his mother), then it looks as if it is not just the
individual bits of Johnny's behavior that deserve disapprobation,

but also his underlying character. If Johnny's lamentable behavior is the product of a fully reflective plan, then Johnny will satisfy (roughly speaking) counter-factuals about what he will do in subsequent cases in which he believes that he can get away with tormenting animals. In addition, Johnny's character is such that he needs to be a different kind of boy before the disposition toward this objectionable type of behavior is finally squelched. This is in stark contrast to the situation, thankfully more likely, where it never occurred to Johnny that animals experience pain and where Johnny might alter his behavior when apprised of that fact. In the latter case, there is disapproval of the action but not Johnny's character. So, it seems to me that the way to distinguish between the two types of cases is by appeal to something like the autonomy variable account.

The last, and perhaps most difficult, step to justify is (H), the premise that disapproval of a person's character provides warrant for holding negative reactive attitudes toward the person with that character. The incompatibilist objection to (H) will be that in a deterministic universe, no one is morally culpable *or* correctly subjective to reactive attitudes, however contemptible one's actions and character may be. On this objection, there may be deplorable actions and deplorable characters, but there are no 'blame-worthy' or even 'resent-worthy' people if determinism is true, since we do not ultimately cause our characters.

In reply to this, some compatibilists distinguish between character traits that were brought about voluntarily and those that were not:

> If a man is not ignorant of what he is doing when he performs acts which will make him unjust, he will of course become unjust voluntarily . . . [;] since an unjust or a self-indulgent man initially had the possibility not to become unjust or self-indulgent, he has acquired these traits voluntarily. (Aristotle, 1962, Book III, Chapter 5, 1114a)

Dennett manifests this line when considering "utterly despicable" persons:

> They *may* not be able to help it *now*, for they may be too far gone (like the drunk who is responsible for having made himself drunk),

but . . . one can be as responsible for one's character as for any other artifact arising from one's past efforts. (1984, 167)

The first objection to these compatibilistic claims is that to hold someone morally responsible for actions simply because the actions were the products of voluntarily chosen character traits seems too harsh. For instance, Aristotle's approval of the principle that "the penalty is twice as high if the offender acted in a state of drunkenness, because the initiative is his own" (1113b) looks barbaric. If my present decisions fail to meet an acceptable compatibilist criterion of free will, then the fact that my previous character-forming decisions may have been free does not make me morally responsible for my present actions. This objection seems well-taken and can be accepted by the compatibilist with equanimity.

A second objection is that not all character-traits are the product of voluntary decisions anyway. Owing to various hereditary and environmental factors, as well as the effects of one's previous unfree decisions, some underlying character traits came temporally prior to anyone's free decisions, and, hence, cannot be viewed as products of compatibilist-style free decisions. To this objection it might be acknowledged that our characters are not entirely a result of our free decisions: to the extent that our characters are not, and we are unable to critically assess them, then we are not responsible for them. Nonetheless, compatibilist free decisions are a constant source of testing for our characters, and if we *endorse* our characters by our decisions, then we have accepted our characters, their etiology notwithstanding, and we are morally responsible for their continuance.

By attending to the autonomy variable view we see the strength of various compatibilist claims that otherwise look unreasonable and hard-hearted. For example, Dennett asks rhetorically "[W]ho more deserves to be despised than someone utterly despicable?" (1984, 167) When we understand *utterly despicable* to entail the exercise of completely reflective free will, this claim looks right. With the same proviso, so does Hobart's claim that "[i]t does not remove our sense of (an act's) vileness to reflect that (the agent) was acting according to his nature. That is very precisely why we are indignant at him" (1934, 85–86). There is, of course, a final incompatibilist objection that says: "Surely you can imagine that because of a deterministic universe you might come to have a character that was completely vile, which you reflectively endorsed, thereby satisfying any compatibilist criterion for free will completely. Yet had the primordial elements been arranged differently you would have rationally endorsed a benign character. So, it was all really a matter of luck. Can you really be morally responsible for your vile character?"

I think that the answer is yes. If I endorse my vile character by making choices in accordance with the autonomy view of free will, then I am both evaluating and molding my character. The fact that such molding is traceable to antecedent events does not negate the fact that I am doing the shaping. It seems that I would warrant both Smartian moral grading and Strawsonian reactive attitudes. Let me illustrate this point by considering an episode that occurred recently in a restaurant. While being shown to a table, my friend and I noticed several clouds of cigarette smoke and asked to be seated elsewhere. While walking away from the smokers, my friend asked indignantly why anyone, especially young persons who began smoking at a time when the health risks of smoking were widely known, would smoke cigarettes? I replied that if determinism is true, then one in principle could predict their choices to smoke by reference to the state of the universe billions of years ago. His indignation unassuaged, my friend replied by asking why these people had to be so stupid. Determinism or not, my friend continued, these people were knowingly hurting themselves and putting others at risk, and deserved his indignation, if not worse!

Now, I do not deny that there is a strong intuitional pull toward saying that if determinism is true, then the justification of our reactive attitudes toward agents is weakened, especially when one remembers that negative reactive attitudes are typically associated with such things as retaliation and vengeance. My claim is rather that my friend's position—that it is correct to feel resentment toward agents who act in morally pernicious ways due to their characters, even if we believe that determinism is true—also enjoys strong intuitional support. The libertarian Kane disagrees, claiming that if determinism is true, then one's reactive attitudes cannot focus on agents in this way, because any resentment we feel toward agents will be "transferred" back to parents, society, or, if one is a theist, perhaps to God (1985, 181). But if an agent's character is disapprobational in the sense given in (G), then I see no reason why the reactive attitudes cannot be fixed on the agent. The point is not that the agent is the best available candidate, but that the agent is the rightful candidate. Does it lessen your reactive attitudes toward Hitler to suppose that determinism is true? Should it?

Consider the separate notions of taking responsibility, holding somebody responsible, and being responsible. To begin, there seems to be no objection to a determinist taking responsibility for, say, a future state of affairs. The determinist, for example, might say: "I take full responsibility for anything that happens to your pet beagle, Mercedes, heirloom crystal, etc., that you entrust to my care." Applying John Searle's speech-act analysis to this case, it looks as if what Searle calls the "sincerity condition" for taking responsibility is the belief that speakers, thereby, are placing themselves in a position where they acknowledge that moral censure may become appropriate (1969, 66–67). I see no reason why the preconditions of this speech act are any different for the determinist than for the libertarian.

One might object that the determinist cannot consistently take responsibility, simply because doing so implies a metaphysical view that determinists logically cannot accept. (One is reminded of arguments that determinists cannot really *deliberate*—cf. R. Taylor, 1964). Maybe determinists are just forgetting their presuppositions. Or maybe determinists are aware of the logical problem and are just being magnanimous.

Not necessarily. It seems to me that determinists who take moral responsibility for future and past events sometimes do so because of their feelings of control over those events. I doubt that incompatibilists will deny that determinists experience the common subjective impression that they are producing their own choices and actions. Now, if determinists can experience these feelings of control, it is a very short distance to the belief that they will be morally culpable should that control produce disapprobational results. So, our feelings of control cause our belief in our own responsibility; but the belief in determinism is consistent with such feelings, so the belief in determinism is consistent with our belief in our own responsibility.

Although my argument starts from the egocentric perspective of our feelings of control, it is easily expanded. If determinists can take moral responsibility, then they can also hold others morally responsible. This is because, if we ignore the magnanimity interpretation, *taking responsibility* is simply the first-person instance of the larger notion of *holding responsible*. One might say that taking responsibility for *a* is, among other things, a way of holding oneself responsible for *a*. Moreover, it would reveal hubris for agents to think that although *they* are morally responsible, nobody else is. Considerations of symmetry seem to require that determinists who take responsibility for their actions also hold other persons responsible for their actions.

What does this discussion prove? If my argument is correct, it shows that it is logically and psychologically possible that we believe both that determinism is true and that people are morally responsible for their actions. This, admittedly, does not prove the logical compatibility of determinism and moral responsibility, any more than the possibility of my believing that I am a man and a woman establishes the logical possibility that I am both. Since my belief may be confused, the inference is not deductively valid. But does the premise provide some *support* for the conclusion? Well, how do we know whether determinism and moral responsibility are compatible or not? It is not as if the answer can be gotten by looking somewhere or by doing conceptual analysis. So, we are reduced to addressing the question by using thought-experiments. And here it seems to me that the fact that determinists who take responsibility evince their belief in both determinism and responsibility is a highly relevant piece of evidence.

There is a final incompatibilist worry that should be addressed. Imagine that you are awaiting execution for a murder committed in accordance with your rationally endorsed, determined character. "But for the position of the primordial elements," you might say, "I would not be executed."[1] Although this intuition is a powerful one, it does not do the work the incompatibilist hopes it will. Execution and other forms of cruel punishment are indeed unwarranted if determinism is true, but they are also unwarranted in libertarianism. The conclusion is not, however, that moral responsibility is a sham, but simply that certain severe forms of punishment are morally wrong. What we need is for *our theory of ethics* to place limits on the severity of punishment that we attach to our ascriptions of moral responsibility. Ethical theory, not metaphysics, is the appropriate branch of philosophy to address the issue of precluding barbarism.[2]

6. Conclusion

The aim of this chapter has been to show how a determinist can accept a stronger sense of "moral responsibility" than Smart's moral grading and to produce a formalist rationale for the ascription of that content. I have argued that given the autonomy sketch of free will from Chapter 2 we can justify the application of Strawsonian reactive attitudes on formalist grounds, although the further question of the degree of punishment must be settled by ethical, not metaphysical, considerations. That is, I have defended this claim: When S performs an immoral act a as the result of a decision d that satisfies our autonomy account, then S is appropriately subject to the range of attitudes from moral disapprobation through resentment and blame to punishment, simply because S performed a, irrespective of the utility of holding S responsible.

If the argument of this chapter is plausible, compatibilism will gain certain advantages. Compatibilism will have avoided the utilitarian scapegoating problems which Smart and to some extent Dennett face. We also will have a more theoretically satisfying justification for ascribing the reactive attitudes than Strawson provided. And we can ignore Dennett's advice that "we mustn't look too closely at the particular micro-details of the accused's circumstances" (1984, 162) when ascribing responsibility. It is only by looking closely at the micro-details that we can know whether a person's determined action was one for which the person may be held responsible, despite its determination.

II

Free Will Unravelled

5

Free Will
as an Exemplar Concept

ABSTRACT The argument of Part I of this book was designed to present a compatibilist view of free will and moral responsibility that is internally consistent and able to stand up to some important incompatibilist objections. Although I believe that the autonomy account is largely successful on that score, I do not believe that it is ultimately acceptable. Compatibilism plays to only some of our intuitions regarding free will. There remain several issues over which the application of *free will* is simply irresolvable. These issues include: (1) whether persons must meet the normative requirements of free will; (2) whether bribes ever reduce our freedom; (3) whether we are made unfree by forces that strongly influence, without absolutely dictating, our choices; and (4) whether being free requires feeling free. In addition, I reconsider the debate from Chapter 2 between the compatibilists and incompatibilists over the internalistic construal of free will, which I argued is required by compatibilism.

The explanation I offer for the conflicting intuitions that these five issues arouse is that *free will* is a paradigm or exemplar concept. An exemplar concept, understood here as in cognitive psychology (Smith and Medin, 1981), is one that we decide applies more or less to an object in virtue of the degree to which that object approximates the paradigm we associate with the concept. *Free will*, I argue, is not a well-behaved exemplar concept (like "bird"), because free will has multiple, conflicting exemplars. I elaborate three of these, and provide some evidence from the social psychological literature on perceived choice that suggests that we may rely on something like my exemplars when we think about our freedom. These conflicting exemplars explain why we can build examples concerning the five issues cited in this chapter (and, doubtless, other issues not considered here) in such a way that intuition moves in opposite directions, thereby making it impossible to provide a consistent free will account.

1. The Normative Problem

The defense of compatibilism in Chapter 2 emphasized that "free will" must be taken as an internalistic concept if it is to have any chance of denoting in a deterministic world. This is because global, non-intervening controllers can always be imagined to be super-added to a deterministic etiology of human decisions, and unless the compatibilist takes the internalistic perspective, such scenarios will be devastating to the compatibilist account of free will.

But even if we decide that free will should be viewed in this way, we still need to specify how satisfactory the reasons and practical reasoning that go into choices must be. Theoretically, one can go either way here. To set out the endpoints of the continuum, shall our compatibilist account say that S decides freely when S decides on the basis of reasons that S accepts, or must the reasons be *good* ones? To consider practical reasoning, does S decide freely when the reasoning process is terrible? Although the autonomy variable account of Chapter 2 places strong normative requirements on the rationality of free decisions, this may be unwarranted. For one thing, maybe free will is not so 'intellectual'. For another, the notion of placing strong normative requirements on free will may appear ill at ease with compatibilism's internalistic predilection. I have heard it expressed in conversation that if it does not matter whether free decisions can be traced back to a global controller, why should it matter how rational our decisions are?

Wright Neely captures the non-normative, subjective element in the free will concept when he cites the following necessary conditions of free action:

> (2) An agent is free with respect to some action which he performed only if it is true that if he had not had a desire to do it, then he would not have done it.
>
> (3) An agent is freer with respect to some action that he performed to the extent that, in doing what he did, he was not thereby frustrating other desires of his own.
>
> (4) An agent is freer with respect to some action which he performed to the extent that the desire out of which he acted was of relatively high priority as compared with any of his desires which he, in doing what he did, thereby frustrated.

(5) An agent is free with respect to some action which he performed only if it is true that if he had been given what he took to be
good and sufficient reason for not doing what he did, he would not
have done it. (1974, 48)

In the classic paper "What Means This Freedom?", John Hospers
uses the efficacy of reasons as a criterion of establishing when
people are responsible in the "upper level" of moral discourse:

There is still another criterion . . . by which a man's responsibility for
an act can be measured: the degree to which that act can (or could
have been) *changed by the use of reasons.* Suppose that the man who
washes his hands constantly does so, he says, for hygienic reasons,
believing that if he doesn't do so he will be poisoned by germs. We
now convince him, on the best medical authority, that his belief is
groundless. Now, the test of his responsibility is whether the changed
belief will result in changed behavior. If it does not, as with the
compulsive hand washer, he is not acting responsibly, but if it does,
he is. It is not the *use* of reasons, but their *efficacy in changing
behavior*, that is, being made the criterion of responsibility. And
clearly in neurotic cases no such change occurs; in fact, this is often
made the defining characteristic of neurotic behavior: it is unchange-
able by any rational considerations. (1961, 31–32)

Hospers does not say, though, whether he thinks that the influen-
tial reasons must be *good* reasons. And this is an important question. With respect to freedom, how much better than no reasons are
bad reasons? For instance, suppose that Hospers's hand washer is
impervious to evidence concerning germs but is sensitive to being
told that some bizarre deity has pronounced that it is OK to cease
the constant hand washing during full moons. The hand washer,
thus, is amenable to some reasons—is not totally sphexish—but the
reasons are extremely poor. What shall we say, and on what principled grounds shall we say it?

Indeed, although the quotation from Neely may suggest that he
takes the non-normative position on this issue, Neely's position is
decidedly normative, as is seen by examining his next condition:

(6) A man is freer not only to the extent that he does as he pleases
and to the extent that his pleasing as he does follows from a coherent

life plan, but also to the extent that this life plan and the character which goes with it have been forged by him through time with due attention to the satisfactions which he may be missing as a result of lacking certain desires, with due consideration of those of his character traits which lead to painful consequences, and with due sensitivity to other types of lives which may serve as ideals for him to follow. (1974, 54)

I think that there is a real dilemma here. Should the compatibilist's account be couched solely in terms of psychological states without commitment to their normative suitability[1] or should the account accommodate the normative aspect? If one says that a free agent's reasons need be rational only to the agent, then freedom risks becoming a matter of subjective willfulness. It would be impossible to reject highly irrational decisions as unfree merely because of their irrationality. This is going to make the free will account too wide. But on the other side of the dilemma, building normative criteria into the free will account entails that much of what prephilosophical common sense takes to be clearly free fails miserably. This would make the account too narrow. This result would seem to undermine the compatibilist's enterprise, since the philosophical account of free will is supposed to reflect prephilosophical notions of freedom to some significant degree, on pain of the charge of redefining *freedom*. So, either way, the going looks rough.

2. Four Cases to Illustrate the Normative Problem

So far, I have claimed that the question of how stringent free will's normative conditions must be poses a serious difficulty for the attempt at a unified account. In this section I give four examples to illustrate two related aspects of that problem. First, I cite at length two cases from the recent social psychological literature of cognitive failure to show that sometimes we feel strong intuitions to say both that an agent is free *and* that the agent is unfree. I then give two other examples to show instances in which, once we adopt a set of normative standards, we can describe some cases in which satisfaction of these standards appears necessary for free will and other cases where those standards seem gratuitous. The upshot of both types of examples is that our intuitions about when to say that someone is free pull in such opposite directions that there is a serious danger that the integrity of the free will concept will be destroyed. Those familiar with Stephen Stich's (1983) argument against the reality of belief will see that my strategy in this chapter is similar to his, which I borrow for my present purposes.

Case (1)

The first case involves some fascinating experiments that demonstrate that experimenters can prompt significant shifts in the attitudes of subjects unbeknownst to them. Experimenters asked a group of subjects to complete a questionnaire giving their attitudes on a number of controversial topics such as capital punishment or abortion (Nisbett and Ross, 1980, 121). Subjects with very strong attitudes toward certain issues were then asked to write essays against their positions, that is, to play "devil's advocate." These subjects were divided into two groups, the "sufficient justification" group, who were paid handsomely for writing the essays, and the "insufficient justification" group, who were paid little or nothing. After writing the essays, the two groups were again asked to complete questionnaires. As evinced by their answers, the sufficient justification group experienced little moderation of their extreme views, but the insufficient justification group experienced a significant shift in the direction of the position they had defended in the essay. Also interesting is the fact that those who had undergone a change in attitude as a result of writing the essay denied having done so, saying that they had always held those beliefs, despite the evidence of the earlier questionnaires.

Psychologically, the interpretation of these results is quite interesting. Why do subjects experience an attitude shift under insufficient justification but not when receiving significant rewards? A cognitivist, non-motivational interpretation is this. Whereas the sufficient justification subjects attributed their writing of the discordant essays to the "situational cause," i.e., the financial reward, the insufficient group were unable to explain their behavior in this way, and wrongly attributed to themselves the "dispositional" cause that they really believed what they were writing in the essays. So, on this view, the insufficient justification subjects made inaccurate self-attributions (Nisbett and Ross, 1980, 121). A motivational explanation is that, given that writing the attitude-discrepant essay was cognitively dissonant, the sufficient group dealt with the unpleasantness by reminding themselves that they were being paid handsomely to do so. The insufficient justification group, however, being unable to use this rationalization, needed some other way to comfort themselves. Because the thought that writing the essay for 'no good reason' was dissonant, the insufficient justification group unconsciously opted to reduce the dissonance by coming to believe that what they wrote in the essay was cogent (Zanna and Cooper, 1976).

For present purposes, the important question is whether the insufficient justification subjects came to their new beliefs on the basis of freely made decisions about the merits of their ideological positions. On the one hand, it seems that they clearly manifested free will. What could be a better example of a free choice than one made as the result of self-conscious, elaborated reasons? The autonomy variable account of Chapter 2 appears to be satisfied. Nonetheless, it is tempting to argue for the other conclusion. Evidently, getting people to write attitude-discrepant essays for small or no rewards may enable us to manipulate their views. The experimenters knew better than the subjects did that an attitude shift would occur. The case in which someone else knows better than you do what you will decide is sometimes held to be a paradigm of lack of freedom. (For a more dramatic example in which experimenters can better predict the decisions of subjects than the subjects can, see Milgram, 1974.) Whatever explanation one prefers to account for the attitude shift—the non-motivated cognitive error view, the dissonance reduction explanation, or some other—it appears that the experimenters have discovered some way to bend our choices in the way they want.

I do not think that we can obviate this conflict by saying that the subjects were partially free. Although that notion seems perfectly reasonable to me, because "freedom" is a continuous rather than discrete concept, I do not think that the notion of partial freedom applies here. Instead, I think that the attitude-shift cases are ones of which we might say both "clearly free" and "clearly unfree" depending on the aspect of the situation we emphasize.

To see this, consider this scenario. Imagine that Professor Manipulator, a respected psychologist at State U, wishes to have capital punishment made legal in the state. The good professor believes that the best way to contribute to this end is to modify the resistance on the part of as many anti-capital punishment students who pass through State U as possible. To this end, everyone who takes Psychology 100, required of all first-year students, is given an attitude questionnaire, and all students who indicate strong resistance to capital punishment are asked to write essays in favor of capital punishment. (We assume that the professor adequately disguises what is being done.) The result of this systematic use of attitude-shift experiments is that after thirty years, a capital punishment law is enacted because it faces very little resistance from the State U-educated people who run the state.

Now, consider the question of who is morally responsible for the students' modulation of their resistance to capital punishment. For instance, suppose that you thought that the shift to accepting capital punishment is immoral and deserving of blame. Upon whom do you affix blame? It might seem that any blame that is affixed in these cases goes to the professor: The professor foresaw the results and purposively set in motion the experiments that would produce them. Without the professor's design, the attitude shifts would not have occurred. At the same time, the students are not blameworthy, inasmuch as they were pawns in the hands of the professor. So, it looks as if the professor, unlike the students, was free.

Nonetheless, we can also argue that the students were free. If we argue that the professor's conscious planning of the manipulation is sufficient to establish the professor's free will, then, by parity of reasoning, the students who experienced attitude shift were also free. Would we conclude that the professor had acted unfreely if we learned that the professor had been a pupil of another professor who had gotten the professor to write insufficiently justified pro-capital punishment essays? The role of the professor notwithstanding, the students who wrote the discrepant essays had better grounds for revising their views on capital punishment than most of us do when we change our views. They were not drugged, coerced, bribed, given misinformation, or otherwise beleaguered. Although we may suppose that they did not know the literature concerning attitude shift, all of us are ignorant about all sorts of things that are pertinent to our decision making, and we do not typically think that we are, thereby, made unfree. All of us should be as free as the subjects who wrote those essays.

The moral to this example is that there seem to be two perspectives from which free will may be assessed—with equal claim to our intuitions—that yield radically differing verdicts on whether the subjects have manifested free will. One perspective emphasizes the professor's control, the other emphasizes the students' rationality.

Case (2)

The second type of case that I wish to consider is a range of instances involving our decisions to entertain information that is contrary to beliefs that we already hold. This discussion will call on some important themes in the recent 'rationality' literature, viz., belief perseverance, bias in favor of existing belief, and subjects' overconfidence regarding their beliefs. Although the free will discussion is typically directed to our decisions regarding less intellectual matters, I think that epistemic decisions, e.g., whether to look for confirming or disconfirming evidence and whether to question one's assumptions, are an important subset of decisions where the question of freedom arises.

Regarding belief perseverance, there is evidence that once subjects get beliefs, those beliefs are very difficult to dismiss, even when the subjects are given overwhelming evidence that the beliefs are false. In one study (Ross, Lepper, and Hubbard, 1975), subjects were asked to distinguish between what they were told were genuine and fake suicide notes. After each guess, the subjects were given false feedback indicating that some subjects were highly successful at detection, some were moderately successful, and some were highly unsuccessful. Thus, during the test, the subjects came to have beliefs about their skills at detection. As soon as the test was completed, the subjects were debriefed and apprised that their feedback had been fabricated, and, indeed, were shown instructions that had assigned each of them to their respective success class. After the debriefing, subjects answered questionnaires on their ability to detect suicide notes: Subjects who had been told that they were highly successful rated themselves as far more successful than those who had been told their ability was average, who in turn rated their ability much higher than those who were told that they were highly unsuccessful.

There are several types of cases that fall in the category of bias in favor of existing belief. For instance, the primacy effect—the process by which "early-presented information has an undue influence on final judgment" (Nisbett and Ross, 1980, 172)—has been demonstrated in several areas. In one case, subjects evaluate persons more favorably when a string of five adjectives is presented to them with the most favorable at the front of the list than they do persons to whom the same adjectives are applied in the reverse order (Asch, 1946). A similar primacy effect was observed when subjects were asked to evaluate the performance of test-takers: among test-takers who correctly answered the same number of questions, those whose correct answers came at the beginning of the test were judged to have performed better than those whose correct answers were concentrated at the end (Jones et al., 1968). In the case of self-attribution, subjects who were told early in a run of thirty guesses that they had successfully guessed whether a coin would turn up heads or tails came to believe they were better guessers than subjects whose false feedback on their successes came largely at the end of the trial (Langer and Roth, 1975).

This bias in favor of existing information—unremarkable given the mutually accommodating demands of physiological feasibility and natural selection—becomes epistemically pernicious when our allegiance to existing belief makes us partial to finding confirming evidence and biased against looking for disconfirming evidence (Wason and Johnson-Laird, 1965). An example of such bias is evident when experimenters show two groups of subjects with strong ideological differences (e.g., on whether capital punishment deters murder) two purportedly authentic studies, one of which gives evidence that capital punishment is a deterrent, and the other that provides statistically equivalent evidence that capital punishment is not a deterrent (Lord, Ross, and Lepper, 1979). Common sense would suggest that subjects exposed to such mixed data would modulate their opinions. Instead, the subjects assigned great weight to the studies that supported their previous position, and ignored the countervailing studies, so that the result was a polarizing of opinion.

On the overconfidence that people have regarding their beliefs (a phenomenon long appreciated by lay epistemologists but only recently documented), subjects were tested on a variety of short-answer formats to determine whether their subjective confidence level correlated with the objective probability that their beliefs were true. Subjects were asked both to select what they thought was the correct answer to a factual question (e.g., What is the capital of Ecuador?), and to express their degree of confidence that their selection was correct. Persons who are ideally attuned to their own epistemic abilities might be expected to display a strong correlation between their levels of confidence and the correctness of their answers. For instance, persons should get approximately one-half of the answers correct for which they are .5 confident, 75 percent correct for those for which they are 3 to 1 confident, 91 percent correct for those that they are 10 to 1 confident, and so on. It turned out that although the subjects' confidence and success levels were closely related when the subjects admitted to being relatively uncertain of their knowledge, in those cases where their confidence levels were greater than 5 to 1 there was a large disparity between confidence level and success. In one experiment using sixty-six subjects, the group collectively was correct on 68 percent of the answers that they considered themselves to be 50 to 1 certain and was correct 81 percent of the time they were confident to a degree of 1000 to 1 (Fischoff, Slovic, and Lichtenstein, 1977).

Now, what do these examples of belief perseverance, bias for existing belief, and overconfidence regarding knowledge have to do with free will? A minimal interpretation would be that *somehow* the normative model of free will that is explicated in the autonomy account is unsatisfied. That model requires that we are impartial seekers after truth who are able to put aside what philosophers like to call "merely psychological" factors like the order in which we receive evidence, its vividness, and the present state of our biases. The above cases suggest that *in the normal case* (and not owing to brain lesions or psychosis) judgment is not made according to our hierarchical paradigm. Thus, our autonomy account faces a problem similar to that faced by a naive use of the Aristotelian mean. Suppose that one held that the path to virtue in selecting actions (or emotions) was to find the two opposite alternatives that are the extremes and then 'average' them. Such an averaging is a sham, because the real work in making the decision is done in selecting what the two extremes are; someone else would find the mean to be different depending on what was assigned to be the extremes. Our attempt at reasoned decision making in the above cases faces a corresponding difficulty. Try as we may to give fair evaluations to competing evidence, if the apparent attractiveness of certain evidence is determined for us by unexamined, non-epistemically relevant factors such as those cited above, our best-intentioned conscious evaluations may occur within such circumscribed limits that the resulting decisions are a sham. Limits that are established by belief perseverance, bias, and overconfidence may narrow what seem to us to be rational alternatives in such a way that our intellectual lives become an exercise in choosing between false dilemmas. All this has the strong appearance of making our epistemic decisions—and any subsequent decisions that depend upon them—unfree.

A second, more ambitious, interpretation of these examples is the theme of this chapter, *viz.*, that there is simply no saying whether poor epistemic agents choose freely or not. We have already suggested why the compatibilist should view our epistemic foibles as destructive of free will: viewed from the outside, the spectacle of our insulating our beliefs from disconfirmation and selecting confirming evidence in a biased way must look, again using Dennett's term, ridiculously sphexish. We appear to be pathetic victims, victimized by our psychological hedonism and laziness. But at the same time, common sense can find reasons to deny this conclusion. After all, where's the compulsion in these cases of epistemic foibles? There is no one to blame for the poor epistemic choices except the subjects themselves. Moreover, why is the choice to discount countervailing evidence or to refuse to look for such evidence any less free than analogous choices regarding one's spouse, country, or religion, that is, other dogmatic choices that typically receive high marks? Finally, on the view that free will is co-extensive with the range of decisions that are "up to you," poor epistemic choices seem to be free choices *par excellence*.

The second aspect of the normative problem that I want to consider in this section is the fact that once we insert normative conditions into our free will account, we will be able to imagine both (a) examples where we remain free despite violations of the normative conditions, and (b) examples where such violations seem to diminish free will. The pessimistic conclusion to be drawn from this would be that the attempt to produce a principled, normative account that will have general application is bound to fail. Since the discussion in Chapter 2 produced several examples of type (b), we need only to produce some instances of type (a). I shall offer two cases to do that.

Case (3)

Imagine the case of a philosophy job-seeker who must decide whether to accept a position at a university in a cold climate or decline it and risk going jobless for the next year.[2] The applicant is undecided even until the fateful phone call comes in which he must give a final answer. While answering the call, he considers his reasons one last time when his most vivid stranded-in-the-cold scenario just pops into his head and on the strength of this thought the applicant decides to reject the offer. Such spontaneity, whether a case of genuine "Valerian" free will (Dennett's word, 1978, 197) perhaps owing to an uncaused subatomic event in the brain (Kane, 1985, 167), or merely an unexpected deterministic recollection, seems to count against Neely's condition (6) cited above and my own notion of the efficacy of the reasoning process. Yet, although the applicant's decision may be *ill-advised*, or in some loose sense, *irrational*, it is arguable that it is free. The point of this example is that 'the liberty of spontaneity' seems to have a significant purchase upon our prephilosophical intuitions as a paradigm of free will, while faring poorly once we add normative conditions to our accounts of free will.

Case (4)

For a final example that reveals the tension between normative and non-normative strains in the free will concept, consider Neely's condition (3) above, which claims that one is freer to the extent that in deciding one is not frustrating one's other desires. We can easily imagine confirming instances by considering situations in which a choice that produces a lower frustration of other desires yields a greater degree of psychological control than situations where one is truly torn between equally desired alternatives (e.g., Buridan's ass; Hamlet; and Slote's (1980) emphasis on the importance of psychological equanimity to freedom in the Stoical and Spinozistic views of freedom). Yet it is easy to select disconfirming instances where reduced dissonance, far from making one freer, might make an agent less free than a more ambivalent counterpart. For instance, there is a strong intuitive feeling that the troubled "savage" in *Brave New World*, who was racked with self-recrimination over enjoying any of that civilization's pleasures, was more free than the other members of the society whose choices almost never caused them to frustrate other desires. A more studied argument for the same conclusion comes from combining two psychological themes. Dissonance theorists have found that choosing between fairly evenly matched alternatives typically creates more cognitive dissonance than does choosing between alternatives where one is clearly more desirable (Brehm and Cohen, 1962, 5). But it has also been found that subjective feelings of freedom are proportional to the degree of perceived similarity of attractiveness of one's alternatives. Great differences correspond to reduced feelings of free choice, whereas small differences correspond to increased feelings of choice (Harvey and Jellison, 1974, 539). Putting these two results together, we conclude that dissonance, *ceteris paribus*, covaries with subjective feelings of choice. Thus it looks as if there are some cases in which increased psychological ambivalence and even distress corresponds to subjects feeling more free, and yet there are other cases in which the opposite is true.

3. The Bribe Problem

The problem question raised in this section is whether bribes ever reduce the free will of the person who is bribed. Slote makes a strong case for saying that bribes may be just as damaging to freedom as threats, given that "some offers are so 'coercive' and humiliating that if we do take advantage of them, we act no more freely than the (threatened) bank clerk . . ." (1980, 131).

Slote supports this claim by pointing out the parity between threats and bribes when viewed from the perspective of utility maximization. Although the spectrum of utility for the results of one's choices is higher for bribes than threats (e.g., plus to even, vs. even to minus), both bribes and threats create a range from which we must choose: "[A]n attractive offer changes our options dramatically, and it seems as reasonable to attribute 'ultimate agency' to someone who makes an effective offer as to someone who makes an effective threat" (130–131).

There are two related themes behind Slote's comparison of bribes to threats. The first is that, viewed mathematically, bribes and threats can be equally seen as creating alternatives that require the same sort of judgment. In a bribe I must choose between retaining my present utility level or accepting an addition, whereas in a threat I choose between my present utility level or risking a reduction. Viewed from the perspective of utility maximization, it is difficult to see why bribes categorically cannot reduce freedom if threats do. The second theme is psychological. Because Slote's explanation of why threats reduce free will is that threats often produce psychological ambivalence in the subject who wishes to resist the threat (discussed in Chapter 2), Slote thinks that bribes can have the same unsettling effect. For Slote, just as the threatened bank clerk might wish to be able to resist the robber, so:

> [E]ven someone who feels that it is rational and worthwhile for him to lick the boots (of someone who offered a million dollar bribe) will also think less of himself for being willing to be rational in this way and wish that he were somehow above this sort of thing. . . . (131)

Although I like Slote's position, I want to contrast to it a view that seems widely reflective of common sense (inasmuch as I get it from almost every student with whom I have discussed Slote's argument). This reply is also suggested by work in psychology that suggests that individuals may ignore the symmetries between bribes and threats, because "anticipation of reward is more conducive to feelings of freedom than is anticipation of punishment" (Harvey, 1976, 81). The response to Slote that I am suggesting is that bribes, unlike threats, *never* reduce free will. Irrespective of the psychological distress that accepting (or rejecting) a bribe might produce, a bribed person is always free to accept or reject the bribe. There is no reason to think that, e.g., in the bootlicking example "embarrassed to choose x" provides any support for "chooses x unfreely." A bribe expands your options in the sense that now you have one more alternative open to you that is (by the lights of the bribe-offerer, anyway) at least as desirable as the alternatives that you had before the bribe. In the worst case, where the bribe is unappealing, you are no worse off than you were before the bribe was presented. So, either way you have an expansion of options or at least not a diminution of options and, thus, cannot have your freedom reduced by the offer.

4. Do Causes That Incline without Compelling Reduce Free Will?

The third difficulty for the free will concept is given by the title question of this section. Here, too, we shall find that we do not know how to answer a difficult question about free will.

Let us imagine two cases in which we can resist intrusions that threaten to influence our choices, but only with considerable difficulty. In the first, I am a struggling dieter with a weakness for desserts. When offered desserts after dinner, if I summon all the 'will power' I can manage, I resist the urge. Let us say that I can manage such strength 20 percent of the time. In the second case I am a manipulatable logic instructor who is prone to yield to my students' demands to give retests for examinations in which the class performed poorly. Here too, suppose that if I really try to resist, I can, but in the normal course of things I do not manage such resolve and give in four times as often as I resist.

What shall we say about the 80 percent of the cases in which I do not manage a strong enough effort to resist? The autonomy variable account seems to yield the answer that in those cases my free will was considerably reduced. In the terms of that account, I have not been efficacious in bringing my decision into line with what the other autonomy variables dictate is the best thing for me to do. Moreover, a slippery-slope argument yields the same conclusion. We can imagine a continuum of cases where the amount of effort I need to make to resist an inducement is increased to the point that, no matter how hard I try, I cannot decide contrary to the inducement. Because I am unfree when my effort to resist is totally inefficacious, surely I am unfree when the effort required is so great that I can manage it only 1 percent of the time, and so on. Thus, although it is a thorny question of just what degree of inclination without compulsion makes us unfree, there is no problem in principle with saying that sometimes we are made unfree in such cases.

The problem is that I do not think that this plausible-looking view has exclusive claim to reflecting our views about free will. Imagine an objector who argues: "As long as it is true that *if* you tried hard enough you could have resisted the inducements, you are free. It was up to you whether to expend the requisite effort or not, and if you did not, then you were effectively electing to submit to the inducements. Thus, causes that incline without compelling do not make us unfree; only compulsion does."

5. Does Being Free Entail Feeling Free?

The fourth problem for the free will concept is the question of whether choosing freely requires that we are aware of ourselves as free agents. Galen Strawson argues that it is conceptually necessary that free agents believe in their freedom:

> [I]t seems *inconceivable* that there should be true free agenthood without belief in freedom. It seems to be a non-causal impossibility: when one imaginatively subtracts any sense of freedom or true responsibility from the agent, its freedom or true responsibility goes too. (1986, 301)

Strawson explicates the sense in which he thinks that free agents must believe in their own freedom:

> [T]he belief that a (potential) free agent must have in its (potential) free agenthood need not be a permanently occurrent belief. . . . Avoiding use of the word 'believe'. . . one might put the central claim as follows: if a being has no *sense* . . . or *conception*, or, most generally, *experience* of itself as a free agent, then it cannot be a free agent. (197)

One way that Strawson supports his claim is by pointing out that being able to choose at all (and, *a fortiori*, being able to choose freely) requires thinking that one can choose:

> In order to be able to choose (at *t*) between performing an X-action and a Y-action, one need not actually be able to put one's choice into effect. . . . But one must (at *t*) at least think . . . both that one can now perform an X-action and that one can perform a Y-action; possession of such a thought or belief is essential to these two courses of action being truly objects of choice for one, now. For if one has no such belief, or thinks that one cannot in fact perform either an X-action or a Y-action, then one cannot mentally determine on either, deciding 'I will perform an X-action (or Y-action)'. One cannot make a choice between them at all.

> Believing you can do something (now) is not a necessary condition of being able to do it (now), but it is a necessary condition of being able to choose or decide to do it (now), in the present sense of 'able to choose'. (137)

A second way that Strawson defends his thesis is by showing the oddness of denying it. Strawson does this by imagining an agent who "acts, and for reasons that she can give," but who doesn't *feel* her own agency in her decisions:

> Although fully self-conscious, the Spectator has no strong particular sense of herself as a decision-making self-governing agent, as we usually (but not always) do. But this very fact appears to preclude her being a free agent. She doesn't really see herself as the decider and rational planner of action (and thus, *a fortiori*, doesn't conceive of herself as a free agent). (235)

Strawson's argument that choosing freely entails believing that one has options available seems obviously true. (It is worth distinguishing this from the incompatibilist argument that freedom entails believing that you can manifest libertarian freedom, which seems to me dubious. See R. Taylor, 1964, for its elaboration, and Kapitan, 1986 and Double, Forthcoming, for a rebuttal.) How can you choose unless you, at least tacitly, believe that you have options?

As attractive as Strawson's position appears, arguments that freedom does not require a sense of freedom are easily produced. First, being free and feeling free seem to be two discrete states. From a psychological perspective, feeling free appears to be a radically different sort of state than the state of being free. Feeling free involves conceptual self-recognition, and, as such, appears linguistic in character. Being free is the way that our choices *are*, and appears not to be linguistic. If this is so, then, by Hume's Law, they must be logically separable. Of course, this case may be an exception to Hume's view, but the burden of proof surely has to be on those who reject it. Second, and related to the first point, Strawson's view does not seem to be accurate phenomenologically. I think that I can imagine myself choosing freely one time without having a sense of my free agency. I may evaluate the merits of options A and not A by rehearsing the various utilities that attend each, e.g., 'A has advantage p, whereas not A has the advantage q', without reflecting on myself. Or, I may choose between the two alternatives without going through any consciously accessible evaluation at all. I may just choose. If I can imagine myself as manifesting free will in such instances, it is difficult to see why I cannot actually do so in the normal course of things.

Strawson perhaps could reply that the sense of freedom that free agents must have does not require any consciously accessible rehearsing of alternatives using the word *I*. The mere fact that free agents must be *able* to self-consciously reflect on their freedom shows that they tacitly represent themselves as free, even in those cases where they do not engage in self-conscious reflection. This hypothesized reply brings the debate to a head. What are we to make of the claim that when we decide freely we tacitly represent ourselves as being free? What does it mean and how shall we determine whether it is sanctioned by the free will concept?

6. Three Exemplars of Freedom

In this section, I elaborate three exemplars of freedom that I believe philosophers implicitly use in deciding whether to count particular cases as instances of free will. The paradigms are intended as idealizations to which individuals' paradigms of freedom at most approximate. So, although the paradigms I describe are broad and fairly imprecise, there will be a lot of room for disagreement among philosophers utilizing them, since the paradigms contain somewhat conflicting threads. There is nothing 'magical' about the number 3:

Perhaps the explanatory job that I seek to do with the three para-digms can be done by dividing them up into more paradigms or by making them conflicting elements within only one or two para-digms. My basic claim is that there is some underlying cognitive explanation for the conflicting free will intuitions cited in the previous sections, and that providing an explanation in terms of three conflicting paradigms is one way in which that deeper *expla-nans* can be adumbrated.

A methodological note. My selection of a taxonomy of three paradigms is an exercise in armchair speculation. My claim that these paradigms have some degree of psychological reality in philo-sophers' thinking about free will is armchair psychology in its baldest form. Although I think that what I say in this section has a decent claim to the truth, I am not happy to be forced to speak to what I take to be an empirical question in such a speculative way. Before one got too excited about these freedom paradigms, one would want answers to a multitude of questions that I have no resources to address. Are these paradigms operative only among Western philosophers? Among Western philosophers only in the analytic tradition? Are there significant differences in the para-digms accepted by logicians and ethicists, blacks and whites, men and women, old philosophers and young philosophers, Democratic and Republican philosophers, and so on? It is not inconceivable that there could be empirical work on these issues, and in the next section I suggest that something like my free will paradigms may have been uncovered in the psychological literature concerning perceived freedom. In any event, for present purposes it is impor-tant to specify the paradigms, since I think they ultimately help to explain an important phenomenon.

(*i*) *The Reasonable Man*

For the first paradigm I borrow, with an important emendation, Edgar Wilson's model of *the reasonable man*, which Wilson thinks plays a crucial role in the determination of just provocation in English law (1979, Chapter 11). According to Wilson, the paradigm of the reasonable man is designed to square legal and moral respon-sibility in the following way. In its simplest form, the question put to juries is: Would the average person, possessing "ordinary intelligence and reasonable prudence" react in a similar way to the provocation that the defendant faced? If the reasonable man would respond as the defendant did, then the defendant is neither legally nor morally culpable. If the reasonable man would have refrained, then in absence of evidence of mental incapacity, the defendant is held legally and morally responsible.

Wilson proposes the following (interesting) list of characteristics of the reasonable man:

1. He is not unusually excitable or pugnacious.
2. He is not mentally deficient or under the influence of drugs.
3. He is neither physically abnormal, nor impotent, nor blind, nor a dwarf, nor scarred by severe injuries.
4. If a woman, she is not pregnant.
5. If his self-control is lost in finding his wife in adultery or his mistress or fiancee unfaithful, it is not when he is merely told.
6. He retains his self-control in the face of words however abusive, except in the case of certain undefined extremes.
7. He remains unmoved if his nose is pulled. (319)

I think that a great deal else goes into the reasonable man paradigm besides these characteristics. Like Aristotle's magnanimous man, the reasonable man seems to be adult, male, and a member of the dominant social group. The reasonable man is not motivated by poverty or intense ideological convictions. The reasonable man is a paragon of commonsense beliefs and tastes, because he is what members of the just-described class take themselves to be.

I think that this paradigm holds that the reasonable man possesses the power to resist the deterministic forces to which unreasonable people are subject, but I do not think that the paradigm is explicit about what is required metaphysically to produce this power. On this point I break from Wilson, who says that the reasonable man paradigm is explicitly committed to the existence of "transempirical" (308) Cartesian-style egos. That is, although I agree that the paradigm views the reasonable man as able to resist the unhappiest, 'clockish' consequences of determinism, I think it does not speak to the question of whether this requires a Cartesian ego, some sort of contra-causal physical entity like a Chisholmian person, or whether the reasonable man is simply a happily situated determined physical entity a la Aristotle. The debate over the metaphysics of the reasonable man's free will is a philosophical one that involves substantial argument and cannot be read off the paradigm directly.

Finally, I think this paradigm contains the idea of free action, as well as free will, and with it the idea of political freedom. The reasonable man resists tampering from political sources and is not manipulatable in the Brave New World fashion. (If people are controllable in this way, then that is conclusive evidence that they do not meet the reasonable man paradigm.)

(*ii*) *The Pure Rational Ego*

The second paradigm that I think colors philosophers' judgments about freedom is that of the *pure rational ego*. This model contains elements bequeathed by the great rationalist philosophers: Descartes' notion of the transparency of all of our mental states, Spinoza's view that reconciling ourselves to determinism enables us to be free, and Kant's notion that the ego that decides *because* it follows the dictates of reason is free. The virtues of the pure rational ego include satisfaction of our highly rationalistic autonomy variable account in Chapter 2: self-knowledge, reasonability, intelligence, efficacy, and unity.

The pure rational ego is a more demanding normative model than is that of the reasonable man. Although the reasonable man possesses average intelligence, the pure rational ego marks a goal to which rationalistic thinkers (and non-rationalists during their rationalistic moments) aspire. For instance, the pure rational ego, which is unaffected by fears and desires that buffet even a reasonable man, is an ideal utility calculator. So, unlike normal human beings, the pure rational ego adopts neither risk-seeking nor risk-aversive decision strategies in cases of uncertainty, always preferring to make choices that are mathematically optimal (Kahneman and Tversky, 1982). This illustrates just one way in which the pure rational ego is even less affected by emotions than is the reasonable man. I do not think that this paradigm requires, in Dennett's words, a "perfect Kantian will which would be able to respond with perfect fidelity to all good reasons" (1984, 49). But it is pretty close. What is important is not that the rational ego is transempirical, for that is again too specific to be part of the paradigm, but that it be highly cognitive, the sort of 'thinking thing' that, irrespective of its ontology, is a truth-seeker. In this sense, it is not concerned with the physical body, even if it is part of the body. The rational ego lies above the merely 'contingent' trappings of the reasonable man, inasmuch as it is nonsexual, nonracial, non-politically oriented—in short, it is removed from the world, if not by ontology, then by interest.

(iii) The Nonegocentric Actor

The third paradigm I want to elaborate is the model of the *nonegocentric actor*. The nonegocentric actor, unlike the pure rational ego, is a complete person actively engaged in the world, and, unlike the reasonable man, is not limited to a preferred age, race, sex, or social class. The nonegocentric actor acts from reasons in a loose sense, but the reasons need not be especially well scrutinized; indeed, too much ratiocination poses a danger to the spontaneous, ebullient freedom of the actor. It is through the nonegocentric paradigm that the important libertarian desideratum "the liberty of indifference" gains a hold on the intuitions of philosophers and laypersons alike. The nonegocentric actor is as "free as the wind" and as unpredictable. The latter characteristic makes the paradigm pretty strongly committed to indeterminism, since determinism would make the actor's choices theoretically predictable. The indeterministic aspect is also supported by the notion that the nonegocentric actor is not controllable, so that even if there were a Kanian covert non-constraining controller, that controller could not determine the actor's behavior (Kane, 1985, 46). Finally, the nonegocentric actor exemplifies the "positive conception" of freedom, and not just the aspect of freedom that is free *from* control. The nonegocentric actor can move in many different directions, is free *to* do a wide range of things.

In popular culture, there are many characters who represent the nonegocentric actor: the characters from *Barefoot in the Park*, the child Pollyanna, 1960s "flower children." In philosophy, there are thinkers who endorse parts of the paradigm, although I cannot think of any philosopher whose idea of freedom corresponds to the entire paradigm. The paradigm's emphasis on free action rather than free will is concordant with the traditional views of Hobbes, Locke, and Hume that take freedom to be the ability to act as one wishes (see Chapter 2), but the paradigm is hostile to the compatibilist aims of the British empiricists. A second element of this paradigm is its notion that individual consciousness is logically and psychologically parasitic on our ability to engage in social intercourse, that the mental arena of self-conscious deliberation is simply social communication turned inward. This is a theme familiar among thinkers as diverse as Marx, Nietzsche, Mead, and Sellars. A third philosophical element is the Eastern notion that freedom requires a relaxation of the impulsive desire to figure everything out, the desire at the very heart of the pure rational ego paradigm. The libertarian Kane expresses sympathy for this Eastern perspective, which he characterizes this way:

> A theme of much Taoist and Zen Buddhist writing is that only when the conscious mind relaxes, and does not try to have complete control over its thinking, does the agent become truly creative and truly free. (1985, 114)

7. Some Empirical Support for the Free Will Exemplars

In the last section I hinted that there may be empirical evidence that subjects use something akin to the differing paradigms of freedom when they assess their degree of freedom under experimental conditions. My suggestion has two parts. First, there is substantial evidence that subjects rate the degree of choice that they have in various experiments according to how well they think that various dimensions or factors have been satisfied. Second, a plausible explanation of why subjects focus on the dimensions they do is that they rely on different paradigms of choice in different situations.

The experiments that I shall cite share a generic format:

> (1) Groups of subjects are asked to choose between two or more alternatives, e.g., the more desirable of two prizes they may receive (Wortman, 1975), or which of a number of college football teams is most deserving to play in a bowl game (Harvey and Jellison, 1974).

(2) Certain variables that the experimenters wish to test for (e.g., similarity of options or time believed to have been taken to make the choices) are varied for the subjects.

(3) Subjects fill out posttest questionnaires in which they evince their impressions about their choices by rating their feelings on a numeric scale. Typical questions were "How responsible do you feel for the fact that you got this item rather than another?" (Wortman, 1975, 288) and "How much choice did you feel in deciding which team to select?" (Harvey and Jellison, 1974, 541).

(4) The experimenters tallied and analyzed the responses.

In addition to a fascinating array of results coming from these experiments (e.g., the widespread belief of subjects that they can control random events like the outcome of a coin toss—Langer and Roth, 1975), Harvey and Weary (1981) focus on three factors that appear to increase subjects' feelings of choice. The first is that perceived choice varies proportionately with the perceived similarity of the attractiveness of the various options. For instance, subjects asked to choose between receiving two equally desirable prizes rated themselves as having a greater degree of choice than did subjects who had to choose between a highly desirable and a relatively unattractive prize (Jellison and Harvey, 1973). A closely related phenomenon is that subjects feel they have more freedom of choice in deciding which football team will win a given game if the two teams are evenly matched—if the teams are mismatched, subjects feel less free in deciding which team will win (Harvey, 1976, 79). The second factor that Harvey and Weary cite as contributing to perceived choice is the desirability of the perceived options. They express this Skinnerian point that people recognize the influence that negative reinforcement has over their behavior (Skinner, 1971), but do not recognize the effect of positive reinforcement by asking "How much choice should a person feel who is faced with the decision of whether to die by firing squad or by cyanide gas" (Harvey and Weary, 1981, 81).

The third factor concerns the amount of time that subjects think they took in making decisions. When subjects believe that they have decided quickly, an increase in the number of options increases subjective feelings of choice, but when subjects believe that they have taken a long time to decide, the same increase in the number of options reduces feelings of choice. In an experiment in which subjects were to choose a football team to play in a bowl game (Harvey and Jellison, 1974), subjects were divided into three groups, *viz.*, individuals who had to select from among three, six, or twelve teams. Each of these groups were in turn divided into two groups, one group of subjects who were told that they had taken half the average length of time that all subjects had taken to make their selections, and a second group who were told that they had taken one-and-one-half times the average length of time to decide. The subjects were then queried about the degree of choice they felt they had exercised, and the results of the six groups were compared. Among subjects who were told that they had decided quickly, those who had only three options rated their degree of choice lower than subjects who had six options rated themselves, who in turn rated themselves as having less choice than did the subjects who chose between twelve options. In other words, perceived choice increased proportionately as the number of options increased, as one might naively expect. The interesting results were among the subjects who were told that they had taken a long time to choose. Among this group, subjects who had six options rated their degree of choice higher than did the subjects who had three or twelve options. Harvey and Jellison expressed this result this way:

> [P]erceived choice is greater the greater the number of options when the individual feels that he has expeditiously evaluated the options; whereas, an intermediate number of options produces a relatively great amount of perceived choice when the individual feels that he has taken a rather lengthy amount of time in evaluating the options. (1974, 543)

Among subjects who had twelve options, those who were told that they had taken a short time to make their choice perceived themselves as having had much more choice than those who were told that they had taken a long time: "The mean (for perceived choice) for the long time/very large number condition was significantly less than the mean for the short time/very large number condition" (Harvey and Jellison, 1974, 541). How can we explain this remarkable result? If the results of the experiment showed that perceived choice increases as the number of options increases, then the results could be understood as a function of the decreased certainty that any individual option is best, as in the case cited above where subjects feel more choice in choosing between evenly matched football teams than mismatched teams. This theme, in turn, is easily understood in terms of the commonsense belief that the liberty of indifference enhances our freedom, which I have characterized above in what I call the nonego-centric actor exemplar.

But perceived choice does not correspond to an increase in the number of options when subjects think that they have taken a long time to choose. It would seem, then, that in evaluating their choice in this case, subjects are not so greatly impressed by the liberty of indifference. Instead, I suggest that subjects evaluated the amount of choice they had relative to a more intellectualized standard, to wit, the sort of standards of rational decision making that constitute the pure rational ego paradigm. When subjects think that they took longer than the average amount of time to make a decision, they ask themselves 'how good a job' of sorting through the various options they did. Accordingly, twelve options were just too many to consider thoroughly, and subjects who had twelve options thought they had not done a very good job at making the intellectually optimal choice. Those with six options, in my view, felt more confident that they had met the standards implicit in the pure rational ego exemplar and rated their choice accordingly. So, depending upon the amount of time that agents think they took to make choices (I assume with the experimenters that *telling* subjects that they had taken more or less time in deciding typically is generally sufficient to get them to *believe* what they were told), we can experimentally manipulate subjects into evaluating their degree of choice relative to something like the non-egocentric actor or the pure rational ego paradigm. Although I do not claim that my explanation is the only possible way to account for the data that Harvey and Jellison have uncovered, I think that the data provide the exemplar view with a degree of credibility that is worth reckoning.

Finally, I want to support the exemplar view by looking at some work by the social psychologist Ivan Steiner (1979), who explicitly distinguishes three kinds of choice that correspond to a somewhat different taxonomy of factors that subjects find relevant to increasing their sense of choice. Subjects experience *evaluative choice* to the extent that the best option available to them is clearly more desirable than their prechoice situations. Having evaluative choice is having a 'good' choice in the sense that it enables subjects to better their situations (and thus corresponds to the Skinnerian line that Harvey and Weary cite, *viz.*, that having desirable options increases our sense of choice) (22). *Discriminative choice* is enhanced when subjects feel that they have what lay persons would call *clear* choices (which psychologists sometimes call *meaningful* choices). Subjects who felt that one alternative was clearly more desirable than another reported their choices as more meaningful than did subjects to whom the relative choices were highly similar in attractiveness (23). Finally, *autonomous choice* increases to the degree that subjects view their options as having incommensurable advantages requiring serious deliberation in order to decide which is best. In a highly autonomous choice,

> The individual's idiosyncratic preferences guide the evaluative process, and the individual, rather than the obvious qualities of the options, appears to determine the decision. He or she can perceive the self as an autonomous decision-making agent. . . . (24)

Steiner's three kinds of choice not only taxonomize choice differently than do the three factors cited by Harvey and Weary; they can conflict among themselves. For instance, it seems that discriminative choice, which calls for clearly discernable differences, and autonomous choice, which emphasizes the role of the individual in decision making, are pretty much at odds with each other. Moreover, Steiner showed the potential clash between evaluative and discriminative choice in the following way. Subjects selected between two topics that they would discuss with a clinical psychologist and then were asked, first, whether the two options provided a *good* choice and, second, whether the two options provided a *meaningful* choice. As was expected, goodness of choice correlated with the degree of desirability of the favored option and not the discrepancy between the desirability of the options, whereas meaningfulness correlated with the perceived difference between the two options and not with the desirability of the preferred option (23).

The moral I draw from Steiner's view is the same that I draw from the work of Harvey and Jellison. Steiner's work suggests that there is no unified concept of choice. Instead, there are various sometimes conflicting dimensions along which we might evaluate our degree of choice; which dimension we use depends on contextual and idiosyncratic factors. Any debate in a borderline case over whether someone *really* has a great deal of choice, thus, needs to be decomposed into more precise questions about types of choice. And this is strongly analogous to the procedure that I shall recommend concerning questions over whether we are free in the difficult cases examined earlier in this chapter.

8. The Three Exemplars and the Unsettled Free Will Questions

It is now time to fulfill the promise of this chapter by showing how our shifting allegiances to the various free will paradigms explain our conflicting intuitions on the questions raised in the first five sections. I think that the free will paradigms incline those who are influenced by them toward differing assessments of the three general free will conditions discussed earlier, *viz.*, the ability to choose otherwise, control, and rationality. Appeal to the pure rational ego supports a one-way interpretation of the three requirements, whereas the rational man and nonegocentric actor exemplars suggest that the conditions must be dually satisfied. Consider first how someone who was strongly impressed by the paradigm of the pure rational ego might proceed. Since rationality is the cardinal virtue of those who satisfy that paradigm, it is likely that those enamored of the pure rational ego would think that a free agent's rationality must be one way. A liberty of indifference that existed between one's practical reasoning and one's choices would strike the pure rational ego as a negation of the ego's most ennobling capacity; only one choice can be the rational product of its practical reason at any one time. But given its commitment to the one-way construal of rationality, the pure rational ego will be strongly committed to a one-way interpretation of control and the ability to choose otherwise. For, to demand that free agents must have either dual control or dual ability to choose otherwise would be to require that free agents have the *capacity* to choose in ways that violate one-way rationality. But agents who in fact manifested dual control or dual ability to choose otherwise would violate one-way rationality. Hence, the pure rational ego's emphasis on rationality dictates its position on all three conditions.

Those who are attracted to the nonegocentric actor or rational man paradigms will reason in the reverse direction. As I have characterized the former, its principal concern is with genuine spontaneity understood as metaphysically open futures, which ensures its preference for the two-way interpretation of the ability to choose otherwise. The nonegocentric actor paradigm's insistence on indeterminism, in turn, commits it to a dual interpretation of control and rationality. These are not problematic commitments to those who prefer this paradigm, since the paradigm places little value on strict, imperialistic satisfaction of either condition. And those who are impressed by the rational man paradigm are likely to reason as the above group does, with perhaps more emphasis on the importance of dual control. Not only do rational men need the categorical ability to choose otherwise, but they need to control their choices whichever way they go. This view also requires that the rationality that the rational man paradigm endorses will be dual.

Now, to the various unsettled disputes discussed earlier. I begin with the residual worries about the viability of the internalistic view of free will. I argued in Chapter 2 that compatibilism requires accepting the internalistic view that, assuming the satisfaction of a strong rationality account of free will, even brains-in-vats could possess free will. Thus, the question of whether brains-in-vats could enjoy free will becomes an important test case for compatibilism.

For philosophers under the sway of the pure rational ego paradigm, the notion of free brains-in-vats is conceivable. The fact that brains-in-vats generate no real actions is no problem for the paradigm, since it manifests benign insouciance to the relationship between the ego and the external world. This indifference extends to the causal history antedating the brain's mental operations, provided, of course, that the causal background does not disrupt the logical integrity of those operations. Thus, the pure rational ego does not care about what went on before it got the input upon which it operates, and this indifference extends to the question of whether the ego's operations are deterministic. The pure rational ego, thus, is the epitome of magnanimity. Like the infinitely forgiving lover or parent, the pure rational ego overlooks all transgressions, even the possibility that its own exercise is determined and, in principle, predictable. Rationality is its supreme value, and if it operates in ways that meet its own demanding standards, then the deterministic hypothesis, which troubles less self-secure egos, is of no concern to it. One might say that the pure rational ego is smug.

The notion of a free brain-in-a-vat is anathema to the nonegocentric actor and the reasonable man paradigms. After all, brains-in-vats cannot *act* freely, they are in principle predictable, they are manipulatable, they are not spontaneous, and, perhaps most importantly, they are not social. "Only a perverse, abstraction of a human being such as the pure rational ego could convince itself that it was free even if all its decisions were ultimately traceable to the power of another being," the nonegocentric actor laughs. For those under the influence of the nonegocentric paradigm, the thought that brains-in-vats could be free in any sense indicates hubris and a pathetic attempt to reduce the cognitive dissonance that naturally arises from the sad thought that determinism may be true, and, hence, that our spontaneity may be only an illusion. The reasonable man paradigm also counts against the solipsistic view of free will. Brains-in-vats do not approximate the reasonable man, since they are not men at all. On this paradigm, free agents may be introspective and even somewhat preoccupied with their own rationality, but they must also be in the world. Moreover, brains-in-vats do not exemplify political freedom; they are too liable to tampering.

Let us turn next to the normative problem, which I have characterized as having two aspects. The first is that we can give examples where our intuitions conflict radically on whether we should say that the subjects in the examples decided freely. The second is that although in some cases the satisfaction of strong normative requirements seems necessary, there are other cases where those standards seem gratuitous.

For both sorts of cases, those influenced by the pure rational ego paradigm are content to keep the rationality demands very high and to apply them widely. After all, the *job* of the ego is to think well (and, as a part of that, to decide carefully and wisely). It had better meet high normative standards, since the pure rational ego has no other source from which to derive its freedom. Thus, in the case of attitude shift, the pure rational ego suggests that the subjects are unfree because there are underlying forces at work that pervert the rationality of their egos. On the attribution-mistake interpretation, subjects prove to have faulty self-knowledge, and any decision made on that basis is, thereby, unfree. On the dissonance-reduction interpretation, subjects manifest hedonistically motivated self-deception, which also perverts the subjects' decisions. Reason should not misfire in these ways, and if it does (a sobering empirical possibility for this paradigm), then the agents lose freedom. The same moral is applied to the case of poor epistemic choices.

The reasonable man and the nonegocentric actor paradigms generally agree that in these first two normative examples subjects are free, despite the cognitive failings. To its credit, the reasonable man paradigm has more difficulty with this verdict than does the nonegocentric actor paradigm: the attitude-shift case raises the worry of manipulation, and the examples of poor epistemic choices are worrisome, since those examples (scandalously) suggest that the reasonable man might not be quite so reasonable as we believe. On the nonegocentric actor view, neither of these cases are problematic for *freedom*, although they may be problematic for *rationality* in some broad sense.

In the third example of disagreement on the normative issue, the 'spontaneous' decision of the philosophy applicant to reject the job offer, the three paradigms issue widely different answers to those who consult them. For the nonegocentric actor, the job seeker was undoubtedly free, since such spontaneity lies at the heart of that paradigm. At the moment of decision, rejecting the offer seemed the obvious choice, and the agent manifested his freedom by acting in the way he wanted. On the paradigm of the pure rational ego, the job seeker was almost certainly a victim to a non-rational event (either a truly indeterminist thought or at least one that was unevaluated), and, hence, unfree. According to this paradigm, free decisions cannot be made on the basis of such psychological quirks. Instead, the imagined stranded-in-the-cold scenario would have to be critically assessed by multiplying its disutility by the objective probability of its happening and the result then compared with the rest of the Bernoulli-style utility calculations. The reasonable man paradigm is ambivalent about this case. On the one hand, reasonable men are not flighty; they should not make important life decisions on the basis of momentary whims, since that is the mark of an irresponsible person. Still, the reasonable man is not an idealized utility calculator, and sometimes acts on 'gut feelings'. I think that this paradigm holds that the job applicant's choice was pretty free, but was not a great example of freedom.

The final normative example involved the suggestion that although increased cognitive dissonance with one's decisions reduces freedom, there are cases, like that of the Savage in *Brave New World*, where dissonance may increase freedom over what it would be if one were less distraught. Although all three paradigms agree that the Savage was freer than the simpleminded alphas, betas, and deltas of his new society, they yield differing assessments of the Savage. The pure rational ego paradigm looks favorably upon cognitive conflict, since it reveals heightened self-awareness, and finds decisions made in self-conscious awareness of conflicting motivations to be a high form of rational decision making. Although this paradigm agrees with Frankfurt that there is a point at which the will can be literally paralyzed in a Hamlet-like state (1971, 75–76), it holds that, short of paralysis, the more conscious of conflicts the will is, the freer it is. The nonegocentric actor also agrees that the Savage is freer than the other members in his society but only because the latter are patently unfree due to conditioning. The Savage, on this paradigm, is not a good example of freedom; he is too intense, too obsessive. He certainly is a poor candidate for satisfying the dictum of Chuang Tzu: "No drives, no compulsions, no needs, no attractions. Then your affairs are under control. You are a free man" (Kane, 1985, 114). The reasonable man objects to the idea that the Savage is free because the Savage kills himself, and it is debatable whether suicide is something that reasonable men would choose to do, at least on the grounds of psychological distress.

The problem regarding bribes was: Can bribes reduce one's freedom? The nonegocentric actor paradigm yields a negative answer, since a bribe, however generous, can be intrusive only if one allows it to be. You cannot bribe an honest politician, and you cannot reduce the freedom of a nonegocentric actor by appealing to desires, fetishes, and compulsions. The pure rational ego finds this analysis charmingly puerile, since the rational ego sees bribes as simply altering the utilities of one's options, and, thus, logically no different than threats. A large-enough bribe can make a choice obligatory from a rational perspective, just as a threat can. Moreover, the adoption of a rule of thumb to ignore all bribes (or threats) would be sheer dogmatism, an abdication of the ego's job of generating rational decisions. The reasonable man paradigm is somewhat ambivalent once again, since the reasonable man sees an asymmetry between threats, which are politically pernicious, and bribes that are tempting without being threatening. Nonetheless, even reasonable men succumb to certain extreme bribes and, when they do, their reduced culpability is indicative that their freedom was to some extent reduced by those bribes.

Let us consider next the problem raised by causes that incline without completely compelling behavior. In the examples given in Section 4, I supposed that we might be able to resist such intrusive causes 20 percent of the time, while giving in the other 80 percent. Interestingly, there is an internal conflict within the nonegocentric actor paradigm, depending on which aspect is emphasized. If you focus on the Taoist aspect, you might conclude that in the 'backsliding' 80 percent of the cases one was victim to desires, and, thus, unfree. But the more commonsensical, Pollyanna, aspect might lead you to conclude that one was free in those cases, because this is simply an instance where one did what one wanted to do at that particular time. The reasonable man paradigm sees causes that incline without compelling similarly to the way it views bribes: if compelling enough, bribes can reduce free will (although, in most cases, giving in marks a misuse of one's free will). The pure rational ego paradigm holds that we lack free will in cases where our effort is insufficient to enable us to choose what we think is best, since one of the ego's most important functions is to ensure that this sort of thing does not happen. In terms of my autonomy account, yielding to pressures counts as a violation of the efficacy variable.

Consider finally Strawson's claim that being free entails having "a sense," "conception," or "experience" of oneself as free. Once again, there are two conflicting themes within the nonegocentric paradigm. The Eastern notion that freedom requires a diminished sense of self seems to count against Strawson's claim, since sense of oneself as free seems to imply awareness of the distinction between self and world. The negative verdict is also supported by the paradigm's commitment to spontaneity at the expense of self-awareness. Truly spontaneous agents might be so involved in the world that self-awareness does not enter into their actions. On the positive side, one might argue that nonegocentric actors typically *experience* themselves as free (even if they need not reflect on their freedom), and that they always feel free except for those times when they are unfree. This latter claim is equivalent in first-order predicate logic to the claim that being free materially implies feeling free,[3] and that is some support for Strawson's view. So, the nonegocentric actor paradigm appears to support conflicting intuitions concerning Strawson's claim.

I think that the paradigm of the reasonable man is broadly sympathetic to the position I suggested that Strawson might utilize, *viz.*, that the mere fact that we sometimes explicitly represent ourselves as being free shows that we always tacitly take ourselves to be free. The reasonable man is typically unlikely to forget the obligations of being a person of temperate wisdom, and, hence, constantly carries an awareness of that role. Any apparent deviation from this stance of self-awareness must be subsumed as an implicit case where that paradigm is satisfied (and, hence, a case of tacit belief in one's freedom) or a genuine deviation, in which case the reasonable man has truly 'forgotten himself' and acted unfreely.

The paradigm of the pure rational ego seems to support Strawson's claim. The Cartesian transparency-of-the-mental-thread of this paradigm suggests that, even while engaged in the most careful ratiocination, the ego is also deliciously aware of its freedom in performing its deliberations. The Kantian thread that maintains that freedom is making one's will conform to the 'dictates' of reason *because* they are the dictates of reason also suggests the need to presuppose awareness of one's freedom in order to be free. And the Spinozistic theme of reconciling oneself to determinism also seems to require an implicit sense of self in the act of acceptance, because resignation requires a sense of self as a resigner.

9. Conclusion

The argument of this chapter may be summarized this way:

1. *If there is a class of entities correctly designated as "free choices," they do not constitute a natural kind relative to either scientific theory or common sense.* Hence, from an epistemic point of

view, "free choices" are not on a par with scientific notions like "hydrogen" or commonsense, observational notions like "table," which have fairly straightforward criteria of application.

2. *Given 1, the only reason for thinking that there exists such a kind would be our prephilosophical or philosophically minded intuitive agreement that such-and-such-types of cases count as examples of free will, whereas others do not.* It is not enough that we find the concept *free choice* useful, since many useful concepts are merely idiosyncratic ones that do not designate classes that constitute the objective furniture of the world (e.g., "good baseball game," "stirring musical performance," "clever idea," "lout," and "wonderful human being"). The best that we can do to save the respectability of the free will concept is to try to reach a Rawlsian "reflective equilibrium" regarding possible cases. This will require appeal to our intuitions about what to say about individual cases.

3. *Given the four issues discussed in Sections 1 through 4, as well as the basic difference between compatibilists and incompatibilists on the internalistic way of viewing free will, we see that we can generate an indefinite number of cases where we feel strong intuitions that pull in opposite directions.*

4. *Therefore, any single account of free will that we offer is bound to be either too narrow or too wide, or both too narrow and too wide. Therefore, no principled account can analyze 'our intuitive notion of free will', since there is no such notion.*

5. *Therefore, there is no class of entities that constitutes free choices.*

The explanation for the intuitional anarchy discussed in this chapter is that *free will* is an exemplar concept that is especially ill-behaved because it relies on multiple conflicting paradigms. In Section 6, I type the conflicting paradigms into three distinct varieties, each having some purchase on our intuitions regarding free will. Depending on which of the paradigms we utilize in any particular judgment concerning free will, we will be likely to give answers that are supported by that paradigm. And we sometimes shift from one paradigm to another at a moment's notice, thereby producing much of the bafflement that is characteristic of the free will issue.

Having engaged in this much armchair psychology, I might as well speculate about why philosophers use the paradigms they do. Using a distinction cited earlier, one might say that our selection of free will paradigms is governed by both dispositional and situa-

tional factors. By the former I include things like this. A philosopher might be more likely to rely on a certain paradigm more often
than another (or to explicitly reject a certain paradigm) because of
chronic traits such as temperament, upbringing, ideological bias, or
related philosophical views. For instance, one can easily imagine
how non-intellectual, 'real-life' influences might prompt a young
philosopher to appeal less to the nonegocentric actor paradigm and
more to the paradigm of the pure rational ego with the passage of
time, or to move in the opposite direction. It is likewise conceivable
that a philosopher who comes to be influenced by cultural plural-
ism or feminism might grow to reject the paradigm of the reasonable man. Also under the heading of dispositional factors is the case
of having received reinforcement for or against using one of the
paradigms. It is easy to imagine how someone who achieves success
in publishing books and articles that exploit one of the paradigms
would be reinforced to continue to rely on that paradigm. Having
expressed this much sensitivity to the mundane motivations that
might govern our paradigm selection, I hasten to add that a philosopher might grow enamored of a specific paradigm because that
paradigm appears fruitful and continues to withstand rigorous
scrutiny.

Under the heading of situational factors, I include a wide range of
logically relevant and fortuitous factors that might contribute to
reliance on a certain paradigm. Having just read a certain novel (or
philosophical work), seen a movie, or having tried to console a
depressed friend might make one more likely to opt for a particular
paradigm. Among philosophically relevant situational factors, the
most important is the particular context in which the question of
free will arises. When we are asking whether an agent manifested
free will when our concern is with punishment, the paradigm of the
reasonable man is likely to play an important role. When punishment is not a consideration, but we are instead thinking in terms of
'comparative ethology', the pure rational ego image is more likely
to come to mind. When our concern is with constraint, the nonegocentric paradigm is likely to be consulted.

6

Meta-Compatibilism

ABSTRACT In the first part of this book, I argue for a compatibilistic theory of freedom and responsibility that I think looks fairly plausible. But in the last chapter I argue that the plausibility of views like my autonomy variable account depends on selective attention to certain free will exemplars, and that conflicting intuitions can be generated by looking at different exemplars. In this chapter and the next, I advance a thesis that is consistent with the theme of Chapter 5 but goes well beyond it. I argue that not only is free will an inconsistent exemplar concept, but that it is a subjective, ultimately attitudinal concept as well. The debate between the compatibilists and incompatibilists can have no resolution because there can be no objective properties of free will or moral responsibility for their accounts to hit or miss. Hence, compatibilism and incompatibilism, contrary to appearances, *cannot* logically conflict, since both positions simply express subjective attitudes. I call this higher level 'compatibility' of compatibilism and incompatibilism *meta-compatibilism*.

Although neither the compatibilists nor incompatibilists give *the* correct account of free will, each side captures an attitude that is strongly attractive to us. We can accept the underlying spirit of the intuitions that drive both views, while denying that either view is correct. In addition, the meta-compatibilist line can be applied to individual cases: given the non-realistic nature of responsibility and freedom, both ascriptions and denials of freedom and responsibility can be plausible with respect to the same agent, for a single action, performed for the same motive. Not only does the meta-compatibilism line seem to be plausible on metaethical grounds, it has a significant explanatory role. Unless we subjectivize freedom and responsibility, the conflict between the so-called agent and observer perspectives seems irresolvable, since the views of persons as free and responsible, and as never free or responsible, both have strong intuitional appeal.

In the first section I elaborate the argument for meta-compatibilism. That argument has three principal components: (1) the premise that freedom and responsibility ascriptions attempt to ascribe moral properties, (2) the premise, argued for in the next chapter, that there are no moral properties, and (3) the meta-compatibilist's interpretation of what we are doing when we try to ascribe freedom and responsibility. In the second section I defend meta-compatibilism against seven objections.

1. The Argument for Meta-Compatibilism

The central aim of this book is to reject the following thesis held by all theorists who affirm the existence of free will and most of those who deny it:

(F) It is logically possible that agents manifest free will in the deep philosophical sense that is believed to warrant moral responsibility.

But much of my discussion is directed to rejecting the following thesis:

(A) There is an answer to the dispute between the compatibilists and incompatibilists over the correct analysis of free will.

(F) and (A) are equivalent. If free will is possible, then some account should be able to describe what it is like, even if it is very difficult for us to decide which account we think succeeds. Conversely, if either the compatibilists or incompatibilists are correct, then it is at least conceivable that agents might satisfy that correct account and manifest free will. Since (F) and (A) are equivalent, I am at liberty to argue against either thesis in order to reject the other.

One strategy for rejecting (F) is to show that the accounts given by the compatibilists and incompatibilists are unacceptable, that is, to reject (A). The first half of this task was attempted in the last chapter, and I try to complete the second half in Chapter 8. If this strategy succeeds, then the aim of this book will be achieved without embarking upon the radical strategy that I develop in this chapter and the next. But I think that a more radical tack is also warranted: Both (F) and (A) require that there could exist objective, non-attitudinally dependent properties of free will and moral responsibility. *Free will* and *moral responsibility* are moral terms that purport to ascribe moral properties. But there are no moral properties. Hence, neither (F) nor (A) is true. Let me develop this argument more explicitly.

The standard free will theories (compatibilism, incompatibilism, libertarianism, hard determinism, soft determinism) presuppose that when we talk about freedom and moral responsibility, we are making statements about the nature of extra-linguistic reality. The hard determinists deny what the soft determinists and libertarians assert, but even that denial is a claim about the nature of a non-linguistic, non-subjective reality. All sides agree that the free will dispute is a debate over whether our choices possess an objective property, specifically, whether our choices are free enough to support genuine moral responsibility. All sides agree that the question is whether our choices meet an objective standard and is not simply a matter of how we 'feel about' our choices.

These presuppositions are clear if we consider the two definitional theses of the compatibilist and the incompatibilist: (i) "Free will and determinism are compatible (i.e., may both exist)." (ii) "The existence of free will entails that determinism is false." This commitment also holds in the case of moral responsibility. This is evinced by the familiar claim that you are morally responsible only if you have free will. For instance, van Inwagen claims:

> [I]f moral responsibility exists, then someone is morally responsible
> for something he has done or for something he has left undone; to be
> morally responsible . . . is to have free will. Therefore, if no one has
> free will, moral responsibility does not exist. (1983, 162)

I think that the above considerations justify the first premise of the argument for meta-compatibilism:

1 *If there is an answer to the dispute between the compatibilists and incompatibilists over the correct analysis of free
   will, then free will (and moral responsibility) are objective
   properties that persons might instantiate under certain conditions.*

The next premise is that free will and moral responsibility are moral properties. I shall defend that claim first for moral responsibility, which I think is pretty straightforward, and then for free will, which may appear less so. First, moral responsibility. Although there is a literature that tries to elucidate the various senses of "responsibility" (Baier, 1970; Hart, 1968), I believe that there is at least a consensus that *moral responsibility* must be defined in terms of whether the subject is appropriately or legitimately subject to some degree of praise, blame, reactive attitudes, and so forth. (Recall the discussion of the two dimensions of moral responsibility in Chapter 4.) As previously mentioned, Fischer claims that "a person is a morally responsible agent when he is an *appropriate candidate* for the reactive attitudes and for such activities as praise and blame and punishment and reward" (1986, 12). Glover thinks that "[t]o say that someone is morally responsible for what he does may be to say that he can legitimately be praised or blamed if either of these responses is appropriate to the action in question" (1970, 19). William Frankena makes the moral character of the notion of moral responsibility even more explicit: "[T]o say that X was responsible for Y is to say something like 'It would be right to hold X responsible for Y and to blame or otherwise punish him'" (1973, 72).

These passages support the claim made in Chapter 1 that moral responsibility, as it figures in philosophical and everyday discussions, is understood as a special sort of property that serves as a norm against which we compare conventional types of responsibility such as legal responsibility. One can always ask of persons whom we deem to be legally responsible whether they really are *morally* responsible, just as one can always ask of actions that promote happiness whether they really are *good* (Moore, 1903, Chapter 1). The appropriateness of this open question regarding moral responsibility supports the conviction that we are treating moral responsibility as the most basic, normative variety of responsibility.

So, I am going to take it as pretty clear that *moral responsibility* is a moral notion. I think that the same thing is true of *free* when it is used by philosophers discussing free will. Because I am not as confident that there is a consensus of philosophical opinion that *free* is a moral term, I shall cast a wider net and produce the following considerations that I think, collectively, make this claim plausible:

1. Freedom, like moral responsibility, is subject to debate over its true nature. The just-noted "open question argument" also applies to the topic of freedom. Just as one can sensibly ask, "Granted, *a* maximizes utility, but is *a* right?", one can ask, "Granted, *d* satisfies the compatibilist's (or libertarian's) conception of a free choice, but was *d* free?" The frequent application of the adjectives *real* and *genuine* to the notion of freedom is a tip-off that the open question argument is applicable. It is true that we can ask open questions using non-moral terms, e.g., William Lycan's example "Is a fortnight really two weeks?" (1986, 91). But, unlike Lycan's example, open questions about *real* freedom appear to be deeply normative, since freedom is taken to have a special gravity connected with human dignity and moral worth.

2. Given that we have seen that moral responsibility is a moral notion, and that its application is generally believed to depend upon whether agents are 'really' free, this provides some reason to think that *free* is also a moral concept. This is not to claim that all properties entailed by moral ascriptions are moral properties (since, e.g., being a right act entails being an act, without thereby showing that being an act is a moral property). But with moral responsibility and free will, the dependency is almost mutual: "S did *a* freely" strongly supports "S is morally responsible for *a*." It seems that any notion that stands in such an intimate relation to a moral notion will itself be a moral notion.

3. A final consideration would be to point out that not only does the applicability of *morally responsible* depend upon the applicability of *free*, but that the same sort of considerations are appropriate in deciding whether to apply either term. For instance, compare "How could Jones be morally responsible for *a* given Jones's deplorable childhood?" and "I doubt that Smith really decided freely, given the strength of Smith's paranoid beliefs about college administrators." In many discussions, considerations regarding responsibility and freedom, although analytically distinguishable, are interchangeable as we appeal to the same factors in speaking to both issues.

The upshot of this discussion is that I believe that premise (2) is acceptable:

2   *Free will and moral responsibility, if they exist, are moral properties.*

And from (1) and (2) we can validly deduce:

3   *If there is an answer to the dispute between the compatibilists and incompatibilists over the correct analysis of free will, then at least two classes of moral properties are objective properties that might be instantiated under certain conditions.*

Step 4 is the most controversial premise of the argument for meta-compatibilism:

4   *There can be no objective moral properties.*

I devote the entire next chapter to justifying (4). My argument is that since there can be no moral properties in this sense, free will and moral responsibility cannot exist either. Strictly speaking, this argument is more ambitious than I require, since it is conceivable that freedom and responsibility might be more vulnerable to the considerations that I present in the next chapter than are moral properties in general. So, it is possible that a reader who rejects the general thesis of that chapter might accept a particularized version that is applied only to freedom and responsibility. Anyone who draws that conclusion is more than welcome. Nonetheless, I think the argument that I provide in Chapter 7 gains its greatest plausibility when applied to the total class of moral claims, and that is the version I give. So, I am hereby issuing a very large promissory note.

Nonetheless, the development of the meta-compatibilist view need not await my efforts to justify (4). For one thing, there may be any number of readers who *already* accept my general meta-ethical view, the doctrine alternatively called *moral non-realism, moral subjectivism, noncognitivism, ethical skepticism, ethical nihilism,* and even *ethical relativism.* For the dialectical purposes of this book, such thinkers could skip Chapter 7. And even readers who reject the view that there are no moral properties may find it interesting to see how the debate between the compatibilists and incompatibilists must be recast if one *were* to accept step (4). So, let me go ahead and finish the argument for meta-compatibilism. On the assumption that (4) is justifiable, we may deduce from (3) and (4):

5   *Therefore, there is no answer to the dispute between the compatibilists and incompatibilists over the correct analysis of free will.*

This step represents the non-realist conclusion that I seek to establish in this chapter and the next. But I want to draw out the implications of this conclusion for the debate between the compatibilists and incompatibilists, and, more generally, between those who accept and reject free will. An important implication will be that since there is no free will or moral responsibility, the disputes between the compatibilists and incompatibilists will have to be radically reinterpreted by the meta-compatibilist. I express this reinterpretation in two final steps that are explanations rather than premises:

6   *Moral responsibility ascriptions and free will ascriptions serve, individually, to convey speakers' attitudes toward agents, and collectively, to convey attitudes that humanity at large holds toward agents. The attitude expressed by such ascriptions has been called the "agent" or "subjective" perspective; the attitude expressed by denying them has been called the "observer" or "objective" perspective (Nagel, 1986). The latter attitude may be intended globally, by those who deny that anyone is free or responsible, or it may be intended only locally where an individual is subject to particular circumstances (e.g., the agent experienced an epileptic seizure).*

The claim in step 6 that responsibility and freedom ascriptions convey attitudes toward individuals is supported by considering the contexts in which speakers discuss these issues. We care about freedom and responsibility because our decision on whether we can ascribe them profoundly affects how we view ourselves and others. These ascriptions reveal our personal, "reactive" attitudes toward the ascribee, whereas a categorical denial of responsibility shows that we feel that persons are less complete—less fully human—than common sense holds. We may not be passionately involved every time we affirm or deny responsibility, but our willingness to ascribe responsibility at all shows that we have a radically different attitude toward persons than we would if we refused to make such ascriptions. This brings us to the final step in the meta-compatibilist's story.

7   *At this point meta-compatibilism divides into a hard and soft line depending on whether the meta-compatibilist believes that attitudes can be more or less reasonable. The hard-liners argue that because there are no objective properties of responsibility or freedom at stake, all attempted ascriptions of these properties are equally reasonable. The idea here is that if there are no such properties, there can be no standard of reasonability for the attitudes and, hence, all attitudes are equally good (or bad). The soft-liners hold that although moral responsibility ascriptions and free will ascriptions ultimately misfire, some ascriptions are more reasonable than others. The soft-liners maintain, though, that there can be cases where two conflicting attitudes are both reasonable. When such cases arise, if there is no objective property to which such attitudes conform or fail to conform, then the reasonableness of one attitude cannot count against the reasonableness of another. Since the attitudes of responsibility and freedom assignment and denial fall into this class, the soft-liners also conclude that there is no general compatibilist or incompatibilist solution possible.*

An interesting question about step 7 is whether the hard or soft line is more plausible. I confess that I am torn in both directions, an understandable enough response from a meta-compatibilist. I prefer the hard line because it assimilates the reasonability of attitudes to the reasonability of beliefs, which I take to be a function of how likely it is that reality answers to our beliefs. By applying this sort of criterion to attitudes, the hard-liner concludes that neither of two conflicting attitudes can be more or less reasonable than the other, irrespective of what other beliefs or attitudes we hold. An objection to the hard line is precisely that by assimilating the reasonability of attitudes to that of beliefs, the hard-liners ignore the fact that the different ways of assessing their reasonableness is the principal way of distinguishing attitudes from beliefs (Stevenson, 1944, Chapter 1). The soft-liners think that the reasonableness of attitudes lies in factors other than their probability of converging on objective reality. The soft-liners may offer suggestions that approximate the views of certain ethical thinkers who affirm the reasonableness of moral debate while denying the existence of moral truth (see Chapter 7.) For instance, soft-liners might say that attitudes concerning freedom and responsibility are reasonable to the extent that they conform to widely held intuitions about freedom and responsibility, or if they are reached in a reflective way that we are prepared to universalize. Although I am skeptical about this non-realist interpretation of *reasonable*, it poses no problems for my view, since even the soft-liners support the central argument of this chapter and the next. So, in the remainder of this chapter I feel free to exploit the resources of both the hard and soft lines, especially in the second section, where I answer objections.

Let me conclude this section by saying why I like meta-compatibilism. The meta-compatibilist believes that the incompatibilist mistakes an unfavorable subjective reaction to the thesis of determinism for an actual characteristic of determinism per se. Consider the following illustration. I recently had lunch with a friend who claimed that her need for warmth and love made her less self-sufficient than she would be without such needs, and, thus, *demeaned* her human dignity. My friend did not single herself out for criticism in this respect, admitting that such needs were practically universal, perhaps ultimately biologically grounded, and at any rate out of her control. Nonetheless, my friend insisted that she was lessened, demeaned by these needs. When I suggested that one might argue that, despite the reduction of self-sufficiency, one is not demeaned by such needs, but enriched or even ennobled by them ("People who need people . . ."), my friend admitted that although someone *could* conclude this, she felt demeaned anyway.

The meta-compatibilist thinks that drawing the unhappy conclusion that we lack freedom and responsibility from the premise of determinism is like my friend's conclusion that our need for love demeans us. Incompatibilism represents an attitude, a pessimistic reaction to the supposition of determinism. (In a well-known article

P. F. Strawson (1962) uses the terms "optimist" and "pessimist" in place of the usual "compatibilist" and "incompatibilist" labels.) Conflicting *attitudes* are not only logically possible with respect to the same object, but to the extent that attitudes may be reasonable at all, they may be reasonably held toward the same entity if one attends to different facts or looks at the same facts in different ways. One may be reasonably optimistic and pessimistic regarding the same thing.

This sort of ambivalence is characteristic of a wide range of heartfelt issues. Sometimes we feel that we should face death with calm, dispassioned dignity; sometimes we feel that we should "not go gentle into that good night." Sometimes atheists feel that death makes our lives "meaningless," while at other times atheists argue that it is only the recognition of our eventual death that gives our lives meaning. The theist's thought that we are "God's children" can be ennobling; it can also prompt embarrassment and despair. One can view one's life both as an exhilarating adventure and as a farce.

Consider what Strawson calls the "personal" perspective that involves the "reactive attitudes" such as indignation, resentment, gratitude, and shame that we typically associate with moral responsibility. Compare these to the attitude suggested by those who deny that responsibility exists—the so-called objective perspective—that exonerates all persons of the reactive attitudes. Unlike Strawson, who defends the "optimistic" acceptance of the personal attitudes at the expense of the objectivist view, the meta-compatibilist sees the compatibility of holding reactive attitudes toward a subject *and* holding the attitude of exoneration. For instance, being indignant toward S and feeling sorry for S because S is a victim of "moral luck" may be reasonable attitudes to hold at the same time.

This will not seem true, if one thinks that holding reactive attitudes toward an agent and exonerating that agent presuppose contradictory assumptions. For instance, one might think that the following statements conflict:

    i. I reasonably resent you for *a* only if I believe that you could have avoided doing *a*.
    ii. I reasonably exonerate you from all reactive attitudes regarding *a* only if I believe that you could not have avoided doing *a*.

But these two do not conflict, and we can see this by appreciating what is valuable in hypothetical analyses of *could*. I may reasonably resent your action provided you planned and rationally endorsed *a* and had control over your desire to *a* in the compatibilistic hypothetical sense of being able to avoid *a* if you had chosen to. If you satisfy a stringent rationality account of free will (such as the autonomy variable account of Chapter 2) in such a way that *a* reflects who you are and who you wish to be, then resentment is warrantable, irrespective of whether your carefully planned decisions can be traced back deterministically. After all, these are still your decisions even if you are not ultimately responsible for the sort of person you are. In effect, this is the line that I defend in Chapter 4. At the same time, however, it would be reasonable for me to take a different attitude toward you. I could elect to view you from the global perspective (Hospers, 1961; Waller, 1987), and decide that since you are not your own ultimate cause, I feel sorry for you for becoming the sort of person who would do *a* in a fully self-conscious, reflective way. That is, I may reasonably hold the attitude of total exoneration toward you because you *categorically* could not have done, or been, otherwise than you did or were. So, the meta-compatibilist feels the attraction of both the traditional compatibilistic and incompatibilistic views.

Of course, this suggestion will not seem plausible if one thinks that freedom and responsibility are unified properties for which there is only one correct account. In that case we would have to choose between the hypothetical and categorical accounts. But once we give up the assumption that freedom and responsibility are objective, there is no conflict between the hypothetical and categorical accounts, since we are now doing the 'moral phenomenology' of our attitudes rather than trying to analyze concepts that capture some objective properties.

Such ambivalent attitudes are disconcerting, and it is natural to take this as indicative of an objective tension. The meta-compatibilist, however, thinks that the tension is merely psychological. Most of us wish to have unified attitudes as well as unified beliefs, and ambivalent attitudes, no less than conflicting beliefs, are cognitively dissonant. Consider the way that a determinist might look upon a moral monster such as Hitler. On the one hand, the determinist might say that since Hitler did not choose the state of the universe before his birth, he is to be pitied for his poor "moral luck." But the determinist could also say that because Hitler's deeds were profoundly reflective of the sort of person he deliberately tried to be, Hitler merits the loathing that he receives. These conflicting attitudes vie for our attention in rapid succession like the two intepretations of Wittgenstein's duck-rabbit.[1] As with the duck-rabbit, neither interpretation is correct to the exclusion of the other, because the same objective stimulus has the power to evoke different reactions depending on how we attend to it. The debate between the compatibilists and incompatibilists comes down to a question of how we *should* feel about determinism, and unless moral realism is true, there simply is no answer to how we should feel.

2.   Objections and Replies

In this section I consider seven objections to meta-compatibilism from various directions.

The simplest form of objection would be to ignore the issue raised by meta-compatibilism. "Let the metaethicists worry about the reality of free will and moral responsibility: I don't have to. We certainly *believe* that people are sometimes free and morally responsible for their actions, and that belief is all that is needed to raise the incompatibility issue. If we waited upon a metaethical solution before embarking on normative ethics, we could never begin."

It is doubtful, though, that ignoring the objection is any more appropriate in this case than in any other philosophical instance. To admit the subjective nature of freedom and responsibility ascriptions is not, *ipso facto*, to give up demanding reasoned grounds for their application, since a non-realist regarding moral properties per se can still do normative ethics. The soft-liners believe that we can talk reasonably about freedom and responsibility. More important, the fact that a philosophical claim runs contrary to prephilosophical belief is never a *philosophical* reason to reject it, even if one could imagine scenarios where it would be morally obligatory to reject it (e.g., if accepting the subjectivity argument would turn one into a moral cretin).

A second objection is from the moral realist. As noted earlier, all the moral realist needs to do to reject meta-compatibilism is to show how there can be moral properties. That attempt is examined in Chapter 7. But, short of attempting that, one can imagine the moral realist claiming that common sense supports the idea that freedom and responsibility are realistic properties. For instance, Galen Strawson claims that "we are deeply committed to the belief that people can be truly responsible for what they do" (1986, 90). To call this a *belief* is to presuppose that moral responsibility can exist, since in general to say "S believes that p" seems to presuppose that "p" represents some state of affairs that may obtain.

This is not evidence for the realist's interpretation, however, if we can provide an alternative wording that captures how people feel about moral responsibility while remaining neutral on the realism question. Suppose we rewrite Strawson's claim as "We typically hold people truly responsible for what they do." This seems to capture what is true in Strawson's claim without creating a bias toward viewing "morally responsible" as an objective predicate, since *holding responsible* does not presuppose that someone *is* responsible any more than finding someone to be charming presupposes the objective existence of the property of charmingness.

A third objection would be to extend non-realism in ethics to our theory of the world in general, claiming in a Deweyian fashion that the good, the true, and the beautiful are simply that which is ultimately conducive to human interests. On this tack, the ascription of freedom and responsibility are devices we use to organize our lives (and the lives around us) in order to live more successfully: we should not worry about whether the ascriptions correspond to non-linguistic reality, since no claims should be evaluated in this realistic sense.

There are two replies here. First, the flight to non-realism in general would be an enormous price to pay in order to put moral judgments on a par with non-moral ones and would be justifiable only on the strongest general anti-realist arguments. Of course, non-realism in general may be the best view. But, second, if it were, then meta-compatibilism is not hurt, since there is no reason to think that attitudes assessed in terms of their ultimate conduciveness to human interests necessarily conflict with each other or with the adoption of the determinist view. If non-realism is the case, then incompatibility becomes impossible. So, if we renounce realism, then we should be even *more* sympathetic to meta-compatibilism.

A fourth objection is a *modus tollens* argument against the hard version of meta-compatibilism, which applies, *mutatis mutandis*, to the soft version: (a) If freedom and responsibility ascriptions are not subject to being more or less reasonable, then one could make an equally good case for their ascription and denial in all cases. For instance, if "this tastes good" is simply a subjective claim, then one can argue equally for and against it in all cases. (b) But one cannot make equally good cases for and against freedom and responsibility ascriptions in all cases. For instance, there are clear cases where *nobody* would think that someone is morally responsible for an action, e.g., if the agent were three years old. Or, for attitudes in general, in the earlier example surely my friend would be unreasonable if she held that she was demeaned by her need for *oxygen*. To amend this argument to apply to the soft version of meta-compatibilism, simply rewrite premise (a) to read: "If freedom and responsibility are not objective properties, then one could make an equally good case for their ascription and denial in all cases."

The meta-compatibilist should resist (a) in both forms, since the subjectivity of these ascriptions does not imply that they may be used with complete promiscuity. The meta-compatibilist realizes that there are purely conceptual limitations on their apt application. For instance, there are conceptual limitations on the applicability of a pejorative term such as *a jerk*. Only human beings past a certain age may be jerks; a dog that eats another pet's food cannot be said to be a jerk without overt anthropomorphism. Nonetheless, "jerk" is a paradigm of an attitudinal word that does not ascribe a realistic property and over which a debate concerning the warrant of its application, given its conceptual constraints, would be frivolous. Likewise, meta-compatibilism recognizes that individuals may select their own idiosyncratic preconditions for the application of attitudinal terms. A traditional compatibilist such as Hobart might opt for determination by reasons, whereas a libertarian such as Kane might demand the categorical freedom to choose otherwise. Yet this goes no way toward establishing the reasonableness of the resulting ascriptions; I might judge persons loathsome if they ever voted for Ronald Reagan. For all this, "moral responsibility" and "free will," like "loathsome," are not elevated out of the realm of the merely attitudinal.

A related objection is an instance of a criticism that can be made against moral non-realism generally: "Within the so-called conceptual limitations that we place upon the application of *moral responsibility* and *free will*, the meta-compatibilist must say that our judgments of whether persons are responsible and free are simply a matter of subjective attitude. This entails that the reasoning that we go through in deciding whether individuals are responsible or free is pointless—we might just as well reach these conclusions by appeal to a Ouija board or by flipping a coin. But this is to say that there is no role for rational discussion concerning the application of these terms: meta-compatibilism eliminates the 'place of reason' in the ethics of free will.

I think that this is an interesting objection. Certainly there is a difference between reaching moral conclusions via rational and thoughtless means, and any view that is committed to denying this must be incorrect. But moral non-realists, including meta-compatibilists, need not deny this distinction. One may value the reasoned discussion of whether individuals or persons generally are free and responsible, even if one thinks that these discussions logically cannot converge on the truth. For instance, one might think that a reasoned discussion of the applicability of moral terms is constitutive of a higher form of life than one that includes the thoughtless application of moral terms or an equally mindless refusal to apply such terms. The discussion of freedom and responsibility has an internal structure that enables discussants to manifest empirical knowledge, inferential acumen, the ability to empathize with other human beings, and so forth. And meta-compatibilists might value discussions of freedom and responsibility *in case* the meta-compatibilistic view is wrong: there is no reason why meta-compatibilists should not be fallibilists regarding their own theory. Granting all this, meta-compatibilists can insist that *if* there are no properties of free will or moral responsibility, then reasoned ascriptions of freedom and responsibility *cannot* be more likely to succeed at this impossible task than can thoughtless ascriptions. As was suggested in Chapter 1, method can take us only so far *if* the subject matter is recalcitrant.

A sixth objection is: "Since meta-compatibilism claims that there are no objective properties of free will or moral responsibility, it entails that no one is free or responsible. But this is just hard determinism, not a meta-level theory that renounces all the standard theories."

I reply that although the meta-compatibilist argument of this and the next chapter encompasses the hard determinist's conclusion, the hard determinist's view is only part of meta-compatibilism. Meta-compatibilism also differs from the disjunctive argument of the 'moral sceptic' that Strawson describes (1962, 59). Hard determinism has two premises, a deterministic one that is fairly unfashionable these days, and one that relies upon the incompatibilist intuition "How can you really be morally responsible or free if determinism is true?" The disjunctive argument, which really is an improvement over traditional hard determinism, relies on the incompatibilist premise plus the Hobart-like intuition "How can you be free or responsible for an undetermined choice?" Thus, the disjunctive argument manages to avoid the empirical premise that determinism is true. The meta-compatibilist fully recognizes the attractiveness of both of these intuitions but feels equally pulled by the compatibilist view that if our decisions are sufficiently rational, then we are free and responsible irrespective of whether determinism holds. One might say that the meta-compatibilist tries to co-opt the intuitions of all of the traditional thinkers. The distinctive thing about meta-compatibilism is that it refuses to opt for any of these intuitions at the expense of the others. And, since on the standard interpretation the incompatibilist and compatibilist intuitions logically contradict each other, the meta-compatibilist is forced to subjectivize freedom and responsibility to avoid self-contradiction. Not only is such a conclusion forced on the meta-compatibilist, but it is welcomed, since it resolves the tension in a way that the meta-compatibilist believes is theoretically sound for moral terms in general.

A seventh objection sees the meta-compatibilist as vulnerable to the utilitarian/justice objection that befalls any theory that denies that people are morally responsible. For instance, if hard determinism were true, then we are not morally responsible for anything and do not *deserve* to be held morally responsible for our actions. Thus, the only grounds for *holding* people morally responsible would be the utility of doing so, not the fact that they *are* responsible, and this ushers in the scapegoating counterexamples that trouble utilitarian ethics. (In Chapter 4, I argue that this problem arises for even a compatibilist who justifies moral responsibility solely on utilitarian grounds.) For instance, in a case where we must decide whether to hold morally responsible the person who actually performed an action or a bystander who did not, our decision would have to be made on the basis of considerations other than whether the person *deserves* the ascription of responsibility, given that neither is morally responsible. And this seems to be morally repellent, not only for hard determinism and some varieties of compatibilism, but for meta-compatibilism as well.

I think that this is a problem, not only for meta-compatibilism, but for any species of compatibilism that interprets moral responsibility in such a way that it must be justified in terms of consequences (Smart, 1961; Dennett, 1984). An uncompromising response given by the hard liners would be to admit that if non-realism in ethics is true, then we simply have to accept the logical possibility of what may seem to us to be morally repellent scenarios, since ethical judgments can be no more than evolutionarily and socially conditioned attitudes. This simply underscores the enormous importance of justifying moral realism. The unhappy results of accepting the subjectivity of moral responsibility would be part-and-parcel of the outcome of accepting moral non-realism in general.

A more conciliatory view, taken by the soft-liners, would be that meta-compatibilism allows for the reasonability of moral-responsibility-attitudes, *viz.*, those justified by the compatibilist view of Part I that sufficient rationality in one's decision making warrants responsibility and freedom ascriptions. That is, the soft liners can avail themselves of the intuition sketched in Chapter 4 that an agent who meets the rationality criteria of free will deserves the attitudes of praise and blame in the strongest sense. It is true, of course, that soft-line meta-compatibilists would acknowledge the reasonableness of the incompatibilist attitude in favor of the complete exoneration of all agents. But there remains an asymmetry between an agent who performed a given act and someone who did not, inasmuch as the former is subject to the intuition that warrants responsibility and freedom ascriptions, whereas the latter is not.

3. Conclusion

I have argued that unless one adopts moral realism one must view the debates between the incompatibilists and the compatibilists and between those who affirm and those who deny freedom and responsibility as ill-conceived, because either (a) all freedom and responsibility attitudes are equally good (the hard line) or (b) conflicting attitudes regarding the same actions are often reasonable (the soft line). I finish this argument by arguing for moral non-realism in the next chapter. Both hard and soft lines appear to resolve the otherwise intractable conflict between personal and objective perspectives. At one point Thomas Nagel seems almost on the verge of viewing free will similarly to the way that the meta-compatibilist does:

> [T]he problem of free will . . . is rather a bafflement of our feelings and attitudes—a loss of confidence, conviction or equilibrium. . . . [T]he problem of free will lies in the erosion of interpersonal attitudes and the sense of autonomy. (1986, 112)

The meta-compatibilist thinks that this sort of insight, if pressed, solves the compatibility issue.

7

An Argument
for Moral Non-Realism

ABSTRACT In the last chapter, I argue that *free will* and *moral responsibility* are moral terms that presuppose the existence of the moral properties of freedom and responsibility. In this chapter, I try to show that there are no moral properties, thus completing the meta-compatibilist argument begun in Chapter 6.

My argument proceeds in two stages. In the first, I reject *Objective Moral Realism* (the view that moral properties exist in agents and their actions independently of anyone's judgment that they exist). In doing so, I consider five varieties of moral realism. In the second stage, I reject a subjective variety of moral realism (*Universal Subjectivism*) that takes moral judgments to be the products of our widely shared disposition to agree about moral matters. I call the remaining view *Anarchistic Subjectivism* because it holds that moral judgments are subjective, but not universally shared, inasmuch as they depend on a disorganized mixture of factors. This theory holds that there are no 'natural kinds' among our subjective opinions about actions that could provide moral truth.

1. Introduction

There is a great deal to be said for the objectivity of morality. The view that moral judgments express "mind-independent facts" (Wong, 1986, 111) has a claim to being part of prephilosophical common sense because it conforms with the way that we often talk about and act in the world. We can cite widely shared paradigms of moral and immoral acts. We can construct elaborate theoretical systems upon our widely shared "reflective equilibrium" concerning

151

many moral questions (Rawls, 1971). And, not the least of our present concerns, the doctrine of the objectivity of morality makes the question of who has the correct analysis of *moral responsibility* and *free will* robustly truth-valued and subject to serious debate between opposing theorists.

But there is a problem. Although it is easy to *say* that there is moral truth (and give supporting examples), to say so justifiably we must be able to produce a coherent picture of *how* morality could be objective. Without such an account, we should take the moralist's claim as simply a pious hope or, perhaps, as an expression of the belief that morality is serious business (which it undoubtedly is). Modes of discourse cannot be taken at face value, and if there is a problem concerning how a certain type of judgment can be objective, then theorists who advance such judgments owe us an explanation. The prephilosophical belief in moral objectivity, to the extent that it is held, is simply the *explanandum* that a theory of moral objectivism must show that it explains better than competing theories.

Since there are many views these days that are labeled "moral realism" in the recent burgeoning metaethical literature,[1] I should say something about what kind of moral realism concerns me. In the last chapter I argued that saying that S freely chooses *a* and S is morally responsible for *a* are analogous to saying that S is right (or wrong) in doing *a*. All three statements purport to express moral truths. But, on my realistic notion of truth, moral claims need to have non-linguistic, non-attitudinal, non-conventional ontological grounding if they are to be true. Moral realism, as I shall view it, is simply an instance of the general realistic doctrine that holds that "statements . . . possess an objective truth-value, independently of our means of knowing it: they are true or false in virtue of a reality existing independently of us" (Dummett, 1978, 146). Such a "hard moral realism" (Wong, 1986, 111) "requires that . . . moral claims literally construed, be literally true" (Sayre-McCord, 1986, 17). Any weaker type of realism, e.g., one that views morality as a "social creation" (Wong) or intersubjective, but not objective (Sayre-McCord), will be too weak to serve my ontological purposes. Actions (and agents) must possess the moral properties they do irrespective of how humans view things, if moral realism is to be on a par with realism in the rest of our ontological theory.

In case my penchant for talking about moral *properties* may seem unsettling to some readers, let me show why my use of the notion is innocuous. I use the notions of *moral truth, moral facts,* and *moral properties* in this way: moral properties are just those features of the world that make moral statements true. That is, there are moral truths (and moral facts) just in case there are moral properties. My use of the latter term is not meant to suggest the notion of properties as Platonic, abstract entities. Indeed, I take a nominalistic view of properties, wherein property tokens or instances are cases of individuals that are a certain way, whereas property types are simply the sum of their property tokens. Although I am not going to argue for his nominalistic assumption, it is one that the moral realist should not resist, since a realistic view of moral properties understood nominalistically will be a more difficult target for the non-realist. If the realist, upon rebutting my challenge, wishes to go on and claim that moral properties possess an abstract existence beyond their tokens, then that is well and good. On the other hand, had I attacked a Platonistic variety of moral realism, the moral realist would be able to object that I had not criticized the central core, i.e., nominalistic moral realism. The realism issue that I care about is not Platonism vs. nominalism, but is analogous to the issue between realists about intentional states (Searle, Fodor) vs. eliminativists (Patricia and Paul Churchland, Stich). So, the question that I am most concerned to ask is: Is there any reason to believe that there are objective moral property tokens? This is the basic ontological question, whether values are, in J. L. Mackie's phrase, part of the "furniture of the world" (1977, 16). The question about the existence of moral types, though, is an important question because our moral reasoning (and moral intuitions) will depend upon what moral types we think exist. As Aristotle said, there is no science of particulars. In my discussion of the Universal Subjectivist and Anarchistic Subjective views, I shall say something about moral types.

Another preliminary concerns the notion of *property identity*, specifically, the question of when a moral property token is identical to a naturalistic or non-naturalistic property token. I am going to treat such identities as possible when the property at stake is designated in non-synonymous language. Hence, I concede that the type identity claim "Moral property M is identical to naturalistic property N" or the token claim "Moral property token M1 is identical to non-naturalistic property token NN1" may be true although they are non-analytic and not knowable a priori. The importance of such identities has been generally recognized in the philosophies of science and mind, as is evinced by the standard examples such as "Temperature is mean kinetic energy" and "Pain is C-fiber stimulation." (Although these were sometimes carelessly called "contingent" identities.) The moral realist should be allowed the resource of non-analytic, a posteriori identities. This is helpful to everyone, because it puts to rest the facile argument for non-realism based on the premise that moral and non-moral language have different meanings.

It has been argued that ethics does not need to presuppose any ontology in the way that science, or even common sense, must. This view is supported by the kindred view that ethics has its own particular methodology. Thomas Nagel suggests that

> [ethical] reasoning, is internal to the subject. It does not proceed by the application to this subject of methods developed in relation to other subjects, or of a general method of problem-solving and question-answering. While there are some extremely general conditions of rationality, they will not get you very far in any specific area of inquiry. Whether it is molecular biology, algebra, or distributive justice, one has to develop questions, concepts, arguments, and principles by thinking about that field and allowing reason and intuition to respond to its specific character. It happens again and again that the methods of one subject are taken as a model of intellectual respectability or objective rationality, and are then applied to a quite different subject for which they were not developed and for which they are unsuited. The results are shallow questions, non-explanatory theories, and the anathematization of important questions as meaningless. (1979, 145)

I do not deny that one can take such a pluralistic view toward ethics, or even the more liberal view that ethics is simply 'a form of life' or that morality is a 'game' we choose to play. My objection to these views that eschew the ontological question about moral properties is that my concern is to answer an explicitly ontological question: Do free will and moral responsibility exist? If the debates between the compatibilists and incompatibilists are in principle to be answerable, then freedom and responsibility must be objective entities that the competing theories may characterize more or less accurately. If freedom and responsibility are merely subject to pluralistic interpretations, then neither compatibilists nor incompatibilists can claim victory. Consider once more the difference between legal and moral responsibility. If moral responsibility could be given no stronger basis than the fact that particular societies recognize certain cases in which people are morally responsible, then different societies could 'create' equally valid conceptions of moral responsibility. But that means that an individual could be morally responsible for a certain action by the lights of one society and not morally responsible by the lights of another. And this would be to admit that moral responsibility is just one more variety of conventional responsibility—exactly what it cannot be if it is to play its normative role as a standard that our specific ideas of legal responsibility should meet.

In this chapter, I am concerned with moral properties and not with the practice of normative ethics. Whether the practice of ethics can be built upon contractarian or relativist grounds (Rawls, 1971; Gauthier, 1986; Harman, 1975) is not relevant to my ontological question, as interesting as those suggestions are for ethics proper. In my discussion of the universal subjective vs. anarchistic subjective theories later in this chapter, I argue that any form of relativistic ethics will fail to provide the sort of ontological grounding that the moral realist needs to resist meta-compatibilism. The opponent of meta-compatibilism needs to argue that moral properties (freedom and responsibility in particular) are universal in the sense that they provide norms against which any ascription of freedom and responsibility can be judged. It is not enough for those who resist meta-compatibilism to point out that we can devise various theories of freedom and responsibility that are pragmatically valuable. We *know* that this can be done; the compatibilists and incompatibilists have been doing this for most of the history of Western philosophy. But if their debate is not merely the attitudinal dispute that the meta-compatibilist thinks it is, then there has to be an external, universally valid standard of freedom and responsibility that is not relative to any society, culture, set of psychological needs, or contract. So, when I attack moral realism in this chapter, I am attacking the view that moral properties have an objective, *universal,* existence outside of any theoretical frameworks devised by ethical thinkers.

By asking how moral judgments could be objective, I am presupposing that the burden of proof is on the theorist who affirms that they are. Is this fair? Nagel suggests that the burden of proof lies on the objector, since prephilosophical intuition lies with the affirmative theory (1986, 143). But that suggestion seems wrong, since the existence of moral intuitions is simply an *explanandum* to be accounted for by all sides, and there is no initial reason to think that the objectivity doctrine explains the existence of our intuitions any better than a mixed (psychological-sociological-biological) account would. The burden-of-proof question is relevant to the debate between theories that hold that moral properties have an objective existence outside of our moral intuitions and the subjectivists. In matters of ontology, the burden of proof always lies on the theorist who claims that certain entities exist. It is this way in the mind–body problem, in the existence of God, and, for that matter, with quarks, leptons, and the abominable snowman, and I see no reason why it should not hold when we consider the existence of moral properties.

Let me emphasize how I shall not argue. My argument has no premises about the meaning of moral terms. I view meta-ethical arguments that are based on analyses of moral language—e.g., those of Ayer (1952), Stevenson (1944), Hare (1952), etc.—with great suspicion. For one thing, analyses of moral language in terms of its use in venting feelings, trying to alter attitudes, or making prescriptions seem to focus on just the illocutionary aspect of the *use* of moral language, rather than its meaning. (John Searle— 1969, Chapter 6—calls this "the speech act fallacy.") Instead, I think that moral statements, when viewed from the perspective of the philosophy of language, generally are propositional. They are structured as if they ascribe moral properties and as if they are truth-valued, an unsurprising fact given that they are thought to be that way by most people who produce them. Moreover, moral statements serve in logical inferences as if they were truth-valued. Consider: "If killing is wrong, then capital punishment is wrong," "Killing is wrong," "Therefore, capital punishment is wrong." Linguistically, this is a *modus ponens* argument, since the atomic sentences that constitute it have the grammar of categorical propositions. Qualms about whether this really is an instance of *modus ponens* arise only when we ask the metaethical question about the apparent property of wrongness; our qualms do not arise on grammatical grounds.

My second objection to linguistic arguments for moral non-realism concerns their overall strategy. If one is going to try to prove a substantial thesis in metaethics, one needs stronger premises than claims about the *meaning* of moral language. Even if the emotivist-prescriptionist claims about the meaning of moral language were acceptable, they would provide scant support for the metaethical conclusion. The moral realist would still have the reasonable option of accepting the linguistic premises while rejecting the non-realist conclusion. Nothing that one could say about the meaning of moral statements precludes the existence of moral properties, because language is one thing and reality is another. So, by my lights, the only plausible way to argue for moral non-realism will be to use non-linguistic premises.

My argument for moral non-realism shall not use as premises the unprovability of moral statements, the existence of moral dilemmas, or the pessimistic possibility that we may not be able to reconcile utilitarian and formalist intuitions into a coherent system (Nagel, 1979, 73). Although these are serious problems, I do not think that they support moral non-realism in a decisive way. There is always an alternative explanation that is open to metaphysical realists generally: although there is a truth to the matter, it is just extremely difficult to know what it is. The moral realist deserves the same courtesy that is accorded to metaphysical realists in other areas. Finally, my argument is not predicated on the relativity of ethical views—whether between individuals, cultures, classes, or over time. The reasonable rejoinder to relativistic arguments is the same that can be given to the argument from unprovability: the presence of disagreements does not imply that there is no truth to the matter. I shall argue, though, that once we have accepted the first half of my non-realism argument, which rejects the objective location of moral properties, relativistic considerations will have a role to play, since the above rejoinder will no longer be available to the realist.

Let me now describe how my argument proceeds. I sketch three possible types of metaethical views: *Objective Moral Realism*

(OMR), *Universal Subjective* (U-S) theories, and an *Anarchistic Subjective* (A-S) theory. I argue that if either of the first two types of theories are acceptable, then moral realism will be vindicated, but if the A-S theory is acceptable, then non-realism wins. In Sections 3, 4, and 5, OMR is rejected by appeal to some methodological considerations concerning the justified acceptance of properties. In Section 6, the U-S hypothesis is rejected; it is also argued that, despite appearances, U-S theories, even if true, could not support moral realism. Thus, my argument proceeds in two stages, the first designed to undermine the objective theory of moral properties and the second to neutralize the case for moral realism based on a universalized subjectivity. So, mine is a divide-and-conquer strategy.

My conclusion does not suggest that moral discourse is pointless or irrational, since such discourse is often principled. As suggested in the last chapter, two discussants may share enough moral intuitions to make their dialogue valuable, and certain individuals may do a better or worse job of drawing out the logical implications of their systems. My position is rather that such ratiocination has no ontological grounding, which I have argued to be necessary to support the existence of free will and moral responsibility. I think that there does not exist the sort of connection between reality and moral language that would enable fundamental conflicts of intuitions, as we have seen arise constantly in the free will debate (e.g., whether one's will is truly *free* in such and such circumstances, or whether one is *morally* responsible under other circumstances), to possess answers.

2. Three Theories of Moral Properties

I begin by adumbrating the three theories that I shall evaluate, relying on an analogy with metaphysical theories about the nature of physical objects. Objective Moral Realism is the analog to direct realism. Direct realism, interpreted as an ontological theory, holds that physical objects possess the types of characteristics that naive common sense ascribes to them. That is, characteristics such as shape, size, solidity, and, especially, the so-called secondary qualities like color, sound, taste, and odor belong to the physical objects and do not depend for their existence on being experienced by any perceiver. To fix on the visual properties, as is usually done in these discussions, direct realism holds that colors exist occurrently, spread out on the surfaces of physical objects, and our judgment that a particular physical object is a certain color is true if and only if that object possesses that color. Thus, the truth-conditions for our judgments about physical objects exist independently of us in the objects themselves.

OMR views moral properties the same way that direct realism views the commonsense characteristics of physical objects. According to OMR, the objectivity of the judgment "S was wrong to do x" or "Action a was wrong" lies in the fact that the truth conditions of the judgments reside in either S or a respectively. The truth of the assertion is determined by the extra-linguistic reality about which the ascription is made, not by any property of the ascriber. This explains why people with moral disagreements can literally contradict each other; reality can at most answer to one of two contradictory claims. The exact nature of the objective moral properties has been debated by moral objectivists historically, some suggesting that moral properties are natural properties (e.g., the utilitarians on goodness as the felicity-producing tendency of actions) and others suggesting that they are non-natural properties (e.g., Moore on goodness). Other non-naturalist views hold that moral properties are, somehow, established by a theological being or by some 'third realm' sort of entity like a Platonic form.

The point behind the comparison of OMR and direct realism is that both views claim that certain properties that might appear subjective are actually ontologically independent of perceivers. This claim is categorically rejected by the next two theories. The Universal Subjective (U-S) theory of moral properties is analogous to the Lockean indirect realist theory of secondary qualities. According to indirect realism, secondary qualities such as colors are not ontologically independent of being perceived. Rather, physical objects that are not colored themselves produce colored sense data or qualia in perceivers, due to the law-like interaction of the molecular surfaces of the objects and perceivers' perceptual mechanisms. The indirect realist gives a sense to the distinction between veridical and mistaken color perception by taking veridical perception to be the having of the same type of color qualia that normal (e.g., non–

color-blind) perceivers would have under standard conditions (eyes open, conscious, white light present, etc.). Misperception is held to be a divergence from that type. The same model can be extracted from common sense's view of pain, since pain is located in the subjects who feel pain and not in the physical objects that cause pain.

The Universal Subjectivist, like the indirect realist on colors, denies that moral properties reside objectively in agents and actions. Instead, judgments about the morality of agents and actions must be viewed in a more subtle way. Just as the indirect realist reinterprets the truth-conditions (but *not* the meaning) of "This cup is red" to be that normal observers under standard conditions would experience red qualia when looking at this cup, the U-S theorist offers a reinterpretation. For the latter, "Action *a* is morally wrong" has the truth-conditions that normal, competent judges of morality, under conditions of accurate knowledge, non-bias, and so on, would judge action *a* to be morally wrong. The U-S theorist thinks that although, strictly speaking, it would be an ontological mistake to impute moral properties to the agents and actions about which we make moral judgments, it would be no worse a mistake than our naive talk of physical objects as if they were occurrently colored. Although the truth conditions of moral judgments must be reinterpreted as shown above, the U-S theory leaves a perfectly good sense in which moral judgments are truth-valued.

The U-S theorist might go on to explain why moral judgments are universal (or nearly universal). The most promising line seems to be based on natural selection. That is, just as nondefective color perceivers can make color discriminations as the result of mechanisms that were selected in evolution, so, perhaps, nondefective morality perceivers might have been selected for having mechanisms of altruism or compassion by their genes (Dawkins, 1976). If the gap between non-cognitive examples like pain and color-qualia on the one hand and highly cognitive moral intuitions on the other seems too great to sanction the evolutionary analogy, the U-S theorist might offer another example that splits the difference. Noam Chomsky's theory of linguistic universals is a variety of U-S theory that suggests an evolutionary explanation of a fairly sophisticated cognitive ability of persons, *viz.*, the ability of speakers of natural languages to give untutored judgments regarding grammaticality.

The interesting thing about the U-S theory is that it gives the moral realist an alternative in the face of the following challenge: If moral properties are not given some sort of objective ontological status, then morality is at best a matter of social convention and, at worst, a matter of whimsy. The U-S theory shows that morality does not need to be objective to be non-arbitrary. In doing so, U-S theories reduce the motivation to claim that morality 'must' somehow be objective as the only reply to the charge that otherwise morality is simply a matter of taste.

Although OMR and the U-S theory differ metaphysically, that difference is not important metaethically, since both views hold that there are well-behaved types of features that exist *somewhere* that provide truth conditions for moral judgments. The Anarchistic Subjective theory, however, contradicts this claim. As does the U-S theory, the A-S view rejects the objective location of moral properties. But the A-S theory denies that moral judgments are controlled in the quasi–law-like way that the U-S theory maintains. The A-S theorist holds that there are no mechanisms for moral judgment that are analogous to the ones that Chomsky posits to account for our linguistic intuitions. Rather, the A-S theory holds that our judgments concerning right and wrong are governed by a welter of conflicting considerations, including biological, sociological, cultural, psychological, contextual, and idiosyncratic factors. Because these factors intrude upon each other differently for each individual, there is no systematic correspondence between objective features of agents and actions and our moral judgments about them. Thus, the truth-conditions for moral judgments are not the universal dispositions of competent moral judges, since there are no universal dispositions. But, since moral judgments are *intended* to express universality, moral judgments do not express moral properties at all. The A-S theory, for obvious reasons, does not correspond to any standard theory of perception, because even phenomenalists commit themselves to the notion that our qualia are produced in law-like ways. The closest analog might be common sense's view of what constitutes our judgments regarding the attractiveness of clothing.

3. The Argument against Objective Moral Realism

It is now time to present the case against OMR. The first premise is this:

1. *The only justification we have for ascribing objective moral properties to agents and actions is our intuitions that agents and actions are morally right and wrong.*

I think that we utilize our moral intuitions in two stages. First, we experience strong intuitions about various salient moral examples, such as those involving cruelty, unfairness, unusual altruism, and so on. Second, we ask whether the strong convictions that we have about these examples can be "just a matter of opinion," or whether the actions and agents in the example are *really* morally wrong, irrespective of anyone's opinion. The second step is best viewed as an instance of inference to the best explanation: The idea is that our intuitions must be based on the objective moral properties of agents and actions, otherwise our intuitions would not be as strong as they are.

Premise 1 is designed to exclude some possible arguments for the objective location of moral properties. The first are the linguistic arguments. Just as the linguistic arguments of the emotivists, et al., are poor grounds for arguing for moral non-realism, linguistic arguments do not provide evidence for realism. Consider, for instance, the argument that speakers can give contradictory moral judgments, and the argument that moral judgments can function in logical inference. Such linguistic arguments do not provide evidence for the objectivity of moral properties, since the non-realist can reply that logical form is determined by meaning, which does not establish the reference of moral terms. Although moral judgments are intended to designate objective moral properties, the question of whether the world actually possesses such properties is a metaphysical one that must be addressed on non-linguistic grounds. This distinction between meaning and reference that I rely on is not a controversial claim in the philosophy of language but simply a consequence of realism. To take an obvious example, the linguistic facts that we can contradict each other regarding the claim "Jones sees blue" and that we can infer "Jones sees a color" from the former claim provide no evidence for a direct realist theory of color. I am going to use this example as inductive evidence that linguistic arguments are disqualified from bearing on the objectivity issue.

A second possible justification for the objectivity of moral properties that the first premise is meant to exclude is one from special epistemic access. Some thinkers have held that you could just 'see' that moral properties exist, whether naturally or non-naturally; but as argued above, I think that such claims must be interpreted less hyperbolically as the view that we have intuitions about particular cases and then infer that morality is an objective property. 'Seeing' moral qualities, to borrow an expression that J. L. Austin used in discussing mirror images, is not like seeing a bun in a shop window (1962, 31). The analogy with realism about colors is once again instructive: the fact that we *see* the color blue does not provide any weight for the direct realist's theory over indirect realism.

A third argument is that the postulation of objective moral properties explains not simply our moral beliefs, but actual historical facts. Nicholas Sturgeon (1984) suggests that one might need to cite a moral fact such as Hitler's moral depravity to explain his behavior. But I think that this line is extremely doubtful, at least if it is used in behalf of objective moral realism, something Sturgeon himself may not do. To begin, the *moral*, like C. A. Campbell's *duty* (1951), cannot influence human behavior unless it works through some psychological mechanism. Just as it is not duty per se that moves us, but our beliefs and desires about duty, so Hitler's depravity must be instanced in depraved beliefs, desires, values, fears, etc., before it motivates his behavior. But once we admit that Hitler's depraved psychological states explain his behavior, then it is the psychological features of these states that do all the explanatory work. The moral quality of those states becomes debatable and explanatorily unnecessary. This is shown by the fact that a moral non-realist could grant that Hitler's behavior is explained by citing his (depraved) psychological states but deny that those states *were* objectively depraved.

Consider the following example. Suppose we explain Sally's altruistic behavior by saying that she is a good girl. Now suppose, for the sake of the example, that Sally's goodness depends upon the fact that she is a conscientious utilitarian. Hence, we can explain

Sally's behavior by reference to her striving to be a utilitarian. But now there is no explanatory work to be done by insisting that Sally not only endorses utilitarianism, but *is* objectively good—even if being objectively good *is* (in Sally's case) identical to endorsing utilitarianism. Even if moral realism is true because moral properties are identical to natural properties, explanations of behavior must cite those properties under their naturalistic descriptions, since it is under these descriptions that moral properties become understandably connected to behavior. This means that moral explanations of behavior, even if they cite the relevant causal properties, could not serve to justify our belief in the objectivity of moral properties.

My argument is similar to a familiar one in the philosophy of mind. Materialists generally have looked askance at explanations of behavior in terms of mental events and properties, unless there are independent grounds for thinking that the mental is the physical, e.g., by some sort of reduction (Smart, Armstrong, or Lewis). Something like this is going on in my argument, though I think with even more warrant. Given the doubtful status of objective moral realism, I think that we should not be happy with moral explanations of behavior in advance of very strong arguments that the moral has objective existence. Before we accept such explanations, we must already think that moral properties are identical to naturalistic ones; otherwise, the explanation presupposes causal interaction between two very different kinds of properties and appears highly suspect. But this means that we need to accept moral realism *before* we acknowledge the explanatory role of moral properties. Hence, arguments like the Hitler example appear to put the cart before the horse, *if* they are meant to show that moral properties have objective existence.

Although he also argues for the explanatory force of moral realism, Peter Railton (1986) actually supports this last claim. Railton thinks that the objective existence of moral properties explains social movements such as those aimed at achieving greater freedom in religion, suffrage, and civil rights. The moral fact that certain societies were unjust explains why these movements occurred (192). But Railton agrees that "facts about the way things *are* do all the explaining there is to be done" (185). Putting these two claims together, Railton infers that "facts about what ought to be the case are facts of a special kind about the way things are" (185). This conclusion may be true, but accepting the second premise seems to me to weaken our warrant for accepting the first. Since facts about what is the case "do all the explaining," we can explain the same facts that moral properties explain without citing the moral properties *qua* moral. From an explanatory perspective, moral properties are 'free riders' on the naturalistic properties to which the moral realist claims they are identical. As I have argued in the Sally example: even if the moral were identical to some part of the naturalistic world, those properties must be cited under their naturalistic descriptions to produce explanations.

There is a fourth argument that the first premise of my argument is designed to reject. Some thinkers have claimed that the objective nature of moral properties is established by divine command. God, this view maintains, makes moral properties an objective quality of agents and actions. This claim does not entail the familiar view known as "theological ethics," which makes the epistemological claim that we can *distinguish* between right and wrong by relying on some theological source. Though theological ethics may be rebutted with the standard point that we must test the purported claims of the theological source against our own moral intuitions, the objectivity claim simply asserts that the existence of moral properties whatever they may be is guaranteed theologically. Thus, it is consistent with the objection that defeats theological ethics. Still, there are other overwhelming objections to basing the objectivity of moral properties on a theological being: (a) The existence of a morally perfect being is problematic. (b) It is unclear how God, logically speaking, *could* make moral realism true. Because God's omnipotence must be understood to include the ability to do only that which is logically possible, we cannot expect God to be able to perform an impossible task. So, before we can use theology to discredit premise 1 by giving an alternative justification for believing in objective moral properties, we will have to examine the theological account of objective moral properties. I do that when we consider step 4.

The next step in the argument against OMR is this:

2. *Therefore, the ascription of objective moral properties to agents and actions is justifiable only as a theoretical postulation*

to explain our intuitions regarding the morality of agents and actions. (from 1)

This appears to follow directly from the first premise. The idea is that, given step 1, we have to view the objectivizing of moral properties as a theoretical postulation, in particular, as an inference to the best explanation of our moral intuitions. But, as with any theoretical postulation, there are methodological strictures that obtain. The most important are captured in step 3:

3. *Theoretical postulations, in ethics as with ontology in general, are justifiable only if: (a) The postulated entities fit into an otherwise acceptable theory of what exists in an understandable way (the conformity condition), and (b) the data that we use to justify the postulation cannot be explained equally well without making the postulation (the simplicity condition).*

The conformity condition captures the notion that postulated entities must not be "danglers" with respect to the rest of one's theory (Feigl, 1958). The simplicity condition is an imprecise version of Occam's razor.[2] Admittedly, if we came to difficult cases (e.g., deciding exactly when the postulation of relativistic space-time became justified in the face of existing Newtonian physics), we would need to be much more specific about these conditions. In the simple case, though, where the question is whether to add moral properties to our existing picture of the world or subjectivize them, these rules of thumb are precise enough to enable us to assess the postulation. We do not have to choose between radically different theories, but rather between only one *kind* of theory, with or without an addition made to it. (I am assuming that by subjectivizing moral properties, we would be saying that the only existence that moral properties have is in the moral intuitions of thinkers, and we already have to include the psychological states of thinkers in our ontology anyway.)

It is worth noting that both the conformity and simplicity conditions are designed to provide constraints on what we may *justifiably* postulate in our ontology. As such, they are epistemic principles for producing good postulations—that is, postulations that we believe have a strong chance of being true. The conditions do not suggest that it is impossible that objective moral properties exist in theoretically 'messy' ways. It is, after all, a basic realist contention that the world may not agree with our best epistemic efforts to characterize it. So, it will not touch my argument to object that objective moral properties *could* exist in ways that defy conformity and simplicity, because my concern is rather with what is reasonable to believe exists.

It would also be off target to suggest that since the notion of *justified* belief is normative, any attempt to undermine moral realism by presupposing a distinction between justified and unjustified belief assumes what it denies exists. My argument against moral realism does not reject the distinction between justified and unjustified beliefs, since my use of the notion of justification can be understood in terms of increasing the probability of one's having true beliefs, and this notion can be satisfied even if moral non-realism is true.

This brings us to the main premise of the argument:

4. *The ascription of moral properties cannot satisfy both the conformity and simplicity conditions.*

Note that this premise is the denial of a conjunction. In defending step 4, I shall concede that certain moral realist theories may satisfy one of the conditions. For instance, a naturalistic theory that holds that moral properties are (non-analytically) identical to non-moral properties will satisfy the simplicity condition, but it will violate conformity. Non-naturalist theories, however, whether postulating the existence of God, 'third realm' entities, or sui generis moral properties, will violate both conformity and simplicity.

Step 4 allows us to conclude the argument with two inferences:

5. *Therefore, the ascription of moral properties to agents and actions is not justifiable as a theoretical postulation.* (from 3 and 4)

6. *Therefore, the ascription of objective moral properties to agents and actions is not justifiable.* (from 2 and 5)

4. Why Non-Naturalist Theories Cannot Satisfy Both the Conformity and Simplicity Conditions

In this section and the next, I try to justify step 4 in the argument against Objective Moral Realism. To do this, I sketch what I take to be the most plausible alternatives available to the moral realist and then argue that each violates either the conformity or simplicity condition (or both). I shall consider five types of realist alternatives. First, there are theories that make the objectivity of moral properties depend upon the existence of non-natural entities. These include theories that make moral properties: (a) depend upon a theological entity, (b) depend upon an abstract entity, or (c) have a non-natural existence of their own that does not depend on entities of types (a) or (b). Second, considered in the next section, there are theories that take moral properties to be part of the natural world of agents and their actions. Among naturalistic theories, I consider two alternatives: varieties of identity theories that take moral properties at some level to be identical to naturalistic properties and theories that view moral properties as additional to the naturalistic properties of agents and actions.

Let us begin to consider the options open to the moral realist by looking at the non-naturalist alternatives. Consider first the theistic option. A moral realist could claim that actions have the moral qualities they do because they are sanctioned or disapproved by God. On this view, the morality of an action turns out to be a relational property, *viz.*, the relation denoted by "is approved (disapproved) by God." Now, this is very puzzling in at least two ways. First, this view bases the objectivity of morality on the subjective whim of God, Plato's worry in the *Euthyphro*. This, doubtless, creates an objectivity for moral properties in the sense that morality is not a matter of the intuitions of *people*, but it hardly seems satisfactory. It does not explain how morality can be objective, since it leaves unanswered the question: "How could God do it?" Certainly you or I cannot *make* an action have a certain moral status merely by deciding that it does. The answer that God has this sort of ability is unsatisfactory, since it is hard to see how *any* entity could do it. Instead of explaining how moral properties could be objective, the theistic option simply pushes back the question one step.

Second, it seems that the very idea that an action's moral worth might be determined by a relation, rather than its own nature (including its causal potential) seems profoundly anti-moral. For instance, if someone said that the relation that makes actions morally right is the relation of being approved by one's society, we would have to object that this turns moral properties into a species of conventional properties, something that is antithetical to the spirit of moral realism. If the theistic option yields an account of moral properties where it becomes a mystery how those properties can possess their moral status, then it cannot claim to provide a theory that makes *moral* properties understandable. If so, the theistic option is not a viable way to ground the objectivity of moral properties. Either the moral properties have been lost from the theist's account or, if one insists that these are still *moral* properties, then our inability to see how they can be moral shows that their postulation violates conformity.

The second non-naturalistic alternative is also unacceptable. Problems similar to those that arise for the theistic view will arise for the view that moral properties depend upon 'third realm entities'. Suppose that the abstract entity is 'thing-like' in whatever way that a Platonic form is supposed to be thing-like. In this case, the moral realist will face some unanswerable questions. Is the abstract entity itself constitutive of objective value, or does the 'conformity' of actions to that abstract entity comprise their values, or do both the abstract entity and actions that conform to them have objective moral value, although in different ways? Suppose that the moral realist says that the abstract entity itself is constitutive of moral value, irrespective of whether any action ever approximates it (e.g., the 'form of the good' is itself good regardless of whether any individual things ever 'participate' in it). This suggestion is unpromising, since it is difficult to see what it means to say that an abstract entity has (or is) a moral property. It is intelligible to ascribe moral properties to actions, agents, decisions, and intentions, only because these depend ultimately upon agency. Agents and their products (including 'faculties' like the Kantian good will) are the logically appropriate subject of moral predicates, not impersonal things.

So, let us suppose that abstract entities are not themselves subject to moral characterization, but rather that they create standards by which agents and actions may possess moral properties, depending upon their relation to the abstract entity. This will also yield an inexplicable 'location' for moral properties. There are, of course, notorious problems to Platonic scholarship about the relationship that is supposed to hold between the abstract entity and particulars that are supposed to possess their characteristics by virtue of 're-sembling' or 'participating' in the abstract entity (Plato, the *Parmenides*). Whatever metaphor one chooses, the basic problem that undermined the doctrine of theistic moral realism is also operative here. How *could* an action's being related to an abstract entity constitute an objective moral property of the action? I do not know whether any moral realist has an answer to the general question of what makes anything have moral value, but it seems to me that "participates in the form of the good" or "resembles justice" are non-answers. Merely conceptual answers are not going to provide the explanatory insight that we need in order to justify the inclusion of the abstract entities in our ontology. To use an example from Fodor, if we want to know why Wheaties are the breakfast of champions, we want to be told a story about vitamins, minerals, and carbohydrates; being told that they are eaten by non-negligible numbers of champions does not answer our question (1975, 6–7).

Here is another argument against the abstract entity interpretation of moral realism. Suppose that agents and actions possess their moral properties in virtue of relations that they have to abstract entities. The hypothesized entities and the individual agents and their actions are, then, two distinct types of entities. By 'Hume's Law', logically distinct existences can always, in principle, be separated. Thus, we must acknowledge that it is logically possible that both the abstract entities and the agents and actions exist without the existence of the other. Now, take a type of action T that has the objective moral property M in virtue of its relation to the abstract entity F. Further imagine what is logically possible for us, if not Plato, *viz.*, that F ceases to exist. On the view that the objectivity of morality is constituted by the relationship of particulars to abstract entities, we would have to conclude that actions of type T no longer have the moral property M. (We could also look at this the other way around and suppose that F comes into existence at a certain time, thereby making T-type actions have moral property M.) Relations, after all, exist only so long as their *relata* exist.

But this conclusion appears absurd. For, in the case that I am imagining, no other characteristics of T-type actions have changed at the time when the abstract entity ceases (or starts) to exist. By stipulation, T-type actions retain all the *other* characteristics that common sense takes to be relevant to their moral status: they, e.g., may remain productive of a certain level of utility or disutility or continue to be motivated by respect for the categorical imperative or a disregard for it. If this is so, then we should *not* say that the moral nature of T-type actions changes according to the existence of F. But this is to say that the objective moral qualities of actions cannot be constituted by their relation to abstract entities.

The same objection holds if we construe the abstract entities at stake to be propositional (like Popper's world of objective knowledge) rather than thing-like. We may grant that viewing the abstract entities as propositional avoids the difficulties that are peculiar to the Platonic view, *viz.*, is the relationship one of participation, resemblance, etc.? If the third-realm propositions maintain things like "Actions of type-T have moral property M," then the relationship between particulars and the abstract entities is simply that of denotations answering to definite descriptions. The basic problem, though, remains: we can make no clear sense of how being related to an abstract entity can constitute the morality of a particular.

The third non-naturalist alternative is the view that moral properties are intrinsic qualities of actions, the most famous example being G. E. Moore's view that goodness is a simple, unanalyzable quality (1903, Chapter 1). By making the moral status of actions depend on their own properties, rather than their relations to external entities, this view obviates the objection posed to theistic and Platonistic-type accounts. Here, at least, it is a non-relational property of the actions, instead of their correspondence to some non-naturalistic Prescriber or abstract entity that gives actions the moral status they have. The question, though, is whether taking moral properties to be non-natural properties of actions ultimately satisfies conformity.

The postulation of such properties is notoriously problematic, since it is not clear what non-natural properties are supposed to be like. One begins by asking *where* they exist. For instance, the tendency of a type of action to produce consequences of a certain type may be understood as a dispositional physical property. The intention to make one's actions conform to the categorical imperative is a type of psychological property, to be 'located' wherever one locates psychological phenomena generally. To learn that an action's moral properties are not 'in' the world in either of these ways makes one wonder *how* they could exist. In addition, one wants to ask how a non-natural property could supervene upon natural properties. How can any combination of natural properties causally influence a property that is not locatable in space? This riddle is certainly as puzzling as Cartesian mind–body interaction.

So, in terms of step 4, the view of moral properties as intrinsic, non-natural qualities of agents and actions stands opposed to both conformity and simplicity. Conformity is violated because of the numerous unanswerable puzzles that non-natural properties raise. Simplicity is violated because the data that we wish to accommodate by postulating non-natural moral properties—our moral intuitions concerning morality—is actually better explained by adopting the subjectivizing strategy of the U-S or A-S theories. Actually, U-S and A-S theories are simpler than the non-natural view on two counts. First, they are ontologically simpler because the subjectivizing of moral properties eliminates their ethereal non-natural existence 'in' actions and 'relocates' them in the subjective, psychological states of persons who have moral intuitions. Since we are already committed to the psychological states, why add non-natural properties of actions, given that this will not increase our ability to explain anything?

Second, the two subjective theories are psychologically simpler. On the U-S and A-S theories, an agent who makes a moral assessment of an action performs two cognitive tasks: the observation of the naturalistic properties of actions and the formation of a moral assessment of the action. On the non-natural view of moral properties, an agent perceives the non-natural moral character of the action and makes a moral assessment of the action. Psychologically, it is simpler for an agent to carry out the tasks required by the subjective theories, because sensitivity to natural properties is a more biologically feasible task than the recognition of non-natural moral properties. To use the analogy of building a machine as Dennett does (1984, 28), it would be much easier to make one that perceives simple physical properties and then reacts differentially than it would be to build one that perceives more complex properties.

5. Difficulties for the Naturalist Alternatives

Let us now shift to the two alternatives where moral properties are taken to be natural properties of agents and actions. The subjectivizing strategy that is used by the U-S and A-S theorists should be congenial to anyone who accepts a Lockean-style indirect realism or a more radical type of scientific realism (e.g., Sellars' Scientific Image sketched in 1963, Chapter 1). If we are sympathetic to the general strategy of 'relocating' some or most of the commonsense properties of physical objects into the sensory experiences of perceivers, then we should also be sympathetic to the subjectivizing of moral properties in the attitudes, beliefs, and moral intuitions of persons. This is because the motivation is similar in each case: simplicity and the avoidance of unanswerable puzzles about the resultant ontological picture, i.e., what I have called *conformity*. This is not to say that the theory of indirect realism entails the subjectivity of ethics, but only that the views hang together nicely. Perhaps the most useful thing for our purposes about the analogy between the two views is that indirect realism gives a model of how persons can 'recognize' the moral properties of agents and actions that, in a realist sense, are not there. The feelings of approval and disapproval toward agents and actions will be the results of psychological and physiological phenomena and are analogous to our experience of sensory qualia caused by physical objects that do not possess them.

Subjectivism will be a harder sell to the direct realist, whose ontological picture of the world imputes to physical objects the whole range of properties that common sense attributes to them. Since I cannot assume that the reader brings the bias of indirect realism to my argument, I shall propose an argument against naturalistic moral properties that I hope even direct realists will accept. Such a theme can be developed from J. L. Mackie's "argument from queerness" (1977, 38–42). Mackie suggests that, ontologically speaking, moral properties fit onto the corpus of the other properties of physical objects in a bizarre, inscrutable way. And, epistemically, our recognition of realistic moral properties would require some strange mode of apprehension that we do not seem to have any independent reason for postulating. So, even if one is a direct realist regarding perceptual properties, there are additional reasons for rejecting realism for moral properties.

Let me expand on Mackie's theme by considering two naturalistic alternatives for the moral realist. Logically speaking, there can be two types of naturalistic views, *viz.*, one where moral properties are in some way identical to naturalistic properties, and another where the moral properties exist in addition to the naturalistic properties. Let us begin with the identity alternative.

There are several sorts of identity theory open to the realist. The view that seems essential to any attempt of showing that the moral is simply part of the natural world is the token identity theory. If moral tokens are identical to naturalistic tokens, then assuming that moral properties are simply the totality of moral tokens, the moral realist will have a completely naturalistic view in hand. A utilitarian might hold that an instance of this action's rightness is simply this action's disposition to promote happiness. A Kantian might identify an action's rightness with its being produced from respect for the moral law. Type identity theories, which are more ambitious, might identify, e.g., the property type rightness with the disposition to promote utility, and so on.

It is even conceivable that the identity theorist might hold that the identity between naturalistic and moral properties might be even 'looser' than that portrayed by the token theorist. For instance, the relation between these properties might be analogous to the one of "weak supervenience" that John Haugeland (1982) suggests holds between physiological and mental states: A true mental taxonomy fits onto the same entities that the physiological one does, but the conceptual schemes are so disparate that even token identities do not always exist. The analog to this view would hold that moral properties collectively fit onto the body of naturalistic properties (and do not exist without them), but moral properties are individuated differently than are naturalistic ones (perhaps because they depend on various contextual, sociological, and psychological factors). This type of view might also look to the example of Searle's (1983, 265–266) claim that water's wetness is "caused by" and "realized in" the molecules that comprise it and Cornman's (1975) "compatible common-sense realism" that takes both secondary qualities and the theoretical particles of physics to co-exist in the same physical objects. I am not sure that the alternative of making the moral exist 'at a higher level of description' than the naturalistic that is provided by the analogies with the view of Haugeland, Searle, and Cornman is going to help the moral realist. The token identity theorist already views the naturalistic tokens that are to be identified with the moral tokens at a high level of abstraction. For instance, the utilitarian takes the relevant naturalistic property token to be an act's disposition to create happiness; the property is not described at the level of bodily movements or quantum mechanics. Nonetheless, I mention this third type of identity view in order to cast a wider net, while I focus my attention on token and type theories.

Both token and type identities, as noted earlier, can be true despite the fact that the identity *statements* expressing them are synthetic. So, on my view, naturalism is not a species of "definism" (*pace* Frankena, 1973, 97–102). Whether, e.g., Mill actually conflated the meaning of *desired* and *desirable* or not, the point is that he need not have done so, because the identity of naturalistic and moral properties does not entail the synonymy of the designating terms (Mill, 1861, Chapter 4).

So, given that naturalism is not undermined by appeal to the meaning of moral terms, how does it fare on the desiderata of conformity and simplicity? First, the good news. Token and type identity theories have no problem satisfying the simplicity condition. To say that moral properties are naturalistic ones does not increase the number of entities in one's ontology. This is true because property identities never usher into our ontology more entities than exist if only one of the expressions in the identity statement denotes. Now, this claim has been resisted by some thinkers in the mind–body identity debate; the view that the existence of mental properties entails the existence of non-physical properties in addition to our materialistic world view has been the motivation for theories as diverse as panpsychism (Nagel, 1979, Chapter 13) and eliminative materialism. I have argued elsewhere that this worry is unfounded when the entities that are being identified are property tokens or types (Double, 1985), and the point at stake is too tangential to warrant a long discussion here. After all, if I am wrong about this, then the case looks even worse for the identity view of moral properties, since an identity of the moral and the naturalistic will mean extra entities, thus threatening to violate simplicity. But let me take two paragraphs to explain why property identity theories seem to me to be ontologically parsimonious.

The belief that property identities require more properties than are required in the case where only one of the two terms denotes results from looking at the identity from the outside in. We hear, e.g., the expression "the property of producing happiness," and certain associations come to mind. We hear "moral rightness," and different associations arise, even if we are theoretically committed to the identity of the two denotations. For instance, hearing the former expression might produce a recollection of eating chocolate or going to the beach, whereas hearing "moral rightness" might bring to mind thoughts about Kant or Rawls. It is natural, though mistaken, to infer from these differing associations that somehow there are extra properties that are presupposed by the identity theory that would not be implied if only one of the two expressions denoted.

This illusion appears if we look at identities from the inside out. Take a humble property token such as that denoted by "the property of being a red teacup in my left hand." Now, suppose that an anthropologist colleague drops by and mentions that in a certain culture a red teacup in one's left hand is regarded as having rich religious meaning. Thus, if I were to adopt those religious beliefs, the teacup would also answer to the designation "the property of having such and such religious import." But irrespective of the fact that these two expressions have wildly different psychological associations, it is clear that the identity of their denotations does not bring into existence any property that did not exist in the first place. The world has no more 'furniture' in it; we simply have one more way of designating the existing furniture of the world.

So, I am prepared to concede that a naturalistic identity theory of moral and naturalistic properties satisfies the simplicity condition. This means that if the identity theorist manages to justify the identity view, we will have no reason to complain about excess ontological baggage. This leaves, though, the logically prior problem of whether we can see how the identification can be made in an understandable way, i.e., whether the conformity condition can be met.

The first objection to this token identity view is a challenge that all identity theories must face: "What *makes* the identity true?" (Not: "How do we *know* that it is true?") For instance, why is this naturalistic property token identical to this particular moral property token (e.g., being morally acceptable) rather than a different one (e.g., being morally unacceptable)? To take an example where we can give an answer, suppose that this token of the color blue is identical to a token of my favorite color. We can explain why the identity holds by saying that we are conceptualizing the same token in two different ways. "Blue" is simply a color term, whereas "my favorite color" is autobiographical. It just turns out that I prefer the color blue and the explanation for *that* lies buried in my psychological history. Note that this psychological account completely explains the identity at stake; if true, it establishes the identity, again, not in the sense that *proves* the truth to anyone, but that it constitutes the truth of the identity. Likewise with the property of being a red teacup and having such and such religious significance.

This theme is repeated in less mundane examples of property identities. We can explain the identity of temperature and the mean kinetic energy of molecules by telling a story whereby a common-sense property is—by appeal to simplicity—shown to be identical to a theoretical property in thermodynamics, rather than parallel to it or 'emergent' from it. The same sort of story can be told for lightning and electrical discharges from clouds, genes and DNA molecules, and so on. Admitted, the identification is less straightforward epistemically in the scientific cases than in the case of blue and my favorite color, because the former require the acceptance of more theory, and might even tempt us to consider dualistic options. But the identity claim is no more puzzling. The point is that in identifications that we are comfortable about making, there is a fully understandable story that we (or, at least, an expert) can tell about why the identity holds. Sometimes we even may be less comfortable in affirming that identities hold, and may be buoyed by the thought that the identity must hold, even if we cannot tell a fully satisfactory story about *why* it holds. For instance, we might claim that X must be the murderer since there was no one else present at the mansion to perform the dire deed even if we do not see how X could have done it. Or, in the philosophy of mind, I am wont to think that qualia instances *must* be physiological property instances, since there is no other plausible niche for them in our ontology.

But none of these rationales seems operative in the case of moral properties. First, the line that the moral "must" be identical to the natural properties of agents and actions because there is no other place to locate them is foreclosed. The subjectivist has a plausible answer to the question of where moral properties could exist if not as identical to objective properties of agents and actions: moral properties exist only as subjective intuitions *about* agents and actions. Second, the identity cannot be defended on the sort of banal grounds that we used to justify the identity of blue and my favorite color. There is no commonsensical psychological account that can explain why moral and naturalistic terms denote the same property as was available in that case. Third, there seems to be no analog to the picture of 'meshing' the denotation of a scientific term into that of a commonsense one. What we have, instead, are two radically different modes of discourse *and* types of properties. The differing properties will be naturalistic, descriptive properties on the one hand, and moral, essentially prescriptive properties on the other. These seem to clash rather than harmonize and certainly do not appear to have the potential for being identified that commonsense nonmoral and scientific properties do. Although we must concede that the identity of the moral and natural is possible, it seems that no answer to the conundrum of how the moral can be the natural is forthcoming.

Although identity theories and the subjectivist theories are equally ontologically parsimonious, the latter have the advantage of obviating this problem. If moral properties are 'relocated' in the psychological states of persons who make moral judgments, *that* identity question does not arise. (We then have to answer how psychological states can be physiological states of persons, but we have to deal with that identity question in the philosophy of mind anyway. And the identity at stake becomes that of identifying two types of *non-moral* properties.) If we did not have the subjectivizing option open to us, then we would have to bite the bullet and accept an identity theory (or, what is worse, some sort of dualistic theory). But, because the subjectivizing option is available, the moral realist cannot reasonably argue this way.

I conclude this section by examining the second naturalistic option, the view that naturalistic moral properties exist in addition to the non-moral naturalistic properties in the world. To borrow some more notions from the philosophy of mind, the relationship between the two different types of naturalistic properties might be epiphenomenal (the moral depending upon the non-moral, but not vice versa), parallelist (non-interacting), or interactionist. The best thing that can be said for any of these views is the same that can be said for their counterparts in the mind–body question: they obviate the problem of having to explain *how* an identity holds by denying that it exists. In addition, the dualistic positions might be attractive to the naturalist who is not persuaded that synthetic property identities are entirely aboveboard. And these theories do preserve the ontological integrity of the moral while avoiding lapsing into Moorean non-naturalism.

Despite these advantages, none of them look promising. The parallelist analog seems as miraculous for moral properties as it does for the mental. The moral realist certainly should *want* the moral to be determined by the non-moral. But once we reject parallelism, the problem of how the non-moral brings the moral into existence arises for both of the other theories, and no explanation seems even conceivable. One could at least understand how, e.g., observing a non-moral action might produce in a subject a feeling of moral approval or disapproval on the subjectivist story. But it is difficult to see how such an action might give rise to a naturalistic moral property that is not someone's subjective reaction to it. This is so, largely because it is very hard to see what it would be like for there to *be* a naturalistic moral property that is not just the naturalistic property under another description.

Thus, the naturalistic non-identity theories seem to have insuperable problems with conformity. And, of course, they radically violate simplicity by postulating moral properties in excess of the treatments suggested by the identity theorists and the subjectivists. The non-identity theories appear to be as weak as Moore's view on this score (indeed, they make moral properties just as mysterious, as well as unnecessary). Because both conformity and simplicity are violated, the fifth option for the moral realist should be rejected.

6. The Universal Subjective
vs. Anarchistic Subjective Theories

If the argument of the last two sections is acceptable, we are not justified in ascribing objective moral properties to agents and actions. In this case, we will need to account for the existence of our moral intuitions by appeal to subjective factors. One way of doing this will be to view moral intuitions as general cognitive features that non-defective human beings experience when perceiving non-moral stimuli (the U-S theory). The alternative will be to view intuitions as much more sporadic, owing to various factors (the A-S theory). In principle, we could imagine varieties of U-S and A-S theories of different strengths in such a way that there is a slippery slope from theories of one type to the other. But I am going to ignore that fact, since the usual disputants in the debate between the U-S and A-S positions typically describe their theories in ways that leave a fairly wide demarcation. (I have in mind U-S theorists like Hume and A-S thinkers like Ayer.)

The moral non-realist might object to my strategic decision to treat U-S theories as a species of moral realism. It might be objected: "Once we renounce the idea that moral properties are ontologically independent of anyone's intuitions about them, then the whole notion of the objectivity of moral truth is surrendered. Who cares if even *all* persons shared the same moral views? Morality, by its very nature, is not something that depends on what anyone thinks about it." The reason I think that U-S theories, if true, might vindicate moral realism is that U-S theories in principle could allow ethics to be a science, albeit a science with a subjective subject matter. There are, after all, psychophysical laws governing the conditions under which perceivers experience visual and auditory sensations (Hochberg, 1964). Anesthesiology is a branch of medicine. Laws have been devised that describe our ability to rotate mental images (Shepard and Metzler, 1971). So, I think that the U-S theory could do a great deal for the moral realist, even if it is a subjective view. I concede, however, that I believe that the refutation of OMR was the harder part of the argument for moral non-realism. The U-S theory is going to prove to be an indefensible last stand for the realist: if the choice is between U-S and A-S theories, as I have argued it is, then the A-S view should win easily.

How might U-S theories be explicated and defended? Perhaps the best examples of U-S theories are the 'sentiment' theories of the British moralists. Hume provides a clear example:

> The notion of morals implies some sentiment common to all mankind, which recommends the same object to general approbation, and makes every man, or most men, agree in the same opinion or decision concerning it. It also implies some sentiment, so universal and comprehensive as to extend to all mankind, and render the actions and conduct, even of the persons the most remote, an object of applause or censure, according as they agree or disagree with that rule of right which is established. These two requisite circumstances belong alone to the sentiment of humanity here insisted on. The other passions produce in every breast, many strong sentiments of desire and aversion, affection and hatred; but these neither are felt so much in common, nor are so comprehensive, as to be the foundation of any general system and established theory of blame or approbation.
>
> When a man denominates another his *enemy*, his *rival*, his *antagonist*, his *adversary*, he is understood to speak the language of self-love, and to express sentiments, peculiar to himself, and arising from his particular circumstances and situation. But when he bestows on any man the epithets of *vicious* or *odious* or *depraved*, he then speaks another language, and expresses sentiments, in which he expects all his audience are to concur with him.
>
> The distinction, therefore, between these species of sentiment being so great and evident, language must soon be moulded upon it, and must invent a peculiar set of terms, in order to express those universal sentiments of censure or approbation, which arise from humanity, or from views of general usefulness and its contrary. Virtue and Vice become then known; morals are recognized; certain general ideas are framed of human conduct and behaviour; such measures are expected from men in such situations. (1777, 112–114)

But it is one thing to say that humans share universal moral sentiments and another thing to prove it. A critic might well agree with Hume that moral language came into existence because people *want* to express sentiments of universal validity but deny that any

sentiments *are* universally shared. Although the 'language of morals', unlike the language of personal sentiment, purports to express
judgments that are universally acceptable, perhaps there are no
moral judgments that are universally held. So, the U-S theorist
needs some empirical support for the claim that moral sentiments
(intuitions) are indeed universal.

One way the U-S theorist might support the claim of universality
would be to appeal to data from cultural anthropology. Such an
appeal would certainly be an improvement over the method of
inferring universality from the unrepresentative sample of the
moral convictions held by well-to-do, white, Anglo-Saxon, male
philosophers, if even that group shares the purported moral intuitions. But anthropological evidence, even if it could withstand
various methodological criticisms, would be unconvincing unless it
were augmented with a general theory to explain the purported
universality. The most likely theory in this instance, as in the case of
the commonality of our color and sensation experiences and the
Chomskian theory of linguistic universals, seems to be natural
selection. So, the Humean U-S notion of the universality of moral
sentiment would be greatly strengthened by adding to it an evolutionary story.

One evolutionary account is that of the 'selfish gene' given by
Richard Dawkins (1976). I venture no claim about how plausible
Dawkins's view is when compared to other selectionist accounts,
but that is not important, because I wish only to use the broadest
outline of Dawkins's theory to suggest the general strategy available
to U-S thinkers. For Dawkins, the proper level to view natural
selection is not the whole species, nor groups of individuals, nor
individual animals, but genes. Genes that produce behaviors that
maximize their chance for replication multiply, whereas genes that
yield behaviors that hurt their chances for replication are reduced in
number and, eventually, die out. Such genetic factors account for
both altruistic and selfish behaviors. The altruistic faked broken-
wing dance of parent birds when their eggs or young are threatened
by predators is risky to the parent but enhances the likelihood that
genes of their type will survive in the bodies of their offspring. The
case is likewise for the individual animal that gives an alarm call to
others of the group when it sights a predator. The selfish strategy of
biting off the head of her male partner during copulation enhances

the female praying mantis's genes' chance to propagate, because the female has gotten an 'inexpensive' meal that in no way hinders her ability to reproduce. The genes of selfish emperor penguins are advantaged when the birds try to push each other into dangerous waters to test whether a predatory seal might be waiting (Chapter 1).

None of these animals are aware of the moral status of their actions; that these behaviors are tropisms is shown by the fact that the animals will go through them even when they are entirely otiose. If the animals *knew* what they were doing, they probably would not perform the altruistic acts. (One could imagine a comedy routine involving a self-conscious, preservation-minded animal in a dialogue with its selfish genes that are trying to make it risk its life.) Nonetheless, if animals are predisposed to act in various altruistic and selfish ways, it seems reasonable to imagine that when humans reached the point at which we could reflect on the moral status of such behaviors, our natural disposition toward them would create a bias in favor of them. So, for instance, altruism would be greatly admired, whereas acting in selfish ways ('acting from self-preservation') would also have a strong grip on our moral sentiments. Our reflective moral sentiments would tend to approve of behaviors for which there were genetic predispositions, and this would affect the type of moral views we adopt.

The last step that the U-S theorist who is telling this story needs to provide is the premise that the sort of behaviors toward which we are universally sympathetic were determined by our genes. Some seem fairly straightforward. Given the considerable length of time between birth and the time when a child becomes self-sufficient, our genes could be expected to be biased in favor of the nurturing of offspring. Incest taboos seem genetically probable, given that genes that permitted reproduction with close family members would find themselves disadvantaged. Biases in favor of fidelity among sexual partners among some humans are predictable given the 'costs' of reproduction (Dawkins, 1976, 162–165). More suggestive than these specifics—and more speculative—is the idea that the relatively small numbers by which human beings reproduce and our dependence on each other might have selected two of the basic intuitions of theoretical ethics: interest in the well-being of other persons and a bias in favor of fairness.

If all this sounds pretty vague, it is meant to be. I am just trying to suggest how the U-S view might be helped. I am not arguing that a selectionist view is the only way that one can support the U-S theory. One could pick and choose from evolutionary considerations and add to them considerations from non-biological, cultural features common to groups of people living in societies. Or one could opt for the cultural view, entirely rejecting any biological story. For instance, maybe we are not genetically predisposed toward, e.g., sympathy; perhaps sympathy is entirely learned. Or maybe sympathy somehow results from feeling pain in our case and confusing our pain with that of others. Maybe fairness is learned from interactions with other persons. Or, for that matter, we could simply refuse to explain the universality of our moral intuitions. The reason why I elect to 'give' the explanation in terms of natural selection to the U-S theorists is that I think that it strengthens their theory more than any other alternative that I can envisage. If the U-S theorist does not want the evolutionary account, that is fine with me. My aim in offering it is to make the U-S view the most plausible it can be.

It is time to criticize the U-S view. The most important criticism is that U-S theories, whether supported by an evolutionary account or not, fail to yield a theory of morality that is truly *normative*. U-S theories do not defend the deep, prescriptive nature of ethics; instead, by construing morality as the subjective moral intuitions of persons, U-S theories emasculate moral properties by turning them into patently empirical properties whose existence has no implications for ethics. I shall apply this criticism to U-S theories that help themselves to natural selection, because I think that the appeal to natural selection makes U-S theories more explicit and the criticism that I offer more vivid. The criticism, however, is designed to apply whether the U-S theorist utilizes the evolutionary theme or not.

Take the evolutionary account of our putatively universal (or nearly universal) positive sentiments regarding sympathy. The U-S theorist must concede that it is at least logically possible that humans might have evolved in such a way that sympathetic behaviors would be held in low esteem. Suppose, for instance, that humans reproduced in the numbers that insects do and that the early elimination of the vast majority of humans who were born was necessary for the survival of the genes of any. Suppose also that, like most insects, care of offspring was unnecessary. Given these conditions, behaviors that manifest sympathy for other humans might actually be dysfunctional for the genes, with the result that we would not feel moral intuitions favoring sympathy. In this scenario other moral intuitions might be changed as well, e.g., intuitions regarding actively harming other persons and being unfair to them. If one balks at admitting that it is even logically possible that *humans* might have evolved in such a 'heartless' way, then let us imagine that this sort of thing has occurred somewhere on another planet—one with very different biological laws than those that hold on Earth.

Now, what should the U-S theorist say about the status of the moral intuitions of those Heartless Beings? There are only two options, and both point to overwhelming problems for the U-S view. Here is the first alternative. Suppose that the U-S theorist said that the moral intuitions of those Heartless Beings would be morally acceptable (since, after all, those intuitions are universal to those beings). The rebuttal to this option is the same (correct) one that is typically made to varieties of relativism: Even if an entire species accepts certain moral views, those views may be wrong. The correctness of moral views is not established by their popularity, and this fact remains even if one extends the size of the group that holds those views to an entire species. Curiously, on this tack, the U-S thinker makes morality arbitrary in a way that is analogous to the problem faced by the theist who envisages God as establishing the difference between right and wrong: instead of morality being dependent upon the whim of God, morality is dependent on whatever way natural selection turns out.

Now, granting for the sake of argument, that *this* planet is one where there are universal moral intuitions, the moral intuitions that we actually have can be viewed as simply one set among indefinitely many *possible* sets of U-S moral intuitions held by various possible evolved beings. But, I have argued in the previous paragraph that we cannot conclude that the views of the Heartless Beings are morally correct merely because they evolved that way. Thus, since there is nothing special about our own case, we cannot make that inference regarding ourselves either. The U-S claim that our purported altruistic moral sentiments are morally acceptable because they are universal to us is likewise dubious. Our basic notions about morality will not allow us to say that *any* form of 'popular opinion'—even at the level of the entire species—constitutes morality.

The U-S theorist might reply at this point with the sort of rebuttal sometimes given by other relativists: Morality simply *is*, in the relativist's view, whatever is believed to be moral by the specific target group that the relativist selects. So, to say that the Heartless Beings as a species have morally wrong beliefs is to beg the question against relativism. To reply to this, one needs only to make a fairly simple reply: Whatever it is that is determined by mass agreement in attitudes, it is not *morality*. Given their biological heritage, we may choose not to *criticize* the Heartless Beings for their heartlessness. But if there is to be any such thing as morals, then right and wrong have to logically stand outside of what individuals believe to be right and wrong. Right and wrong could not simply be a function of the way we evolved, because in every case the question arises whether we evolved into moral or immoral creatures. At least this is the question to ask if there is anything such as morality in the first place. Relativistic theories, including U-S theories, are from the standpoint of metaethics not accounts of morality at all but varieties of ethical non-realism.

Let us now consider the second alternative. Suppose that the U-S theorist agrees with the argument just rehearsed and concedes that even evolved universality does not establish moral correctness. Although this seems to be the correct stance to take, it is a disaster for the U-S theorist. Since the U-S theorist claims that universal acceptance of fundamental moral views is *constitutive* of the difference between right and wrong, the U-S theorist has no grounds for taking this stance toward the views of the Heartless Beings. Since on the U-S theory morality just is that which is universally accepted by one's species, the Heartless Beings *must* have morally acceptable intuitions. The only way that we can reject the moral views of those beings is by embracing some variety of OMR, which the U-S theorist disavows.

(Obviously it would not do for the U-S theorist to reject the moral views of the Heartless Beings by appeal to our Earthling sentiments in favor of sympathy. For the Heartless Beings could adopt the same strategy to conclude that they are right and we are wrong, and there would be no way to adjudicate the disagreement within the U-S framework. Again, only an appeal to an objectivist theory would do.)

Finally, I should say a word about attempts to 'construct' U-S principles from psychological premises about self-interest, e.g., Rawl's and Gauthier's notions of basing general principles of morality on what egoistic individuals would find prudent in various contractual situations. For the purpose of defending the U-S theory, such constructions can be no stronger than the evolutionary story, which we have found reason to reject. Even if it were true that humans universally share self-interest, any theory of morals that is constructed on such a psychological premise remains subject to the objection that refutes all forms of relativism, including U-S relativism. Why should we think that the resulting theory is one of *morality*? If it is, then it cannot be simply because it conforms to what egoistic individuals would select, but because it is actually (read *objectively*) morally acceptable. Endorsement of an ethical construction is no more constitutive of the constructed view than is a universal endorsement of the basic moral intuitions on which the construction is based. Contractarian views do their work while holding the fundamental metaethical question that we have considered in this chapter at arm's length; by the same token, they do not help justify any particular metaethical conclusion.

7. Conclusion

In the last section, I tried to make the strongest case that I could for U-S theories. For me, that meant suggesting an evolutionary mechanism by which moral intuitions could be reasonably held to be universal or at least as nearly universal as is the ability to distinguish colors or feel pain is for humans. Although this suggestion was sketchy, it seemed to lend some plausibility to the U-S view expressed by philosophers who talk about moral sentiments. But with or without an evolutionary addendum, U-S theories remain relativistic—albeit at a higher than usual level of generalization—and subject to the standard objection to relativism. Thus, even if moral intuitions are universal, U-S theorists cannot support the doctrine of moral realism.

Although U-S theories cannot support the objectivity of moral judgment, I should say something about why I think that Anarchistic Subjectivism is true. In retrospect, the analogy between U-S

theories of morality and theories involving color perception, sensations, and linguistics was quite strained. It is true that animals can
behave selfishly and altruistically in a tropistic way, and, hence,
approximate universality among the individual members of a species. But human moral intuitions, although undoubtedly influenced
by genetically controlled mechanisms, are highly cognitive. And
this means that our moral intuitions are alive to multifarious factors that do not influence the behavior of less cognitive beings.
These factors include such things as individual-specific beliefs and
desires, collateral information about the particular situation to be
judged, memory and memory-lapses, inference and inferential errors, and so on. All these factors open the door to social, cultural,
contextual, and psychological influences that mitigate even strong
genetic dispositions. Dawkins points out that genes must be viewed
as *influences* but not *determinants* of individual behavior: "[I]t is a
fallacy . . . to suppose that genetically inherited traits are by definition fixed and unmodifiable" (1976, 3). So, although U-S theories
cannot be rejected prior to investigation, we should be very scrupu-
lous in demanding evidence before we accept a U-S theory.

There are other problems with U-S theories. U-S theorists do
not tell us exactly what the moral intuitions common to all persons
are supposed to be. We are sometimes told that sympathy and
kindness to others is a universal moral sentiment, but surely these
traits are not universal, indeed, not even nearly so. This is especially clear when we raise the question of whether people abrogate
their claim to kindness by doing certain deeds. The Christian belief
in loving one's enemy, e.g., scarcely looks like a candidate for
universality. I suspect that U-S theorists are guilty of gathering
their data selectively. I also suspect that, when criticized, the U-S
theories are going to be reformulated in verbal ways that make
them trivial.

The A-S view is dialectically in a stronger position than U-S
theories, because the A-S claim is so much weaker. Although U-S
theories are naturally driven to postulate some sort of biological
determinism, the A-S theorist is free to pick and choose explanations for our moral intuitions from various sources in the biological
and social sciences. The non-universal or 'anarchistic' nature of
moral intuitions can be defended by this line of reasoning:

i. The only reason to believe that moral intuitions are universal is the existence of some variety of biological, social, or psychological determinism. (If there were an interplay of these factors, then it is unlikely that universality or near-universality would be approached, since the mode of interaction would probably differ for various individuals.)

ii. Determination by any one source is undermined by the existence of the others. In addition, the holistic and non-modular nature of higher cognitive processes (Fodor, 1983) militates against any simplistic determination by any single source.

iii. Hence, it is unreasonable to believe that there is a universality or even near-universality of our moral intuitions. To the extent that there is an appearance of near-universality, then it must be an illusion created by the biased selection of cases.

As a subjective theory, the A-S view shares the advantage that the U-S view had over OMR in offering explanations of moral phenomena that satisfy the conformity and simplicity requirements regarding theoretical postulations. We have already seen that there is no explanatory gain to be derived by positing objective moral properties in addition to the moral intuitions of individuals. This is not to deny that it is understandable that people should come to view morality as objectively founded. As Hume and Mackie (1977, 43) point out, we not only *want* our moral judgments to have interpersonal validity, but we are naturally biased toward viewing them this way. The moral characteristics of actions and agents *seem* to reside in their objects, and it is only with some effort that we can resist this prephilosophical conviction. But, given that there are no theoretical gains to be enjoyed by the objectivizing view, and the considerable theoretical minuses of objectivizing, the subjective views look better. And between the U-S and A-S theories, I think the choice is clear.

8

Troubles
with Libertarianism

ABSTRACT The argument of Part II so far has been that no account of free will can succeed, not even the compatibilist account of Part I. But there are, no doubt, readers who believe that libertarianism, or maybe libertarianism supplemented with some rationality constraints, can vindicate the notion of free will. So, it is to libertarianism that I turn directly.

In this chapter, I argue that a libertarian conception of free will must satisfy the three conditions of the ability-to-choose-otherwise, control, and rationality, interpreted as dual abilities. I then look at two broad classes of libertarian theories, Nonvalerian theories that satisfy the first condition at the expense of the other two, and Valerian theories, none of which does better than compatibilist theories at satisfying the dual abilities. My conclusion is that the deep reason why no libertarian view can satisfy all three conditions is that the conditions are logically incompatible. Hence, libertarianism, despite its intuitive appeal, turns out to be incoherent, although it captures enough of the way we feel about freedom to rule out compatibilism. I conclude by suggesting that libertarianism has no resources of its own for dealing with rationality objections and must help itself to something like the compatibilist's account from Part I, which we have already seen reason to reject.

1. Three Libertarian Conditions

In the first chapter of this book, I claim that any account of free will must produce an interpretation of how free agents might satisfy the three conditions regarding rationality, control, and the ability to choose otherwise. Part I developed the compatibilist's one-way interpretation of these conditions, but in Chapter 5 I argued that the compatibilist's picture relies upon a biased examination of our free will paradigms. Implicit in Chapter 5 was a similar criticism of the incompatibilist's dual interpretation of the three conditions, but I did not focus on particular libertarian theories. In this chapter, I hope to show that a libertarian account of dual rationality, control, and the ability to choose otherwise also fails, thereby concluding the argument begun in Chapter 5.

The most important of the three conditions for the libertarian is the requirement that free agents have the ability to choose otherwise under the exact conditions that obtain at the moment of choice. The libertarian's interpretation of this requirement signifies the clearest demarcation between the incompatibilists and the compatibilists and is probably incompatibilism's greatest selling point. The compatibilist's argument that the concept of "can choose otherwise" is analytically definable in terms of the hypothetical notion that agents would have chosen otherwise had some condition been different seems dubious to me. Chisholm rejects the hypothetical analysis by arguing that the categorical statement (a) "He could have done otherwise" is not logically equivalent to the hypothetical statement (b) "If he had chosen to do otherwise, then he would have done otherwise":

> . . . (b), it would seem, could be true while (a) is false. That is to say, our man might be such that, if he had chosen to do otherwise, then he would have done otherwise, and yet *also* such that he could not have done otherwise. Suppose, after all, that our murderer could not have *chosen*, or could not have *decided*, to do otherwise. Then the fact that he happens also to be a man such that, if he had chosen not to shoot he would not have shot, would make no difference. For if he could *not* have chosen *not* to shoot, then he could not have done anything other than just what it was that he did do. (1964, 27)

I think that Chisholm is correct in his rejection of the compatibilist's claim when viewed as linguistic analysis. Beyond this technical criticism, incompatibilists are more closely attuned to the sort of freedom that we *think* we have. Even if we renounce indeterminism on theoretical grounds, many of us retain the belief expressed by the libertarian Castle in *Walden Two* (Skinner, 1948, 258) that alternative choices seem to be available to us at an instant, without the need for conditions to be different. This so-called feeling of freedom leads some to think that we *have* libertarian-style categorical freedom; at the very least, it helps persuade us that we *need* to have it to be free. In addition, there is the familiar incompatibilistic intuition that moral responsibility requires categorical freedom.

As noted in Chapter 1, the libertarian's commitment to indeterminism guarantees a dual interpretation of the control and rationality conditions. For the libertarian, free agents not only have the ability to choose in two directions, but they must be in control of either choice. This consequence could be deduced from the demands of moral responsibility. If an agent is to be truly responsible for either choice, A or not A, then both outcomes are under the agent's control. The case is likewise with rationality, although a predictable amount of strain is likely to arise. Libertarians, at the very least, need to show how indeterministic choices *can* be rational whichever way they turn out. Ideally, libertarians will show us how such a dual ability might be, contrary to appearances, a desirable or even necessary element of rational choices.

2. Nonvalerian Theories

Any libertarian theory needs to suggest some vehicle by which indeterminacy enters into human choices, given the initially plausible assumption that human decisions are the result of deterministic events in the same way that other macroscopic events are. Many libertarians posit a special metaphysical entity—e.g., a Cartesian nonphysical mind, a Chisholmian person, or a Kantian transempirical ego—that produces choices, but is not determined to produce those choices. Such maneuvers have seemed extravagant to some libertarians, who wish to suggest a way that indeterminism might enter into decision making without postulating either non-natural entities or entities with an obscure metaphysical status (Kane, 1985). For some, the most promising candidate has seemed to be a model in which indeterminacies at the quantum level are "amplified" to allow for indeterminacies to occur at the level of brain states. Dennett (1978, 287) mentions this view in quoting from David Wiggins (1973). Kane discusses at length Sir John Eccles's amplifier model of how micro-indeterminacies could be propagated to affect the brain (1985, Chapter 9). My "delay libertarian" view given later also presupposes such quantum amplification.

The issue of the psychological reality of such quantum models is, of course, a thorny problem for those who propose them and is worrisome enough to make philosophers think twice about accepting any view that is committed to them. Besides the question of whether such amplification occurs, there are other puzzling questions, notably why the amplified quantum effects coincide with libertarian choices. Moreover, the postulation of such indeterminacies makes any theory committed to them in principle disconfirmable to the extent that the indeterminacies cannot be discovered. But, despite that, such indeterminacies are empirically possible; and because I think that the more ontologically daring theories are at least logically possible, libertarianism has at least another vehicle for indeterminacies besides quantum amplification. So, for present purposes, I ignore these reservations about the empirical assumptions of libertarian theories, although I say something about that in the final chapter.

Among libertarian theories, it is useful to distinguish between those in which the indeterminacy is postulated to occur at the moment of choice, making that choice indeterminate relative to the totality of the agent's psychological and physiological history, and theories in which some element of indeterminacy occurs prior to the choice. Examples of the former include the theories of Chisholm, Taylor, van Inwagen, Campbell, and Kant. Examples of the latter include a view suggested by Dennett (1978, Chapter 15), Kane's subtle theory, and a view that I devised, which I call *delay libertarianism*. Extrapolating from some terminology used by Dennett and Mark Bernstein,[1] I call the former theories *Nonvalerian* and the latter *Valerian* libertarian theories. In this section, I shall consider how well the Nonvalerian theories satisfy the three libertarian conditions sketched in the last section. In subsequent sections, I pose the same question to the three different types of Valerian theories.

In evaluating the Nonvalerian theories, I am ignoring the specifics of how the indeterminacy is supposed to take hold, e.g., whether the theory is Cartesian, Chisholmian, or relies on quantum indeterminacy. My reason for this omission is that those specifics will not bear on my argument that Nonvalerian theories cannot show how the three libertarian requirements can be met. For instance, if my argument against the coherence of dual rationality is sound, it will count against the dual rationality of Cartesian souls, Chisholmian persons, or physicalistic persons who choose as a result of quantum indeterminacy. The ontology will not matter. Given this simplifying fact, I am free to select any Nonvalerian view as a focus of my discussion, and I shall use that of van Inwagen, since his view is admirably explicit.

It seems pretty clear that satisfying the categorical interpretation of the ability to choose otherwise is the strong point of the Nonvalerian theories. After all, that is what these theories were designed to accomplish, and unless one worries about the *quality* of the control and rationality of Nonvalerian choices, as I shall do presently, it looks as if Nonvalerian agents have exactly what free agents need in the way of categorical freedom. On these theories, an agent like van Inwagen's thief (cited in Chapter 1 earlier) could actually have chosen either way in the exact circumstances in which he found himself, without needing any of his psychological states to be different. This is a selling point for Nonvalerian theories that I shall argue Valerian theories cannot match. Still, this ability to choose otherwise might not be worth much if it is purchased at the expense of control or rationality. I shall discuss at length the problem that Nonvalerian theories have with the latter and briefly mention control at the end of this section.

I know of no better statement of the problem that Nonvalerian theories have with rationality (indeed, one-way, let alone dual rationality) than that provided by Kane:

> If the agent might either make a choice or do otherwise, given all the same past circumstances, and the past circumstances include the entire psychological history of the agent, it would seem that no explanation in terms of the agent's psychological history, including prior character, motives and deliberation, could account for the actual occurrence of one outcome *rather than* the other, i.e., for the choosing rather than doing otherwise, or vice versa. . . . [T]he outcome may be different . . . though the psychological history is the same. (1985, 53)

> . . . [W]hat I cannot understand is how I could have reasonably chosen to do otherwise, how I could have reasonably chosen B, *given exactly the same prior deliberation* that led me to choose A, the same information deployed, the same consequences considered, the same assessments made, and so on. (57)

Kane's point makes one wonder: why bother to deliberate if you are just as likely to opt for either of two contradictory alternatives? This point most forcefully counts against a Nonvalerian theory that embraces the so-called liberty of indifference by placing the likelihood of each alternative at .5. For instance, in van Inwagen's earlier cited case of the thief experiencing Nonvalerian freedom in his decision to steal, van Inwagen imagines the thief's total psychological state to include two conflicting pairs of beliefs and desires: (a) the desire to keep his promise to his mother not to steal, (b) the belief that the best way to keep his promise is to refrain from robbing the poor box, (c) the desire for money, and (d) the belief that the best way to get money is to rob the poor box. Van Inwagen suggests that if God were to "reset" the world to its identical state at the moment of the thief's decision thousands of times, then "on about half these occasions" (a) and (b) would produce the thief's decision to refrain whereas "on the other occasions" (c) and (d) would produce the decision to steal (van Inwagen, 1983, 140–141). Although the Nonvalerian theorist is not committed to claiming that this perfectly balanced liberty of indifference holds for all free choices, I show presently how the objection can be amended to apply to cases where the two alternatives are not equally likely.

Let me try to illustrate why a perfectly balanced liberty of indifference will mean that neither choice can be rational. Consider two cases. In both I am a student trying to learn the inference rules of sentence logic. My task is to identify the rule that was used to produce a certain line in a proof, a common exercise in elementary logic books. Alternatively, my task can be described as deciding which rule I think was used or deciding what answer to give. In Case 1, let us imagine a determinist scenario where each step in my deliberative process is the causal result of earlier steps. For simplicity, we may suppose that no logically irrelevant factors causally intrude into my deliberations, and that my deliberations proceed through consciously accessible states for which I produce an accurate protocol. For instance, my 'thinking out loud' might go: "Well, the previous line was a conditional. What rules of inference use conditionals? *Modus ponens* does, but that doesn't look right. How about *modus tollens*? . . ." Although I may or may not decide on the correct answer, each step is determinate.

In Case 2, I am faced with the same problem, but here I exercise Nonvalerian free will. My reasoning process has delimited my choice of an answer to either *modus ponens* or *modus tollens*, but my continued reflections do not uniquely determine which rule I shall select. That is, I can adduce reasons for selecting each, but my will is not determined in either direction by my deliberations. In an instant I select *modus ponens* owing to an indeterministic emission of a beta particle from an atom in my brain. Had the particle been emitted a nanosecond before or later I would have selected *modus tollens*. That is to say, in van Inwagen's words, "there are possible worlds in which things were absolutely identical . . . with the way they are in the actual world" up until the decision, and yet the decision was *modus tollens* (1983, 128).

The first question I wish to ask about these cases is: *In which case do I display more rationality in reaching the final answer?* In Case 1, my reasoning process is rational if the causal sequence of inferences is itself logically well-founded and otherwise not. The fact that my deliberations were related between themselves causally neither establishes nor counts against the rationality of the deliberations. This is not true of Case 2. Since, by hypothesis, my choice between the two inference rules was not caused by some logically salient reason, my choice cannot be reasonable. This obvious fact might tend to be obscured by the possibility that afterwards I might ardently defend the rationality of my decision by citing my reasons for selecting *modus ponens*. To all observers (including myself) my selection seems reasonable; after all, I did have my reasons. But, in response to this, we must note that the stipulation that my choice did not causally depend upon my reasoning process demonstrates that such post facto rationalization is worthless. In real-world cases, there is abundant evidence from social psychology that we should be extremely wary of individuals' attributions of the causes of the behavior of themselves and others. The moral is that the fact that the subject's choice in Case 2 *seemed* reasonable to the subject provides no evidence that it was.

The Nonvalerian might adopt a fallback position here, pointing out that the decision in Case 2 was *pretty* reasonable because it was *circumscribed by*, if not caused by, our reasoning. This reply is unacceptable because it takes a perspective that is too narrow. We may grant that if I have narrowed my choice to *modus ponens* or *modus tollens*, I have done something commendable—at least it is better than having no clue as to which inference rule to select. But if each of the subsidiary decisions that I made en route to limiting my final selection to one of these two had manifested Nonvalerian free will, then there is no reason to believe that I would have reached that penultimate position with any more probability than I would have reached any other mathematically possible position. That is, if at every step along the way my subordinate decision had been indeterministically free of the dictates of my reasoning process, then who knows where I would have ended up? My decision process would have been an exercise in anarchy. So, when one cites the partial reasonability of my final choice between *modus ponens* and *modus tollens*, the reasonability that brought us to the final choice was the rational determinism involved in the previous decisions. The final indeterministic choice merits no 'credit' for the rationality of the prior decisions: instead, with respect to rationality, the final choice is a 'freeloader' on the previous deterministic decisions that delimited the range of the final choice.

The second question is: *In which case, if either, do I deserve credit for getting right answers or criticism for wrong answers?* To answer this question, let us concern ourselves with what might be called *epistemic credit* and *epistemic criticism*. It seems that one deserves epistemic credit for getting the right answer only if one knows, or at least justifiably believes, the right answer, and it seems that any plausible account of these notions excludes one's arriving at the answer 'just by luck'. Regarding epistemic criticism, it seems that it is applicable only if appropriate epistemic criteria are not invoked, and if this failure was under the control of the agent. The second part of this necessary condition implies that one is not subject to epistemic criticism if failure to meet appropriate epistemic criteria was a matter of luck.

If these claims about the necessary conditions for epistemic credit and criticism are correct, then in Case 1 I am at least in principle subject to both credit and criticism. Determinism per se counts against neither possibility. But these conditions do count against the possibility of credit and criticism in Case 2. Now, it might be objected that if libertarianism is true then I am criticizable for making decisions under conditions of inappropriate evidence. A good epistemic agent in the Case 2 situation where one has equal reasons for *modus ponens* and *modus tollens* would suspend judgment rather than opt for either. But this point is confused. In Case 2 I did not decide to choose arbitrarily between the two equally attractive alternatives. Instead, my deliberations took me up to the point of equilibrium between *modus ponens* and *modus tollens* and then 'chance intervened'—the next thing I knew I had chosen the former. Thus, I should not be criticized for reaching the wrong answer.

The preceding discussion was directed against Nonvalerian theories that ascribe to free choices a perfect liberty of indifference, and my conclusion was that under such conditions *neither* choice will be rational. But Nonvalerians do not have to accept the doctrine of the liberty of indifference, however congenial that assumption seems to be to their view. Let us suppose that Nonvalerian agents can make choices with a likelihood other than .5 each way. For instance, let us suppose that the probabilities of the two alternatives are, say, .7 and .3 or .81 and .19. In this case, one might argue that the agent's reasoning contributed to the greater likelihood of the more probable choice and, thus, was not impotent in the way I have imagined in the logic example. Fine. The problem for the Nonvalerian is that the above argument still demonstrates that the alternative that was less than .5 probable would represent an irrational choice had it been actualized. But this means that the choice could not be dually rational, thus violating the libertarian's own condition. The compatibilist is happy with choices that are one-way rational, but the libertarian needs dual rationality.

Let me conclude this section by considering how well Nonvalerian theories do on the dual-control requirement. The familiar compatibilist arguments that free will requires determinism (e.g., Hobart, 1934; Ayer, 1954) seem to claim that both control and rationality require determinism. This is not surprising, since the notion of choosing rationally seems to entail control. That is, the sentence (i) "I rationally choose A" seems to mean (ii) "*I* pick A (have control over the selection of A)" and (iii) "*I* do so for good reasons." I think that the notion of control is also contained in the ability-to-choose-otherwise condition. Here, (iv) "I have the categorical freedom to choose otherwise" appears to entail (v) "*I* have control over which of two alternatives will be selected."

The problem with this intuitive notion of dual control is that if indeterminacy is allowed into the picture, then it looks as if we cannot have two-way control, because the alternative selection will not be strongly enough attached to the agent. *I* do not control that which is indeterminate, since indeterminate events are not under the control of anyone or anything.

Let me support this claim. Being in control of a choice seems to require the presence of the appropriate background psychological states that lead in the direction of that choice. Determinists and indeterminists agree that controlling our choice of A requires a congeries of beliefs, desires, values, character traits, and so on that point toward A. It is, thus, conceptually suspect for the Nonvalerian to maintain that if we were to 'freeze' all of these the way they actually are, give the agent another chance to make that choice, and have the agent choose not A, then the agent would *control* that choice. I doubt that such a hypothesized event would warrant the designation *control*. I am buoyed in this conviction by the fact that Kane, who tries to save the strongest variety of dual control that he thinks indeterminism allows (by making the indeterminate element the degree of effort that the agent musters), concedes that dual control can only be partial (1985, 95).

Moreover, despite the highly sophisticated attempts to defend the notion of agent causation by Chisholm (1964; 1976) and R. Taylor (1966), the most that I have gleaned to assuage my worries over dual control is the suggestion that agents have the power to initiate changes that theologians sometimes ascribe to God—the power to bring about events without themselves undergoing change (Chisholm, 1964, 32). This is scarcely comforting. The problem is not that it is inconceivable that there should be a type of metaphysical entity that we stipulate to be able to 'produce' in some way either A choices or not A choices at an instant of time; for all I know, this is how many people think that human choice operates. The problem is that even if such entities were to exist, it would be conceptually suspect to maintain that they had control over their choices.

3. Dennett's Valerian Theory

The type of indeterminacy that Dennett suggests 'giving' libertarians—in order to show that indeterminacy is no improvement over determinism—is one in which genuinely random thoughts occur to agents during otherwise determinate deliberations (1978, 286–299). Dennett imagines a philosophy job applicant deciding which of two job offers to accept by running through a list of six determined considerations. The occurrence of a seventh consideration, however, is undetermined; if it occurs, then she chooses one way and if it does not occur, she chooses otherwise. According to Dennett, if the undetermined consideration occurs, then the applicant decides as rationally as she would have decided had the extra consideration been merely unforeseen, though determined. This is because the agent's "intelligent selection, rejection, and weighing of the considerations that do occur . . . determines which microscopic indeterminacies get amplified . . . into important macroscopic determiners of ultimate behavior" (295).

Valerian theories like that suggested by Dennett go a long way toward answering the charge that the occurrence of indeterminacy within the deliberation process necessarily yields irrational decisions. Unlike van Inwagen's thief, whose psychological states seem to be impotent in arriving at the choice, once Dennett's agents get their randomly generated considerations, their decisions could be a determined function of their deliberations. To use Dennett's analogy, a deliberator could be like a computer performing mathematical operations on a randomly generated number. This would guarantee hegemony for the agent's deliberative process, even if the decision could not be *entirely* explained, because of the earlier indeterminacy.

The compatibilist could object that any indeterminacy in the deliberation process would make the resulting decisions irrational, but that objection would evince an unrealistically stringent demand. We must admit (on pain of infinite regress) that reasons sometimes 'pop' into our heads without being summoned, and it is hard to see why a truly indeterminant 'popping' would be more destructive to the rationality of the resulting decisions than would an unexpected deterministic occurrence of reasons. Dennett's view does enable our deliberations rationally to control our choices, which was the major objection to van Inwagen's view.

The problem with Dennett's Valerian theory, according to a libertarian, is that it is just determinism with a randomizer attached. Dennett's theory does not capture the spirit of the conditions of categorical ability to choose otherwise, dual control, or dual rationality, since it does not locate the indeterminacy where the libertarians want it, *viz.*, at the final choice. This means that although such Valerian decisions can be one-way rational, they cannot be dually rational. In the case Dennett gives, the job applicant decides rationally one way if the seventh consideration occurs to her, and decides rationally the other way if it does not. This yields a compatibilist-style one-way rationality, but does not satisfy the libertarian who demands a theory whereby we choose rationally *either* way given the exact state of affairs that obtain. The case is likewise, *mutatis mutandis*, for dual control.

Finally, Dennett's Valerian view provides an ability to choose otherwise that fails to meet the spirit of the libertarian requirement. To see this, compare Dennett's and standard compatibilist accounts. The latter hold that agents are free to decide otherwise, provided they would decide otherwise if they are so inclined. As we have already seen, the libertarians think that this hypothetical freedom is a sham. Now, Dennett's Valerian view holds that we do enjoy a categorical freedom to decide otherwise, since the appearance of some considerations on which we base our choices is literally indeterministic—that is, there are other physically possible worlds in which our decisions would have been different. But this sort of categorical freedom, no less than the hypothetical freedom provided by the compatibilist's account, is too weak to satisfy the libertarian. The libertarian thinks that, even if it is physically possible that other thoughts *could* have popped into, e.g., a murderer's head, the murderer is not morally responsible provided the murder was a determined product of the thoughts that occurred. For the libertarian, it looks as if here, too, the agent becomes a victim to 'fate', understood now in an indeterministic sense. If the considerations that I use in deliberating may or may not occur, and my decision is determined by them, then I am just as much 'victimized' by them as I am if determinism is true. Libertarians want the freedom to decide either way, given the conditions that in fact obtain. So, although Dennett's view does an admirable job at producing one-way rationality—an unsurprising fact given that Dennett is a compatibilist—it fails to provide dual rationality, and it fails to produce the sort of indeterminacy that libertarians want.

4. Kane's Theory

In this section, I consider how the sophisticated multiply-Valerian view of Robert Kane fares on my construal of the conditions of dual rationality, dual control, and the categorical ability to choose otherwise.[2] Kane's theory includes the sort of indeterminacy that Dennett hypothesizes but also places indeterminacy at a second level that produces a much more interesting picture. Kane applies his theory to three distinct types of choices. In practical choice (where I am solely concerned with satisfying my present desires), I may delimit my receptivity to reasons for and against a choice deterministically, and yet I may remain open to the nondeterministic influence of thoughts that, when interpreted, provide reasons for one of the alternatives. For instance, suppose I have decided to live in either A-land or B-land, but the recollection that B-land has pleasant beaches just occurs to me, tipping the scales in favor of the latter (1985, 104). Although indeterministic, my choice was rational because I had already decided not to count factors in favor of C-land, and the recollection would have had no effect on my decision unless I liked pleasant beaches. Indeterminacy enters the picture, for Kane, not only regarding whether chance thoughts, recollections, and so forth occur to the agent during deliberation, but also in the amount of effort the agent makes to continue deliberating and, thus, remain open to such considerations. So, the indeterminism involves both cognitive *and* volitional states. In prudential choices, the second type of indeterminacy takes the form of the degree of importance that I assign to my future states (i.e., whether I regard my future well-being on a par with my present satisfaction) (159). In moral choices, the additional indeterminacy lies in the degree of effort that I make to take the moral point of view in serious cases where inclination and duty collide (149).

Kane believes that if agents satisfy his libertarian sketch, they will gain "ultimate dominion" over their choices by satisfying what he calls the *Condition of Ultimate Dominion* (CUD):

> An agent's power (or control) over a choice at a time t satisfies the condition of sole or ultimate dominion if and only if (i) the agent's making the choice rather than doing otherwise (or vice versa, i.e.,

doing otherwise rather than making the choice) can be explained by saying that the agent rationally willed at t to do so, and (ii) no further explanation can be given for the agent's choosing rather than doing otherwise (or vice versa), or of the agent's rationally willing at t to do so, that is an explanation in terms of conditions whose existence cannot be explained by the agent's choosing or rationally willing something at t. (1985, 46)

To focus on the case of moral choice, for Kane, condition (i) will be satisfied because the selection of either alternative can be explained by citing the agent's reasons for the decision. Condition (ii) will be satisfied since the indeterministic occurrence of factors in the agent's deliberations (the occurrence of relevant ideas and/or the degree of effort made to take the moral point of view) will preclude the possibility of a deterministic explanation of the agent's choice.

If we take Kane to mean true explanations, then his view will allow (ii) to be satisfied, because any libertarian theory will succeed on that score. I wish to object, however, that Kane's view will not permit (i) to be satisfied. We should note that the first condition of CUD that the agent's choice "can be explained by saying the agent rationally willed at t to do so" should be interpreted as "can be explained *truly*" or "can be *adequately* explained." If the first condition does not mean this, then CUD could be satisfied by persons whose indeterministic choices are entirely unconstrained by reasons, provided that there is some confabulated explanation of that person's choice in terms of rational willing. Thus, CUD would entail that everyone whose choices satisfy condition (ii) exercises ultimate control, since we can always make up rational explanations for any choice via post facto attributions of beliefs and desires.

So, I think that CUD must be understood to require true or adequate explanations. The question of what constitutes an adequate explanation is, of course, one of the foremost topics in the philosophy of science, the disputants being advocates of the deductive-nomological model and those who believe that not all adequate explanations must make the *explanandum* a logical consequence of the *explanans*. There is a minimal principle, however, that I believe is so weak that both sides to the debate would accept it. I call it "The Principle of Rational Explanation (PRE)":

Citing a person's deliberative process *P* rationally explains a choice *C* only if the probability of *C* given *P* is greater than the probability of not *C* given *P.*

For example, if citing Smith's deliberative process concerning smoking is to truly explain Smith's decision to smoke a cigarette, then a very minimal condition needs to be met, *viz.,* that the deliberative process make it more likely that Smith decide to smoke than decide not to.

PRE is not committed to any particular view of the logical form that rational explanations must take, nor to the type of *explanans* (causal, teleological, functional laws) permitted. PRE does not even claim that a good rational explanation must make the *explanandum* highly probable, but only more likely than its negation. To see how innocuous PRE is, imagine what one would have to say to reject it. Let 'P' designate the entire deliberative process of a subject prior to a particular choice C. Suppose that the occurrence of P makes C no more likely than not C. PRE is false only if P explains C. But under the stipulated condition, it is difficult to see how P *explains* C; instead it seems that the occurrence of P was irrelevant to explaining why the choice was C rather than not C. The temptation to believe that P is explanatory owes, I think, to the fact that in a 'normal', that is, non-libertarian, scenario we *would* count P as a viable candidate for being an adequate explanation. But we should be careful not to let our commonsense acceptance of rational explanation, which I think is at least broadly deterministic, spill over into a case where, ex hypothesi, the *explanans* is debarred from making the *explanandum* more likely than not.

PRE counts against the satisfaction of CUD in this way. In a case in which an agent satisfies Kane's account, the totality of the agent's deliberative process—including the amount of effort that the agent expends to remain open to new alternatives, to view the future on a par with the present, or to take the moral point of view—can at most make only one of two alternatives more than .5 probable. (If there were a perfect liberty of indifference, as with van Inwagen's thief, neither alternative is more than .5 probable.) But, then, citing the totality of the agent's psychological processes would allow us to explain at most one alternative, not the two alternatives that CUD requires be explained. So, although on PRE one alternative could be rationally explained, a *dual* satisfaction of Kane's requirement would be foreclosed.

This argument may be explicitly set out this way:

> a. An agent's deliberative process cannot make two complementary choices more than .5 probable.
> b. If PRE is true, then citing an agent's deliberative process cannot explain a choice unless that choice is made more than .5 probable by that process.
> c. PRE is true.
> d. Therefore, citing an agent's deliberative process cannot explain each of two complementary choices.

In a published reply to an article of mine (Double, 1988a), Kane (1988) concedes that PRE would cause embarrassment to the dual rationality of libertarian choices, but argues that the cases that exemplify his conception of freedom show that my principle is unacceptable. This is because, e.g., in the case of a moral dilemma, both the choice that yields to temptation and the choice that rises to duty could have resulted from the identical prior state of the agent's character and motives, even if the probabilities of those two occurrences were, e.g., .7 and .3. PRE is false because, given the indeterminate nature of the degree of effort that the agent musters, an alternative that is less probable than its complement might have resulted from the same character and motives:

> [S]uch choices *whichever way they go* can satisfy the conditions of dual rationality. . . . But this means that *PRE can fail for these cases* whenever the choice is made that is less probable (but still possible) given the agent's prior character and motives—because the prior character and motives embodied an inner conflict that could have been resolved either way (even if the chances of its being resolved either way were not equal). (1988, 456)

As I understand this proposal, Kane imagines a person engaged in a difficult choice (e.g., a case involving moral temptation) in which that person's character, motives, and conflicting welter of cognitive attitudes do not uniquely determine the strength of effort that will be made to resist temptation. In such a case, either choice is rational, even though the choice made may be less than .5 likely, since it may be less than .5 likely that the person's will power is strong enough to produce the choice it does. Hence, for Kane, citing the character, motives, and cognitive states of such agents explains or rationalizes whichever choice is made, thus guaranteeing dual rationality.

Kane argues that this picture saves the dual rationality of libertarian choices by claiming that it shows how the following Conditions of Dual Rationality (DR) can be satisfied:

> (DR) The choice of A by an agent is *dual rational,* if and only if, *whichever way it goes* (i.e., whether the agent chooses A or chooses otherwise), the outcome is (a) the intentional termination of an effort of will that is the agent's effort of will, (b) the agent has reasons for the choice (whichever occurs), (c) the agent does it *for* those reasons, and (d) given the agent's character and motives, it is, all things considered, rational for the agent to do it at that time for those reasons. (1988, 446)

I think that this very elegant move by Kane diminishes the problem of dual rationality for Kanian agents. Kane shows that if the indeterminacy is gingerly located in the deliberative process by way of the effort that the agent musters in making the choice, libertarian choices need not be wildly capricious as compatibilists have often charged. Nonetheless, I doubt that Kane's move ultimately saves dual rationality. My objection can be expressed as a dilemma for Kane's paradigm of free moral choice where the choice an agent makes depends on the indeterminate strength of the agent's effort to select the moral option over the self-serving one. Consider, first, the alternative of not counting the degree of effort the agent manages as a part of the deliberative process. If we do not count the degree of effort, then it will be a mystery as to why the agent makes either choice, since, *ex hypothesi,* it is the effort that makes the difference between which outcome is selected. As Kane points out (1988, 451), in Kanian free choices, character and motive do not explain why choices are made; hence, if we do not count the agent's effort as part of the deliberative process, then citing the rest of the deliberative process cannot satisfy the antecedent of PRE. Thus, no counterexample to PRE is produced if we discount the degree of effort expended.

So, consider the second alternative of counting the degree of effort expended as a part of the deliberative process. It will not suffice simply to point out that whatever effort is made will decide the choice. In order to explain why the actual choice that was made is selected, we need to specify how strong the will actually is at the instant of choice if we are to have an explanation of why *that* alternative, rather than its complement, was chosen. But once we specify the strength of will that is actually operative, then only the option that that strength of will selects will be explained. It will be clear that, relative to all the psychological factors *plus* the actual strength of will exerted, the complementary choice will be inexplicable. So, dual rationality is lost if we count the amount of effort expended as part of the overall deliberative process that leads to choices.

Let me clarify my point with an illustration. To take a case of a Kanian prudential choice, suppose that I am struggling against my addiction to smoking cigarettes. I have reasons for smoking (my desire for nicotine), and reasons for resisting (concern for my health); my choice whether to smoke a particular cigarette will be made on the basis of whether my indeterministic will power is strong enough to allow me to choose in accordance with my long-term prudential reasons. Suppose that I do resist in this instance, and we explain my decision by citing my health-minded reasons. That this cannot be a satisfactory rational explanation of my choice is demonstrated by the addition of two counterbalancing details to the story. First, I am a notoriously weak-willed individual, who almost never musters enough will power to resist strong temptations. (We may suppose that I do so only one of every ten times.) But, second, in this instance I do manage to resist temptation in one of those unlikely 10 percent of the cases, because of the strengthening of my will power ultimately as a result of quantum indeterminacy. It seems clear to me that the initial explanation that cited my reasons without referring to the actual degree of effort expended to select the prudential choice is incomplete and inadequate. Given the rest of the story we see that the most important part of the explanation has been omitted. Hence, even a weakly adequate, PRE explanation of my smoking needs to include the exact degree of will power that I managed. But once we cite this, then only the actual choice that my degree of will power produced is explained, and it is not true that citing the same psychological facts explains both the actual choice and its unchosen complement.

In terms of Kane's Conditions of Dual Rationality, my objection is that Kanian free agents do not satisfy condition (c), the requirement that agents make whichever choice they do *for* the reasons favoring the choice that actually is made. It is true that, depending on the degree of effort that agents muster, we can say that they chose 'for' the prudential or weak-willed reasons. For Kane, the strength of will decides which set of reasons will be operative and, in this sense, either outcome can be rationalized. So, Kanian free agents are not capricious, arbitrary, or irrational. And maybe showing that is as much rationality as Kane feels his theory needs to impute to free agents. Certainly, Kane's picture helps us to understand a great deal about Kanian free agents:

> [P]rior character and motives provide (i) the reasons and dispositions that account for the agent's trying to resist moral or prudential temptation, but they also provide (ii) the self-interested reasons, inclinations and character traits that explain why it is *difficult* for the agent to resist temptation in the situation. In other words, the complex of past motives and character explains the inner *conflict* from *both* sides. It explains why the agent makes the effort *and* also why it is an *effort*. (Kane, 1988, 449–450)

But despite the insight provided by Kane's sketch, I do not think that two logically contradictory choices can be explained even weakly by citing the degree of effort of the will that 'sided' with the reasons that support one of the choices. Suppose that given my character (c) and motives (m), my indeterminate exercise of will power, wp1, produces self-serving alternative A, and had I managed a stronger exercise of will power, wp2, I would have chosen altruistic alternative not A. Also suppose that relative to a specification of c, m, and wp1, we have a rational (not necessarily deterministic) explanation of choice A. That is, given my character, motives, and momentary weakness of will, A is understandable without being determined. Now, surely citing c, m, and wp1 would not produce a rational explanation of not A had that alternative been selected. Why would my weakness manifested in wp1 result in not A? Thus, to explain not A, a different set of *explanans* is needed, namely, one that includes wp2. So, one cannot cite my actual psychological condition (c, m, and wp1) to explain the two contradictory outcomes. Instead, the situation is this: given that a strong degree of will power is exerted, not A is explainable and, given a weaker degree, A is explainable. But citing just one degree of will power cannot do double duty. And we have already seen that citing the degree of will power exercised is necessary, since Kane agrees that character and motive alone fail to explain Kanian free choices.

Let me turn to the question of whether Kanian free agents satisfy my construal of dual control. It seems at first blush that Kanian free agents are unlikely candidates for dual control, given that they do not even enjoy one-way control. The reason for the latter claim is that one cannot have control over that which is indeterminate. Consider once again Kanian agents in moral dilemmas who will choose altruistically only if their indeterminate degrees of effort manage to be strong enough to resist the egoistic temptations. Although Kane is correct to point out that whatever efforts the agents muster will be *their* efforts, the fact remains that which degree of effort is made is not under their control. This is a trivial consequence of the hypothesis that the amount of moral effort that such agents manage is indeterminate.

Let me illustrate this claim by again using the scenario where I am a smoker trying to resist this particular cigarette and, depending on the amount of will power I manage, I shall or shall not smoke. Now, suppose that a purely deterministic state of affairs (e.g., the condition of part of my cortex at an instant) dictates the strength of my will when I make my decision. *No one* would judge that I have two-way control, and most incompatibilists would deny that I had even one-way control. But, now, it is hard to see why my control is increased once we hypothesize that the actual strength of my will at that moment is indeterminate relative to the rest of my life's history rather than being determined by my cortex. In terms of control, it is difficult to see what I have gained by Kane's supposition that my will power is indeterminate that I failed to have if the determinist's hypothesis is true. If this is correct, then Kanian agents do not fully satisfy the dual-control requirement.

In fairness to Kane, I hasten to point out that he admits that placing indeterminacy into agents' choices guarantees that agents will have only partial control over their choices (1985, 95). Kane suggests that the desire for complete control is a bad idea, a Western obsession that Taoism and Buddhism teach us to rise above (114). One might object that there is a familiar incompatibilist intuition that holds that without complete control an agent cannot be fully morally responsible for choices, but Kane answers appropriately: agents exercising Kane-style freedom fail to be totally responsible, precisely because of the role of the indeterminate effort they make (154). Elsewhere Kane suggests that, although our control is limited, it is still good enough to salvage what is worth saving in the prephilosophical model. Kane points that the 'ownership' of the will cuts some ice:

> [T]his effort of will, though it is indeterminate, is the *agent's* effort of will. It is not somebody else's will, nor is it an alien force. It is the agent's own doing and the agent feels it as such phenomenologically. (1988, 454)

Although I agree that the effort of will is the agent's, I do not think that the agent's ownership satisfies the demand that the typical libertarian theories make on the relation between agents and their wills. That notion demands imperialistic control, not mere ownership. Of course, Kane is quite explicit that his theory is not designed to give libertarians everything they hope for, and for him this is not a criticism but rather a strength of his theory.

Let me finally consider how successful Kane's view is at satisfying the libertarian requirement of a categorical ability to choose otherwise. As was the case with Dennett's view, I doubt that Kane's theory fully satisfies the spirit of the categorical requirement, although, unlike compatibilism, it does make the ability to choose otherwise a physical possibility. For Dennett, agents could have chosen otherwise had other indeterminate thoughts occurred during deliberations. For Kane, the same sort of indeterminacy is present, plus the indeterminacy at the level of effort. But this additional sort of indeterminacy makes the indeterminacy of the choice conditional in a way that yields only a weak sense of the ability to do otherwise. Kane's agents could have decided otherwise, *had the indeterministic micro-events that resulted in the occurrence of certain thoughts or the level of effort expended been different.*

But such freedom is not good enough for the sort of incompatibilist whom I have tried to sketch in this chapter. As remarked in discussing Dennett's view in the previous section, the incompatibilist does not see what good it is to know that quantum indeterminacy *could have* changed the murderer's effort to resist temptation, if, in fact, the murderer's effort of will was not strong enough to resist. Kane's variety of the ability to do otherwise seems as unlikely to satisfy what the hard-minded libertarian wants as is the compatibilist's account or Dennett's Valerian view.

5. Delay Libertarianism

I now want to sketch another Valerian theory that relies on the possibility of quantum indeterminacies, which I call *delay libertarianism*. This theory makes the possibility of time gaps a common feature of our decision making, and, to the extent that is empirically warranted, an ubiquitous feature of the rest of our cognitive and biological lives. On this view, for most decisions it is indeterminate whether the decision will follow the deliberation immediately or whether it will be delayed a small fraction of a second. (I leave this imprecise, because the length of the delays needs to be specified empirically.) Sometimes delays may occur in sequence, producing longer delays between the deliberations and the resultant decisions.

Delay libertarianism locates indeterminacy at the point where our deliberations are followed by our decisions. (To make this more psychologically realistic, we could suppose that not all deliberative processes are conscious, but that supposition is tangential to understanding the delay concept. The important thing is that delay theorists want to focus on the point at which the determinists *believe* that deliberations cause decisions.) The delay theory holds that, in the case of free choices, the deliberations "set the stage" for the ensuing decision in the sense that the former establish which decision will be made *if any decision is made*. The deliberations do not, however, make the decision physically necessary, since the decision is indeterminate, and may either occur or not occur. If the indeterminate decision occurs, then it immediately follows the deliberation and *appears* exactly as it would if it were caused by the deliberation. If the indeterminate decision does not occur, there is a delay. In this case, there are two possibilities. First, since most of the psychological factors that went into the deliberation that led up to the initial indeterminate decision remain intact, the stage remains set for the same decision to be made. (Metaphorically, the deliberative state of the agent has another chance to push the decision across the threshold.) If, on the next try, the decision fails to occur (thereby producing an iterated delay), the same process may be repeated, and so on. The second possibility is that during any of the delays brought about by the failure of the indeterminate decision to occur, agents may think of some other considerations that prompt them to extend their original deliberations, possibly leading them to different decisions than they would have made had no delays occurred. Thus, at no single instant are the two alternatives, e.g., decide A and decide not A, physically possible; yet in free decisions the alternatives of deciding A and not deciding A (that is, having one's decision delayed) are physically possible.

There are some reasons why a libertarian might prefer delay libertarianism to the theories considered above. First, it has always been difficult for libertarians who try to avail themselves of quantum indeterminacy to explain why the sub-atomic indeterminacies occur *just when* we manifest libertarian freedom. It cannot be, for instance, that when we prepare to make a decision, the sub-atomic particles 'know' that they should 'go on a spree'. So, is it not miraculous that the sub-atomic and macro-levels correspond in any significant way? Delay libertarianism answers this objection. Because the possibility of delays is a common feature of our mental lives, there is no problem in seeing how they correspond to free decisions. They are always, or almost always, there.

A second, related, advantage of delay libertarianism is that it allows free will to be as frequent a phenomenon as common sense believes it is. (The libertarian should not claim that delays are sufficient for free will, since unfree agents will also experience delays.) It has always seemed to me that theories like those of Campbell, Kane, and Kant, which make free will realized only under the greatest of efforts, were not really accounts of "free will," but of a much narrower concept. Delay libertarianism does not deny that the moral phenomenology that these theories describe occurs, but it explicates free will at a broader, more mundane level that cleaves more closely to the prephilosophical notion of freedom.

Delay libertarianism makes free will more "egalitarian," since you do not need Taoist/Buddhist receptivity (Kane) or an especially keen sense of duty (Kant, Kane, Campbell) to enjoy it.

Third, more so than the other views examined, delay libertarianism satisfies the intuitive demands of rationality. It clearly does this better than Nonvalerian theories. It is even slightly better on this score than Dennett's or Kane's theories, because delay libertarianism's indeterminacy does not apply to the considerations generated or to the degree of effort expended. The delays simply give agents more time to deliberate. Thus, agents who are especially subject to delays are not, ipso facto, as whimsical or flighty as agents who are particularly prone to the occurrence of new considerations in their deliberations or to having their will power fluctuate. Such agents would simply be *slower*. One might say that the indeterminate possibility of delays constitutes the difference between rational decision making (if the delays fail to occur), and even *more* rational, one-last-chance-to-reconsider decision making (if they occur).

All this notwithstanding, the hard question is whether delay libertarianism enables us to satisfy the libertarian requirements any better than the previous theories did. Ultimately, I think that delay libertarianism fails. Although it is better at providing one-way rationality than van Inwagen's, Dennett's, or Kane's view, it fails just as clearly at dual rationality. It shows how one choice could be rational provided the delays occur and another could be rational if the delays do not occur, but it does not show how we could rationally select either choice given the actual occurrence or non-occurrence of the delays. The delay theory also fails to produce a sort of indeterminacy that libertarians want. An agent's ability to choose otherwise is, on this theory, dependent on whether the delays occur. But this condition creates the same type of situation that libertarians find objectionable in Dennett's and Kane's view. Indeterminacy needs to be located at the instant of the choice—keeping all previous factors the same—if it is to satisfy the libertarian notion of genuine categorical freedom. Thus, it seems that only a Nonvalerian view such as van Inwagen's can satisfy the desire that motivates the could-have-chosen-otherwise condition. The story is similar for the dual-control requirement. Delay libertarianism satisfies one-way control much the same way that Dennett's theory does. The 'randomizer' that the delay theory adds to the deterministic one-way control is simply the possibility of time gaps that enable agents to deliberate longer, but such delays do not give agents control over both possible outcomes. A chance to change one's mind that is contingent upon delays does not provide control over the alternative choices that are *not* made if the delays fail to occur.

6. Libertarianism's Problems with Rationality

In the debate over who has the better account of the notion of freedom, libertarians have tended to emphasize the could-have-chosen-otherwise condition, whereas compatibilists have stressed the rationality requirement. This is not surprising. The former are motivated by our abhorrence of the idea of determinism, with its threat to our dignity, moral responsibility, and its susceptibility to the power of Kanian covert nonconstraining controllers (including God). The compatibilists, on the other hand, are 'soft on' our ability to choose otherwise and try to assuage our worries on that issue by suggesting that, since determinism does not count against rationality, if our choices are rational enough, then maybe we should not *mind* being without categorical freedom. Now, if libertarianism does as badly on rationality (and control) as I have argued it does, and if freedom requires both the categorical ability to choose otherwise and rationality, then the concept of freedom at best becomes fragmented into libertarian and compatibilist varieties, neither being wholly acceptable. That is the thesis of this chapter so far.

Not only does the libertarian's categorical freedom to choose otherwise not touch the issue of rationality, it does not even free us from the freedom-defeating power of a covert non-constraining controller. Suppose we attempt to treat the satisfaction of Kane's Dual Rationality condition cited earlier in this chapter as sufficient for libertarian free will. (I am not sure that Kane does this, but it is certainly a line that would appeal to many libertarians.) DR is satisfied if both choices would result from an agent's intentional effort of will, if the agent selects the alternative *for* reasons and if the choice is rational for the agent "given the agent's character and motives."

Of course, there is nothing built into DR that *stipulates* away the power of would-be controllers; rather their power is to be emasculated by the indeterminacy in Kane's account. Let us imagine, then, that a would-be controller tries to destroy my Kane-style free will. To make this a case of practical choice, suppose that the controller places in me each day a different pair of conflicting desires, e.g., to try to look as much as I can like two celebrities. So, on Monday my desires are to try to make myself look as much like Johnny Carson and as much like Raisa Gorbachev as possible. On Tuesday my conflicting desires are to look like Dan Quayle and Margaret Thatcher, and so on. My choice between these two alternatives may be imagined to follow Kane's recipe—my receptiveness to reasons supporting each is ultimately indeterminate, and even indeterminate thoughts regarding each pop into my head (e.g., I recall that my father used to look like Johnny Carson).

It seems pretty clear that I might satisfy DR, especially when we recall that condition (d) of DR requires only that the choices I make are rational given my character and motives. If my character is such that I think that trying to look like celebrities is a good idea, and each day I find myself with a new pair of motives, I do not see any way to deny that the last condition of DR is satisfied. Nonetheless, it seems that in this scenario I am clearly unfree. My choices, even though they enjoy libertarian freedom, are ultimately due to the manipulation of the controller. The fact that indeterminacy would prevent the controller from being able to dictate the exact choice that I make is of little moment, given that either choice is unfree.

This illustrates, I think, that indeterminacy, even if it is necessary for free will, far from being sufficient, does not even *address* the rationality problem. Throughout this book I argued that the only way to make one's compatibilist account alive to the rationality issue is to build normative requirements explicitly into the account. The moral here is likewise: if libertarianism is to be a complete account of free will, the libertarian account must explicitly address the rationality issue.

Now, I see no reason in principle why libertarians cannot help themselves to the compatibilists' normative conditions such as those given in my autonomy variable account, not as sufficient conditions, but as necessary conditions added to their own preferred conditions. By doing so, libertarians could try to obviate objections (like that just offered) based on rationality, although I am convinced by the arguments given earlier in this chapter that libertarians cannot produce an account that provides for dual rationality. But, within the larger dialectic of this book, this strategy appears unpromising for the defenders of the reality of free will. In the previous chapters I argued that adopting compatibilism is an implausible way to save free will and turned to libertarianism as a last-ditch effort to save the day. On inspection, though, libertarianism not only seems predicated on three incompatible theses, but requires the resources of compatibilism to enable it to cope with the rationality objections. But compatibilism has no resources to manage this. So, the attempt to save realism by an eclectic use of compatibilistic and libertarian theory seems unlikely to succeed.

7. Conclusion

In this chapter, I give the dual interpretations of three conditions—the could-have-chosen-otherwise, control, and rationality conditions—that I believe make up the core of libertarianism and pre-philosophical common sense's views of free will. I then tried to see whether various libertarian theories could show how these conditions could be met. It turned out that Nonvalerian theories like those of van Inwagen were the purest libertarian theories, satisfying the first condition admirably. Unhappily, Nonvalerian theories proved unable to show how dual control or dual rationality could be satisfied. The three Valerian theories that were examined turned out to make all the libertarian conditions unsatisfiable, although they seemed capable of satisfying compatibilist one-way demands on freedom. Thus, the libertarian would seem to face a dilemma: opt for an ideologically pure Nonvalerian theory, which fails on dual control and dual rationality, or select an impure Valerian theory that yields one-way rationality, control, and a weakened sense of ability-to-choose-otherwise. If libertarians take the Nonvalerian option, they have bought into all of the problems that make libertarianism problematic to students in Philosophy 101. But if they opt for the latter, then why not be a compatibilist, since indeterminacy does not do anything for agents that determinism cannot? In addition, the libertarian's emphasis on indeterminacy obscures the fact that rationality is an insoluble problem, for the incompatibilist as well as the compatibilist. To the extent that libertarianism was the last great hope for free will, that hope is dashed.

9

Conclusion

ABSTRACT In this book, I have tried to show that there can be no such thing as free will and, hence, that both compatibilists and incompatibilists are mistaken. The incompatibilist argues that in a deep sense being free is incompatible with determinism, and, hence, if anyone is free in this sense, then determinism is false. The compatibilist argues that people can be deeply free within a deterministic universe, despite the fact that their ability to choose otherwise is only hypothetical. My view is that although both of these positions derive considerable strength from the way that we think about freedom, they are both wrong because there is no deep sense of "free will" to be explicated. Although one can conceive of many varieties of freedom, there can be no single, deep sort of free will to be found. The argument is the same regarding moral responsibility. There is no more profound sense of "moral responsibility" than 'caused-by-your-character-responsibility,' which, although different from mere causal responsibility, does not closely resemble what philosophers mean by "moral responsibility."

In Chapters 2 through 4, I tried to augment some familiar compatibilist accounts in order to construct the best account that I could. In Chapters 5 through 7, I developed two lines aimed at refuting all views of free will, including that of Part I. In the last chapter, I attempted to undermine the specifics of the libertarian view of freedom, thereby providing a third reason to reject libertarianism in addition to the two general criticisms of free will already given.

In this chapter, I want to summarize the results of my investigation by listing six conditions that I think that any acceptable account of free will should meet; I then argue that no account meets them. This strategy directly supports the conclusion of the book that although there are many senses of "freedom" that one might articulate, there is no deep sense of "freedom." This leaves the enormous practical problem of how we might view each other if there is no free will and no moral responsibility. I address that problem by arguing that what we have left after giving up free will and

moral responsibility is enough to sustain what is legitimate in commonsense views of human freedom.

1. Six Conditions for an Account of Free Will

Any attempt to explicate a philosophically interesting concept must
meet general conditions of adequacy, as well as criteria that are
specific to the subject in question. In this section I propose three
general and three content-specific criteria for *free will*.

(1) *The conceptual clarity condition*

Any attempt to explicate a concept—whether that explication is done
by means of the traditional reductive analysis that aims for a group of
simpler logically necessary conditions that are jointly sufficient for
the application of the term, or a looser list of characteristic features,
or even an exemplar or paradigm—needs to be understandable. We
must be able, in principle, to tell whether an imagined case would fall
under the extension of the explication, without having to first ascertain whether it falls within the extension of the analyzed concept. The
explication should utilize familiar, understandable concepts or, if it
uses new ones, it should explain them by relating them to previously
understood concepts. There should be no doubt about the logical
coherence of the explication.

(2) *The empirical plausibility condition*

Beyond being conceptually acceptable, a philosophical theory
should, if satisfied, fit harmoniously into the rest of what we *think*
that we know about the world. Thus, given the rest of our world
view, we should ask how reasonable it is that any particular philosophical account of the denotation of a term might be satisfied
when compared to the satisfaction of competing accounts. Does the
account need a one-in-a-million shot to be satisfied? To take a
simple example, if one held that dreams are real events occurring to
people while traveling in 'astral-bodies' (Halverson, 1981, 104), the
empirical implausibility of that account would seriously count
against it.

(3) *The extension condition*

If the explication is one of analysis, then the *analysans* must match the *analysandum* in extension, with only a little room for slippage. The greater the slippage, the more likely it is that we are revising the concept. This is especially important when principled counterexamples are possible that point to radical differences between *analysans* and *analysandum*. The same principle holds for explications that purport to be rough characterizations or to offer exemplars.

Although these three general conditions are fairly bland, naming specific conditions for the explication of "free will" is quite controversial. The controversy is due to the fact that there are conflicting exemplars that we associate with "freedom," "free will," and "moral responsibility," and our selection of conditions will be influenced by the paradigms that affect us the most. When compatibilists and incompatibilists disagree on the content-specific conditions of adequacy, there will be no higher court of appeal to settle the disagreement—certainly not common sense, nor philosophers' "reflective equilibrium," since these are themselves pulled in various directions by the competing paradigms. This inability even to agree on the playing rules of the game portends unfavorably for the prospect of any side providing a generally acceptable account.

As argued throughout the book, I think that "free will," as a philosopher's term of art, has at least three necessary elements.

(4) *The ability-to-choose-otherwise condition*

That compatibilists and incompatibilists are committed to the view that any acceptable sense of "free will" must entail that free persons could have chosen otherwise is shown by the extensive twentieth-century debate over whose account of this notion captures 'the' prephilosophical notion (Moore, 1911; Austin, 1961; Chisholm, 1976; Aune, 1967; Lehrer, 1968). Even those compatibilists who, with admirable candor, announce that they do not *need* to argue that determinism is consistent with the ability to do otherwise (Dennett, 1984,b), agree that in a determined universe one can do otherwise, *if* what you mean is "would have done otherwise, if you had wanted."

If the main theme of this book is correct, then the attempt by both sides to give a single correct analysis of the notion of choosing otherwise is fruitless, since there is no single *analysandum* to be captured. Doubtless, we could get most people who reflect on freedom to admit that free agents, in a general sense, could have conducted themselves differently than they did. But if you pin the question down to that it addresses the compatibilists' and the incompatibilists' debate over whether it is necessary that one be able to choose differently than one does under the identical conditions that obtain in every aspect of one's psychological history, then I doubt that there would be any consensus forthcoming. Hence, philosophers, lacking any bedrock prephilosophical intuition to appeal to, provide answers to this question that are theory-laden, if not by their compatibilist and incompatibilist biases, then by appeal to things like the free will exemplars of Chapter 5. My conclusion is that although any account of free will must hold that free persons 'could have chosen otherwise', that notion may be understood either categorically, as the incompatibilists do, or hypothetically, as most compatibilists do, and that there is no way to adjudicate the dispute about who is right.

(5) *The control condition*

The same sort of disagreement that arose over the ability-to-choose-otherwise condition also breaks out over control. Compatibilists think that agents manifest one-way control over their choices when the determined micro-events that cause their choices are identical at a macro-level with commonsense psychological states that satisfy the specifics of their free will accounts. The doctrine of one-way control maintains that we could control alternative choices only if we had undergone different psychological states; libertarians think that control must be dual. Again, there is no way to adjudicate the dispute over whether one-way or dual control matches *the* prephilosophical view, because there is no such view.

(6) *The rationality condition*

We have already seen that both sides think that freedom requires a certain degree of sensibleness in one's choices, and I have argued that any specification of that degree is bound to produce counterexamples that show it to be too stringent or too liberal. So, the rationality condition is also a problem for the attempt to find a central locus of free will. Moreover, the same sort of dispute that broke out over the previous two conditions is bound to break out between the compatibilists and incompatibilists over one-way vs. dual rationality (see Chapter 8).

2. Rating the Free Will Theories

Libertarian theories generally do pretty badly on the three general conditions. Those that rely on Cartesian or Kantian egos or Chisholmian persons run afoul of the conceptual clarity condition, risking what Kane characterizes as "the emptiness of postulating obscure or mysterious forms of agency or causation" (1985, 74). Such theories also have great difficulties with empirical plausibility. Libertarian theories like those of Kane and the others examined in Chapter 8 that rely instead on the possibility of the amplification of quantum indeterminacies are less subject to the conceptual objection but face weakened empirical plausibility. The question of why quantum indeterminacies should occur just when we manifest libertarian free will strikes me as unanswerable. Different libertarian theories have their own particular difficulties with the extension condition. Theories that hold that free will is co-extensive with the class of libertarian choices without narrowing the range of the latter by adding rationality requirements seem to make the class of free choices too broad, by allowing deeply irrational choices to count as free. Theorists who build into their accounts the proviso that free choices are those made from moral duty, like Kant and Campbell, reduce the range of what they count as free choices, but this makes their conception of free will too narrow to be an account of pre-philosophical notions. This strategy also fails to address the rationality issue. Even Kane's view, which makes free will depend on practical and prudential effort as well as the effort to be morally conscientious, is at once too demanding (with respect to effort) and too lax (regarding rationality). But even if libertarians were to append to their accounts rationality constraints like those developed in Chapter 2, the extension condition would be met only weakly. No set of normative conditions could be elastic enough to conform to the vicissitudes of how rational we think free will must be.

Regarding the three content-specific conditions, which the libertarians are committed to interpreting as dual conditions, the argument in Chapter 8 yields the conclusion that no theory can satisfy them all. Hence, if 'the' prephilosophical conception of free will were committed to this libertarian picture, I could rest my conclusion about the non-reality of free will on this argument alone. That would have made this a much shorter book. But since there is no *one* prephilosophical view, as I argued in Chapter 5, I cannot claim to have rejected free will simply because I have rejected libertarianism. We have seen, however, a reason to reject a strong thread that runs through commonsense views of freedom.

This brings us to the compatibilist theories. By distinguishing between normative and non-normative, and hierarchical and non-hierarchical views, we can divide compatibilist theories into the three types examined in Chapter 2. These include non-normative, non-hierarchical theories (e.g., Hume's), non-normative hierarchical theories (e.g., Frankfurt's), and normative hierarchical theories, like the autonomy variable view. (I have not considered normative non-hierarchical accounts, because those seem somewhat odd to me, and I do not know of any historical thinker who held such a theory.)

First, the general conditions. Regarding the conceptual clarity condition, all compatibilist theories enjoy the advantage of avoiding the postulation of any new types of entities or events to our ontology. This means that no new conceptual puzzles arise, since compatibilists do not have to explain any new ontological candidates. And with the empirical plausibility condition, all compatibilist theories share the empirical plausibility of existing physical theory. These views do not require any additions to the rest of our physical theory, nor any fortuitious quantum amplifications in order to make room for human freedom. Concerning the extension condition, it appears that the three types of compatibilist theories fare increasingly well at meeting prephilosophical notions of freedom, although even the best compatibilist account does not do terribly well. The non-normative, non-hierarchical view fails for the standard cases of psychological compulsion such as addiction and kleptomania, and the non-normative, hierarchical views like those of Frankfurt fail due to irrational choices, as was argued in Chapter 2. Normative, hierarchical views such as those like the autonomy variable account enable the compatibilist to rule out irrational choices but go too far by ruling out choices that are made on the basis of cognitive weaknesses that common sense views as free though irrational. Given the enormous range of our demands on how rational free choices must be, I doubt that any compatibilist account can even remotely approximate those demands.

All three types of compatibilist theories do fairly well on the one-way interpretation of the abilities to choose otherwise and somewhat less well on control—the crucial question is whether the one-way interpretation is adequate. But we have seen in Chapter 5 serious reason to doubt that the one-way interpretation has a general purchase on how we feel about freedom. Concerning the final condition, one-way rationality, the more cognitive theories do better than the less cognitive ones, but the vagaries of the notion of rationality prevent even the most cognitively oriented accounts from being more than modestly successful.

I have tried to think of some hybrids of the libertarian and compatibilist views in order to envisage another alternative that meets these conditions and have been unable to do so. The best strategy that I can see is to admit that there are at least this many partially adequate notions of freedom, and indeed as many types as we find useful to distinguish. But since there is no single overriding sense of "freedom" to be found, i.e., there can be nothing about non-linguistic reality that constrains our efforts to taxonomize freedom in one of the various ways rather than the others, the central theme of this book is established. There can be no such thing as free will.

3. What Is Left

Even if this is true, the underlying questions that drive philosophers to the free will problem remain. If "free will" and "moral responsibility" are incoherent, we still need answers to the following questions. Is it intellectually defensible to distinguish between actions that we control and events that we do not control? If there is no free

will, can we make any sense of the idea that agents can be autonomous in their behavior? Does the conclusion that there is no free
will entail fatalism? Does it make sense to look at our past actions
with remorse? Given our conclusion regarding moral responsibility,
is it reasonable to hold Strawsonian reactive attitudes toward persons, or must we view all persons from the detached, 'objective'
perspective that we take toward infants and lunatics? In the broadest terms, how much of our prephilosophical ways of viewing each
other should we give up if we accept the arguments of this book
concerning freedom and moral responsibility?

Let me address these questions by indicating some of the ways that
the conclusion of this book counts against some prephilosophical
ways of viewing ourselves and then suggest ways that my conclusion
does not. Generally speaking, I think that my view is revisionistic
regarding some of the more idealized prephilosophical views about
freedom and responsibility. First, my view counts against the excesses
encouraged by common sense's sometime flirtation with the doctrine
of the supremacy of the will 'against all odds'. Although I have not
purported to show that a libertarian metaphysics *cannot* obtain, I
think that I have shown that *if* it did, the result could not be the
satisfaction of the widely advertised incompatibilist *desiderata* of the
categorical ability-to-choose-otherwise, dual control, and dual rationality. Thus, with classical compatibilists such as Schlick, Hobart,
and Ayer, I maintain that a libertarian metaphysics of human choice
would not yield what the libertarians want. If I am right about this,
then the hyperbolic strain in common sense that maintains that
people are 'free to be anything they want to be' must be rejected, for
the simple reason that nobody can have that 'sort' of freedom. I
consider the rejection of the unreflective doctrine of the supremacy of
the will a desirable implication of my view.

Second, like hard determinism, the view developed in this book
undercuts the following retributive strain in the justification of
punishment that the belief in free will suggests to some: "You have
misused your free will, so you deserve to suffer for it." Whether one
thinks that there is no free will because one is a hard determinist or
because of the reasons given in this book, one should reject the idea
that freedom justifies retribution. If supportable, retribution would
have to be justified on other grounds, and I cannot imagine what
those grounds might be.

But to deny that retribution can be justified is not to imply that we must renounce the "personal," "reactive attitudes" that we typically hold toward each other. Such attitudes, although unjustifiable by reference to free will and moral responsibility, can be reasonably applied to agents who make self-conscious, rational choices. As I argue in Chapter 6, even if we deny the existence of objective moral responsibility, we still have two alternatives open to us. We may give up the personal attitudes when we view persons from a global perspective, or we may continue to hold those attitudes toward persons who choose reflectively. Either perspective is reasonable. We do not need the metaphysics of free will and moral responsibility in order to justify our taking the personal stance toward each other, since we logically merit these attitudes simply in virtue of the fact that we are persons. The abilities to feel pleasure and pain, to form plans and have fears, to evaluate the quality of our behavior in light of our conception of the good—all make the personal stance appropriate irrespective of whether we enjoy freedom and responsibility. We do not fall from the grace of personhood simply because the theoretical prize of freedom turns out to be illusory, any more than we would if it turned out that a malevolent being has the power to force us to act the way we actually do if we were ever to decide to act otherwise (Frankfurt, 1969).

Third, my view requires a different way of looking at the past than a libertarian might adopt. Consider the case of reflecting on a tragedy and feeling remorse that we had not tried harder to prevent it. To libertarians, the idea of blaming ourselves for past acts and omissions is reasonable, provided that we were in a position to have acted otherwise by manifesting our 'free will'. On my view, one would have to say: "If determinism is the case, then it is both sad and ironic that this tragedy and my inability to prevent it were determined to be just that way. If the metaphysics of the libertarians is true, then it was perhaps not physically necessary that that tragedy occur. But any transition from the series of events that actually occurred to an alternative course of events where the tragedy did not occur would not have been a transition that I directed through the utilization of my 'free will', given that there is no such thing. I *wish* that one of the non-tragic alternative courses of events had obtained rather than the one that actually obtained, but it was not 'up to me' to ensure that it did."

I think that this way of looking at the past reduces the tendency of individuals to blame themselves for past events and is, thus, somewhat revisionistic of common sense in this respect. I do not think that it undercuts the feelings of *remorse* regarding the past. Blaming oneself, like retribution, seems reasonable only to one who believes that there is free will, but remorse in the sense of regret and sorrow that things have been a certain way is sensible even without free will. For instance, we can regret our eventual deaths and wish that persons were immortal without believing that anyone has the power to prevent death from overtaking us. Since regret seems to me to be one of the most reasonable attitudes we can take, it is a good thing for my view that it leaves room for it.

Let me now shift to the aspects of prephilosophical common sense that are compatible with the conclusion of this book. To assert that there is no freedom or moral responsibility is consistent with the rejection of fatalism, understood as the doctrine of the impotence of human choices. In order to show that fatalism is false, we simply need to show that our choices can influence the outcome of events, and we can establish this by moving our fingers or deciding what words to say. We do not need libertarian or compatibilist-style free will to be able to do these things. All we need is one-way control, which we often manifest, although it is clearly not tantamount to freedom.

It is tempting to say that one-way control is sufficient for *autonomy*, if not free will and, thus, that on my view autonomy is ensured by the same sort of considerations that refute fatalism. In one sense, this is true, because autonomy can be viewed as simply the type of one-way, rational control that we enjoy when we satisfy something like my autonomy variable account of Chapter 2. The trouble is that "autonomy" is a richly paradigmed term, much the same way that the word *freedom* is, and my autonomy variable account focused on only part of what we take autonomy to be. The Chisholmian notion of a person as an undetermined, unmoved mover has a strong purchase on our views about autonomy, and the account in Chapter 2 goes no way toward establishing that persons who satisfy it enjoy Chisholmian autonomy. Thus, my denial of the reality of free will is consistent with the assertion that we have the sort of autonomy that the satisfaction of the autonomy variable account yields, but it is not consistent with all types of autonomy.

But isn't one-way autonomy good enough to sustain free will? Compatibilists think so. Why isn't the correct conclusion to be drawn from this book that of compatibilism instead of the non-reality of free will? Dennett asks whether we can "even conceive of beings whose wills are freer than our own?" (1984, 172). Dennett thinks that since we cannot, we are as free as we *can* be. And surely this is tantamount to having free will.

There is an ambiguity in the notion of conceiving of beings who are freer than us. Hierarchical theorists like Dennett are correct to hold that highly reflective beings who satisfy the one-way interpretations of the free will conditions are as free as is reasonable to demand. I should be happy to learn that I satisfy the autonomy variable account of Chapter 2 most of the time. Nonetheless, there is a rough, inchoate notion of beings who *are* freer than determined agents who satisfy compatibilistic accounts of free will. Much of naive common sense holds that *we* are such beings. There is a strong libertarian strain in common sense that sees freedom as the satisfaction of the ability to choose otherwise, to control those choices, and to choose rationally in either of two directions. Prior to explicitly going through the logical difficulties involved in the dual satisfaction of these conditions, most people see no problem with the idea that these conditions can be met. For this reason, most persons view themselves, most of the time, as freer than the most ardent compatibilists view themselves.

If I am correct in the argument presented in Chapter 8, the dual interpretation of these three abilities is ultimately incoherent. But this does not mean that common sense, as muddled as it might be, does not have a notion of beings who are freer than deterministic agents who satisfy compatibilistic accounts. And it is this part of prephilosophical views of freedom that libertarians and compatibilists need to capture if their accounts are to capture what common sense thinks free will is. Short of succeeding at this, libertarians and compatibilists at best provide only partial accounts of a fragmented concept—and have failed to vindicate *the* notions of free will and moral responsibility.

If this is true, maybe I should be more pessimistic than I have been prepared to admit. I concede that it is tempting to think that if we lack libertarian-style autonomy and free will then we are helpless and forlorn, because we have lost a commodity of immeasurable value. But the aim of this book has been to show that there cannot be any such precious jewel. Given that "free will" is an incoherent concept, we should not fret over the fact that free will eludes us. (Compare with Dennett, 1984, 172.) What exists, and what we can reasonably hope to maximize for ourselves, is the demythologized version of autonomy. Although this is not equivalent to the welter of things we have come to associate with freedom, it enables us to overcome fatalism. Whether or not determinism is true, our rational decision processes are enough a part of the etiology of our behavior so that without those processes our behavior would be different. The presence of our beliefs, desires, and values within the causation of our behavior is enough to dispel the fatalistic doctrine of the impotence of our wills, regardless of whether determinism is the case.

In my view, we should replace the question "Was S free in doing *a*?" with the question "Was *a* reflective of S's character?" This replacement of one concept with a non-equivalent one has much to recommend it. First, while the former question is unanswerable, as the thesis of this book maintains, the latter question is in principle answerable. At the very least, the autonomy variable account explicates what it is for an act to be reflective of one's character. Second, attending to the latter question enables us to address the underlying issues that drove us to *care* about freedom and responsibility, even given the non-realist conclusion of this book. The point, after all, in worrying about freedom and responsibility was to reach a conclusion on how to view each other. But we can address those concerns by asking whether persons' behaviors are deliberate manifestations of their characters or aberrations. Although knowing that a certain act belongs in the former category is not equivalent to knowing that it is 'free', it is enough for us to decide how to treat the agent who performs the act. As Schlick (1939, 151–154) and Paul Churchland (in correspondence) suggest, knowing whether agents are acting according to their characters enables us to know whether there is any point to trying to modify their behavior. On this view, if I have a stable, reflectively endorsed disposition to do *a*, then it is sensible to hold me responsible for *a*, and there is no need to ask the further question of whether I did *a* freely. Although this sort of 'character-responsibility' is not equivalent to all prephilosophical notions of moral responsibility, it is stronger than the notion of causal responsibility and enables us to make the distinctions that we want to make regarding human behavior.

The doctrine of the non-reality of free will is revisionistic with respect to the quasi-magical and retributivist elements of common sense's ideas about freedom and moral responsibility. But it retains what I think are the best parts of the prephilosophical view, i.e., a practical sense of autonomy, rational choice, and the distinction between acting from and acting not from one's character. These notions permit us to continue to view persons *as* persons, while avoiding unsupportable and internally inconsistent views regarding freedom and responsibility. This demythologized way of looking at persons is consistent with the humane treatment of each other, without buying into a pair of concepts that we do not need and cannot justify.

Notes

Chapter 2

1. Other important hierarchical accounts include those by Wright Neely (1974), Michael Levin (1979), Keith Lehrer (1980), Daniel Dennett (1984), and Susan Wolf (1987). Frankfurt has developed his original account further in (1987). The accounts of Neely and Wolf seem the closest to the view I present, because they have the greatest normative commitment.

2. In a later discussion of his 1975 paper, Watson appears to place more emphasis on the normative requirements of self-evaluation than he did in the original paper:

> Free will involves the capacity to reflect critically upon one's values according to relevant criteria of practical thought and to change one's values and actions in the process. To be free is to have the capacity to effect, by unimpaired practical thought, the determinants of one's actions. (1982, 7)

3. I am assuming that determinism implies that there is only one physically possible course of events for the universe (van Inwagen, 1983, 3). On this assumption, there will be only one physically possible alternative for each of an individual's choices, and, hence, only one way for an individual to respond to the environment. Thus, any controller who causes individuals to choose contrary to the way that they would have chosen if determinism-without-controllers were the case must be interrupting the otherwise normal deterministic progression of events.

4. Charles Taylor (1976) claims the propensity for critical self-assessment to be essential to our status as person.

5. I owe this suggestion to George Schlesinger.

6. Compare with van Inwagen, 1983, 111.

7. For a similar example designed to show that ancestral determination does not, ipso facto, defeat compatibilist analyses of our ability to do otherwise, see Lehrer, 1976, 264–266.

Chapter 3

1. My juxtaposing the existentialist view and the Kantian theme is not meant to suggest that neo-Kantians are particularly likely candidates for the role of obedient torturers. Certainly one's Kantian reflection over the application of the categorical imperative or the principle of treating persons as ends may well counteract mindless fulfilling of promises. I think that Kantians would agree that rule worship is a potential danger to our freedom.

2. I owe this term to Robert Kane (1988).

3. Throughout I have called the first argument that freedom requires morality *neo-Kantian* because it borrows the language of autonomy vs. heteronomy and uses it in a way that Kant perhaps did not intend. What I mean by "the heteronomous will" is one that is pulled in more than one direction by desires, in contrast to a will that desires to maximize a single aim. So, in my terms, a will that desires above all else to maximize knowledge is not heteronomous, even if *Kant* would call such a will heteronomous because it is influenced by the condition of its own desire, i.e., "if you want to maximize knowledge, then choose in such and such a way." For Kant, choosing to satisfy *any* desire rather than choosing due to the moral law appears to be a form of constraint and an instance of heteronomy (1785, second section).

My rationale for addressing the neo-Kantian rather than Kantian conception of heteronomy is this. The neo-Kantian argument strikes me as fairly intuitive, since we all experience instances where conflicting desires seem to threaten our freedom. So, I think that this argument certainly needs to be answered. But the Kantian line that desire, ipso facto, destroys freedom is far less intuitive. It presents a model of free will that is psychologically unrealizable for real ("phenomenal") persons existing in space and time, who I take to be the appropriate subjects of free will accounts.

4. The usual way of addressing this predicament is to distinguish between the morality of actions and agents. We might then say that although the gardener performs an immoral deed, the agent is not morally culpable because of ignorance concerning the real nature of weeds. This distinction does not help Wolf, however, since her view appears to be that the freedom of the will depends not only on the moral quality of the agent (something we have rejected), but on the actual moral quality of the action.

Chapter 4

1. It is widely noted that we do not have the strong intuitions against deserving moral praise in a deterministic universe that we do regarding

punishment. This raises the suspicion that our uneasiness regarding the latter may be due to some factor besides the alleged incompatibility of determinism and moral responsibility per se. To indulge in some psychological speculation, a possible explanation is that we feel abhorrence of punishment per se, and transfer that abhorrence to the notion of punishment in a determined universe. If one can rule out severe forms of punishment on utilitarian grounds (see note 2), one may feel less resistance to the compatibility of moral responsibility and determinism.

2. Glover (1970) argues that punishment must be constrained by the utilitarian view that we are justified in punishing only if (1) there is good reason to believe that we are bringing less harm into the world than we are preventing, and (2) punishment causes less harm than any other equally effective method (153). Hobart (1934) claims in a like manner "That which is moral in moral indignation . . . will not permit us to take satisfaction in seeing (the criminal) . . . tortured, merely for the torture's sake" (89). Hospers (1961) makes a similar point.

Chapter 5

1. There is a widely accepted view associated with Donald Davidson and Dennett that any organism that satisfies a belief-desire psychology is, ipso facto, rational. That line, even if accepted, does not help settle the debate over the normative aspect of free will, however, because the degree of rationality I am concerned with in this dispute is much greater than the minimal sort of rationality defended by the Davidson–Dennett line.

2. This example is a hybrid of ones given by Dennett (1978, 293–294) and Kane (1985, 104).

3. That is, given 'F1x' stands for 'X feels free' and 'F2x' stands for 'X is free,' then (x) (F1x or not F2x) is logically equivalent to (x) (F2x then F1x).

Chapter 6

1. Compare with the following observation:

We may be able temporarily to view William Calley . . . as a phenomenon—a repulsive and dangerous bit of the zoosphere—without condemning him . . . But it is next to impossible to remain in the attitude of inability to condemn Lieutenant Calley for the murders at My Lai: our feelings return before the ink of the argument is dry. (Nagel, 1986, 124)

Chapter 7

1. Important recent work includes that of Railton (1986); Sturgeon (1984); and Brink (1984); as well as the articles in *The Southern Journal of Philosophy* (1986), Supplement (Spindel Conference on Moral Realism); Sayre-McCord (1988); and Copp and Zimmerman (1984).

2. James Cornman provides a more rigorous treatment of simplicity in this way:

> *If* there are no empirical reasons or evidence for the existence of any entities of kind K, no scientific theoretical reasons and no metaphysical reasons to assume any entities of kind K, no linguistic reasons for entities of kind K, and fewer recalcitrant philosophical problems without any entities of kind K, *then* it is more reasonable to deny than to assert that there are any entities of kind K. (1975, 26)

Chapter 8

1. Bernstein uses the term *Valerian libertarianism* (Bernstein, 1989), there following Dennett's citation of a claim by the writer Paul Valery that "invention is the intelligent selection from among randomly generated candidates." (Dennett, 1978, 297)

2. It is important to emphasize that Kane, himself, does not attempt to give a theory that would entirely satisfy what I call the prephilosophical demands for absolute, two-way rationality, control, and ability-to-choose-otherwise. He frankly concedes that Kanian free agents will enjoy less than the complete satisfaction of these *desiderata*, but thinks that his theory yields the greatest satisfaction of these conditions that is reasonable to demand. Thus, my discussion of Kane's view is designed to show that it cannot produce everything that *I* think that a libertarian theory should seek to provide. My resistance to Kane's theory, besides the problem with dual rationality sketched in this chapter, is of the systemic sort that compatibilists hold toward libertarian views generally, and is sketched in the last chapter.

References

Aristotle. (1962). *Nicomachean Ethics.* Translated by Ostwald, M. Indianapolis, Ind.: Bobbs-Merrill.

Asch, S. (1946). "Forming Impressions of Personality." *Journal of Abnormal and Social Psychology*, [vol. 4], 258–90.

Aune, B. (1967). "Hypotheticals and 'Can': Another Look." *Analysis*, [vol. 27], 191–95. Reprinted in Watson (1982), 34–41.

Austin, J. L. (1961). "Ifs and Cans." In his *Philosophical Papers.* Oxford: Clarendon Press.

Austin, J. L. (1962). *Sense and Sensibilia.* New York: Oxford University Press.

Ayer, A. J. (1952). *Language, Truth and Logic.* 2d ed. New York: Dover.

Ayer, A. J. (1954). "Freedom and Necessity." In his *Philosophical Essays.* London: Macmillan. Reprinted in Watson (1982). Page references are to Watson anthology.

Baier, K. (1970). "Responsibility and Action." In Brand, ed. (1970), 100–16.

Bernstein, M. (1989). Review of Kane's *Free Will and Values. Nous.* [vol. 23], 557–59.

Berofsky, B., ed. (1966). *Free Will and Determinism.* New York: Harper and Row.

Bouwsma, O. K. (1965). "Descartes' Evil Genius." In his *Philosophical Essays.* Lincoln: University of Nebraska Press.

Brand, M., ed. (1970). *The Nature of Human Action.* Glenview, Ill.: Scott, Foresman.

Brehm, J., and Cohen, A. (1962). *Explorations in Cognitive Dissonance.* New York: Wiley.

Brink, D. (1984). "Moral Realism and the Sceptical Arguments from Disagreement and Queerness." *Australasian Journal of Philosophy*, [vol. 62], 111–25.

Burge, T. (1979). "Individualism and the Mental." In French, P., Uehling, T., and Wettstein, H., eds. *Midwest Studies in Philosophy*, vol. 4, 1979. Minneapolis: University of Minnesota Press, 73–121.

Campbell, C. A. (1951). "Is 'Free Will' a Pseudo-Problem?" *Mind*, 446–65. Reprinted in Berofsky (1966), 112–35.

Cherniak, C. (1986). *Minimal Rationality*. Cambridge, Mass.: MIT Press.

Chisholm, R. (1964). "Human Freedom and the Self." In Watson (1982), 24–35.

Chisholm, R. (1976). *Person and Object*. LaSalle, Ill.: Open Court.

Copp, D., and Zimmerman, D., eds. (1984). *Morality, Reason, and Truth*. Totawa, N.J.: Rowman & Allanheld.

Cornman, J. (1975). *Perception, Common Sense, and Science*. New Haven: Yale University Press.

Davidson, D. (1984). *Inquiry into Truth and Interpretation*. New York: Oxford University Press.

Dawkins, R. (1976). *The Selfish Gene*. New York: Oxford University Press.

Dennett, D. (1978). *Brainstorms*. Cambridge, Mass.: MIT Press.

Dennett, D. (1984). *Elbow Room*. Cambridge, Mass.: MIT Press.

Dennett, D. (1984,b). "I Could Not Have Done Otherwise—So What?" *Journal of Philosophy*, [vol. 91], 553–65.

Double, R. (1985). "Phenomenal Properties." *Philosophy and Phenomenological Research*, [vol. 65], 385–92.

Double, R. (1988a). "Libertarianism and Rationality." *Southern Journal of Philosophy*, [vol. 26], 431–39.

Double, R. (1988b). "Meta-Compatibilism." *American Philosophical Quarterly*, [vol. 25], 323–29.

Double, R. (1989). "Puppeteers, Hypnotists, and Neurosurgeons." *Philosophical Studies*, [vol. 56], 163–73.

Double, R. (Forthcoming). "Determinism and the Experience of Freedom." *Pacific Philosophical Quarterly*.

Dworkin, G., ed. (1970). *Determinism, Free Will, and Moral Responsibility*. Englewood Cliffs, N.J.: Prentice-Hall.

Dummett, M. (1978). *Truth and Other Enigmas*. Cambridge, Mass.: Harvard University Press.

Feigl, H. (1958). *The "Mental" and the "Physical."* Minneapolis: University of Minnesota Press.

Fischer, J., ed. (1986). *Moral Responsibility*. Ithaca: Cornell University Press.

Fischoff, B., Slovic, P., and Lichtenstein, S. (1977). "Knowing with Certainty: The Appropriateness of Extreme Confidence." *Journal of Experimental Psychology*, [vol. 3], 552–64.

Fodor, J. (1975). *The Language of Thought*. New York: Crowell.

Fodor, J. (1981). "Methodological Solipsism Considered as a Research Strategy in Cognitive Psychology." In *Representations*. Cambridge, Mass.: MIT Press.

Fodor, J. (1983). *The Modularity of Mind.* Cambridge, Mass.: MIT Press.

Frankena, W. (1973). *Ethics.* 2d ed. Englewood Cliffs, N.J.: Prentice-Hall.

Frankfurt, H. (1969). "Alternate Possibilities and Moral Responsibility." In Fischer (1986), 143–52.

Frankfurt, H. (1971). "Freedom of the Will and the Concept of a Person." In Fischer (1986), 65–80.

Frankfurt, H. (1987). "Identification and Wholeheartedness." In Schoeman (1987), 27–45.

Fromm, E. (1941). *Escape from Freedom.* New York: Holt, Rinehart, and Winston.

Gauthier, D. (1986). *Morals by Agreement.* Oxford: Clarendon Press.

Glover, J. (1970). *Responsibility.* London: Routledge & Kegan Paul.

Goldman, A. (1968). "Actions, Predictions, and Books of Life." *American Philosophical Quarterly,* [vol. 5], 135–51.

Goldman, A. (1978). "Epistemics: The Regulative Theory of Cognition." *Journal of Philosophy,* [vol. 85], 509–23.

Halverson, W. (1981). *A Concise Introduction to Philosophy.* 4th ed. New York: Random House.

Hare, R. M. (1952). *The Language of Morals.* New York: Oxford University Press.

Harman, G. (1975). "Moral Relativism Defended." *Philosophical Review,* [vol. 74], 3–22.

Hart, H. L. A. (1968). "Responsibility and Retribution." In Hart (1968), 210–37.

Hart, H. L. A. (1968). *Punishment and Responsibility: Essays in the Philosophy of Law.* New York: Oxford University Press.

Harvey, J. (1976). "Attribution of Freedom." In Harvey, Ickes, and Kidd (1976), 73–96.

Harvey, J., Ickes, W., and Kidd, R., eds. (1976). *New Directions in Attribution Research,* vol. 1. Hillsdale, N.J.: Lawrence Erlbaum.

Harvey, J., and Jellison, J. (1974). "Determinants of Perceived Choice, Number of Options, and Perceived Time in Making a Selection." *Memory and Cognition,* [vol. 2], 539–44.

Harvey, J., and Weary, G. (1981). *Perspectives on Attributional Processes.* Dubuque, Iowa: William C. Brown Publishers.

Haugeland, J. (1982). "Weak Supervenience." *American Philosophical Quarterly,* [vol. 19], 93–103.

Hobart, R. (1934). "Free Will as Involving Determinism and Inconceivable Without It." In Berofsky (1966), 63–95.

Hobbes, T. (1841). "Questions Concerning Liberty, Necessity, and Chance." In *The English Works of Thomas Hobbes,* vol. 5, Sir William Molesworth, Bart., ed. London: John Bohr. Reprinted in Morgenbesser, S., and Walsh, J., eds. (1962). *Free Will.* Englewood Cliffs, N.J.: Prentice-Hall.

Hochberg, J. (1964). *Perception.* Englewood Cliffs, N.J.: Prentice-Hall.

Honderich, T., ed. (1973). *Essays on Freedom of Action.* London: Routledge & Kegan Paul.

Hospers, J. (1961). "What Means This Freedom?" In Berofsky (1966), 26–45.

Hume, D. (1748). *An Inquiry Concerning Human Understanding.* Hendle, C., ed. (1955). Indianapolis, Ind.: Bobbs-Merrill.

Hume, D. (1777). *An Enquiry Concerning the Principles of Morals.* In *Hume's Ethical Writings.* (1965). Edited by A. MacIntyre. New York: Macmillan.

Huxley, A. (1932). *Brave New World.* New York: Harper and Row.

Jellison, J., and Harvey, J. (1973). "Determinants of Perceived Choice and the Relationship between Perceived Choice and Perceived Competence." *Journal of Personality and Social Psychology*, [vol. 28], 376–82.

Jones, E., Rock, L., Shaver, K., Goethals, G., and Ward, L. (1968). "Pattern of Performance and Ability Attribution." *Journal of Personality and Social Psychology*, [vol. 10], 317–40.

Kahneman, D., and Tversky, A. (1982). "The Psychology of Preferences." *Scientific American*, [vol. 246], no. 1, 160–73.

Kane, R. (1985). *Free Will and Values.* Albany: SUNY Press.

Kane, R. (1988). "Libertarianism and Rationality Revisited." *Southern Journal of Philosophy*, [vol. 26], 441–60.

Kant, I. (1785). *Foundations of the Metaphysics of Morals.* New York: Bobbs-Merrill.

Kapitan, T. (1986). "Deliberation and the Presumption of Open Alternatives." *Philosophical Quarterly*, [vol. 40], 230–51.

Langer, E., and Roth, J. (1975). "Heads I Win, Tails It's Chance: The Illusion of Control as a Function of the Sequence of Outcomes in a Purely Chance Task." *Journal of Personality and Social Psychology*, [vol. 32], 951–55.

Lehrer, K. (1968). "Cans Without Ifs." *Analysis*, 29–32. Reprinted in Watson (1982), 41–45.

Lehrer, K. (1976). "'Can' in Theory and Practice: A Possible Worlds Analysis." In Brand, M., and Walton, D., eds., *Action Theory.* Dordrect-Holland: Reidel, 241–70.

Lehrer, K. (1980). "Preferences, Conditionals and Freedom." In van Inwagen, P., ed., *Time and Cause.* Dordrect-Holland: Reidel, 187–201.

Levin, M. (1979). *Metaphysics and the Mind–Body Problem.* Oxford: Oxford University Press.

Lindley, R. (1986). *Autonomy*. Atlantic Highlands, N.J.: Humanities Press.

Locke, J. (1974 [1690]). *An Essay Concerning Human Understanding*. Yolton, J., ed. New York: Dutton.

Lord, C., Ross, L., and Lepper, M. R. (1979). "Biased Assimilation and Attitude Polarization." *Journal of Personality and Social Psychology*, [vol. 37], 2098-109.

Lycan, W. (1986). "Moral Facts and Moral Knowledge." *Southern Journal of Philosophy* (Suppl.), 79-93.

Mackie, J. L. (1977). *Ethics: Inventing Right and Wrong*. New York: Penguin Books.

Milgram, S. (1974). *Obedience to Authority*. New York: Harper and Row.

Mill, J. S. (1861). *Utilitarianism*. Many editions.

Moore, G. E. (1903). *Principia Ethica*. Cambridge: Cambridge University Press.

Moore, G. E. (1911). *Ethics*. London: Williams and Norgate.

Nagel, T. (1971). "Brain Bisection and the Unity of Consciousness." *Synthese*, [vol. 22], 396-413.

Nagel, T. (1979). *Mortal Questions*. New York: Oxford University Press.

Nagel, T. (1986). *The View from Nowhere*. New York: Oxford University Press.

Nathanson, S. (1985). *The Ideal of Rationality*. Atlantic Highlands, N.J.: Humanities Press.

Neely, W. (1974). "Freedom and Desire." *The Philosophical Review*, [vol. 83], 32-54.

Nisbett, R., and Ross, L. (1980). *Human Inference: Strategies and Shortcomings of Social Judgment*. Englewood Cliffs, N.J.: Prentice-Hall.

Nisbett, R., and Wilson, T. (1977). "Telling More than We Can Know: Verbal Reports on Mental Processes." *Psychological Review*, [vol. 84], 231-59.

Perlmuter, L., and Monty, R., eds. (1979). *Choice and Perceived Control*. Hillsdale, N.J.: Lawrence Erlbaum.

Popper, K. (1965). "Of Clocks and Clouds." Arthur Holly Compton Memorial Lecture. St. Louis: Washington University.

Puccetti, R. (1981). "The Case for Mental Duality." *The Behavioral and Brain Sciences*, [vol. 4], 93-123.

Putnam, H. (1987). *The Many Faces of Realism*. LaSalle, Ill.: Open Court.

Railton, P. (1986). "Moral Realism." *The Philosophical Review*, [vol. 95], 163-207.

Rawls, J. (1971). *A Theory of Justice*. Cambridge, Mass.: Harvard University Press.

Ross, L., Lepper, M., and Hubbard, M. (1975). "Perseverance in Self-Perception and Social Perception." *Journal of Personality and Social Psychology*, [vol. 32], 880-92.

Sartre, J. (1956). *Being and Nothingness*. New York: Philosophical Library.

Sayre-McCord, G. (1986). "The Many Moral Realisms." *Southern Journal of Philosophy* (Suppl.), 1–22.

Sayre-McCord, G., ed. (1988). *Essays on Moral Realism*. Ithaca: Cornell University Press.

Schlick, M. (1939). *Problems of Ethics*. New York: Dover.

Schoeman, F., ed. (1987). *Responsibility, Character, and the Emotions*. New York: Cambridge University Press.

Searle, J. (1969). *Speech Acts*. Cambridge: Cambridge University Press.

Searle, J. (1980). "Minds, Brains, and Programs." *The Behavioral and Brain Sciences*, [vol. 3], 417–24.

Searle, J. (1983). *Intentionality*. Cambridge: Cambridge University Press.

Seligman, M. (1970). *Helplessness: On Depression, Development and Death*. San Francisco: Freeman.

Sellars, W. (1963). *Science, Perception and Reality*. New York: Humanities Press.

Shepard, R., and Metzler, J. (1971). "Mental Rotation of Three-Dimensional Objects." *Science*, [vol. 171], 701–3.

Sidgwick, H. (1907). *The Methods of Ethics*. New York: Dover.

Simon, C. (1988). "On Defending a Moral Synthetic *A Priori*." *Southern Journal of Philosophy*, [vol. 26], 217–33.

Skinner, B. F. (1948). *Walden Two*. New York: Macmillan.

Skinner, B. F. (1971). *Beyond Freedom and Dignity*. New York: Knopf.

Slote, M. (1980). "Understanding Free Will." In Fischer (1986), 124–39.

Smart, J. (1961). "Free Will, Praise and Blame." *Mind*, [vol. 70], 291–306. Reprinted in Dworkin (1970), 169–213.

Smith, E., and Medin, D. (1981). *Categories and Concepts*. Cambridge, Mass.: Harvard University Press.

Steiner, I. (1979). "Three Kinds of Reported Choice." In Perlmuter and Monty (1979), 17–27.

Stevenson, C. (1944). *Ethics and Language*. New Haven: Yale University Press.

Stich, S. (1983). *From Folk Psychology to Cognitive Science: The Case Against Belief*. Cambridge, Mass.: MIT Press.

Strawson, P. (1962). "Freedom and Resentment." *Proceedings of the British Academy*, [vol. 48], 1–25. Reprinted in Watson (1982), 59–80.

Strawson, G. (1986). *Freedom and Belief*. Oxford: Oxford University Press.

Sturgeon, N. (1984). "Moral Explanations." In Copp and Zimmerman (1984), 49–78.

Taylor, C. (1976). "Responsibility for Self." Reprinted in Watson (1982), 111–26.

Taylor, R. (1964). "Deliberation and Foreknowledge." In Berofsky (1966), 277–93.

Taylor, R. (1966). *Action and Purpose.* Englewood Cliffs, N.J.: Prentice-Hall.

Taylor, R. (1974). *Metaphysics.* 2d ed. Englewood Cliffs, N.J.: Prentice-Hall.

van Inwagen, P. (1983). *An Essay on Free Will.* Oxford: Oxford University Press.

Waller, B. (1987). "Just and Nonjust Deserts." *Southern Journal of Philosophy*, [vol. 25], 229–38.

Wason, P. C. and Johnson-Laird, P. N. (1965). *Psychology of Reasoning: Sructure and Content.* London: Batsford.

Watson, G. (1975). "Free Agency." Reprinted in Fischer (1986), 81–96.

Watson, G., ed. (1982). *Free Will.* New York: Oxford University Press.

Wiggins, D. (1973). "Towards a Reasonable Libertarianism." In Honderich (1973), 31–6.

Wilson, E. (1979). *The Mental as Physical.* London: Routledge & Kegan Paul.

Wolf, S. (1980). "Asymmetrical Freedom." In Fischer (1986), 225–240.

Wolf, S. (1987). "Sanity and the Metaphysics of Responsibility." In Schoeman (1987), 46–62.

Wong, D. (1986). "On Moral Realism without Foundations." *Southern Journal of Philosophy* (Suppl.), 95–113.

Wortman, C. (1975). "Some Determinants of Perceived Control." *Journal of Personality and Social Psychology*, [vol. 31], 282–93.

Young, R. (1984). Review of van Inwagen's *An Essay on Free Will. Philosophical Books*, [vol. 25], 41–43.

Zanna, and Cooper, (1976). "Dissonance and the Attribution Process." In Harvey, Ickes, and Kidd (1976), 199–218.

Index